BOCCONI
UNIVERSITY
PRESS

Federica Marchionni

ENVISIONING
THE UNOBVIOUS

A Playbook to Build Your Future

Cover: Cristina Bernasconi, Milano
Typesetting: Laura Panigara, Cesano Boscone (MI)

EGEA S.p.A.
Via Salasco, 5 - 20136 Milano
Tel. 02/5836.5751 – Fax 02/5836.5753
egea.edizioni@unibocconi.it – www.egeaeditore.it

First edition: April 2025

ISBN Domestic Edition	979-12-80623-58-4
ISBN International Edition	979-12-81627-39-0
ISBN Digital International Edition	979-12-81627-56-7
ISBN Epub Edition	979-12-229-8007-2

Stampa: Geca - Divisione Libri di Ciscra Spa, Arcore (MB) - www.gecaonline.it

To the good people.
They inspire and will save humanity

Table of Contents

Zero: On the Road to Envision
Human Pillar: Core Strenght

Welcome to a powerful place. The level zero. Each of us starts at a sort of a level zero every day, because every day begins with a Zero Hour. It is the launch of a new stage in the course of life. It brings many possibilities to imagine and explore. We all have, within us, the resources to go much further than where we are now, expanding our vision exponentially. Starting from zero does not mean you are starting from scratch. Quite the opposite. Every day, even on the darkest days, we wake up with energy and capability, just like a rocket on the launch pad. It may appear to be rooted to the ground like a tower, without the wings to fly, when in fact it is loaded with fuel and tools that can carry it high into space. And like a rocket leaving the Earth behind, it's important that we leave something behind our limited preconceptions about what we think is possible. Too often we underestimate ourselves and settle for a limited view of what is possible for our lives, families, communities, and even humanity.

My level zero, as a young girl, was this: A remote small Italian town of few people. An uncertainty called home, filled with strife. Very limited means with which to make a living or build a life. Not far from my home, there was a place I used to go to take refuge in my imaginary world, the medieval Castle of Santa Severa. A solid fortress with a history of war, with the sea echoing, as if in a long corridor. In front of such strength, I could talk to my alter ego, Fedy, my heroine. With her, I would exercise our right to dream as a protester marching for change. Together we would make it, together we would laugh, and together we would overcome. There was always great comfort in knowing that Fedy had the superpower of being a visionary. It didn't matter that glimpses of the future were coming true just as we were playing. What mattered was that I continued to use my alter ego to stay creative and not leave anything to circumstance. No! I was going to use the muscles of life to let myself be pulled forward as if I had a powerful engine inside.

As a child, school was my saving grace. There I was highly valued for my commitment and excellence. My local public school, the only one in our hamlet, was a tiny house with five rooms, one for each of the five elementary classes. There was a small backyard where during playtime at recess, we would pretend to make tomato sauce like our relatives in aprons bent over giant steaming cisterns, we would stir our giant imaginary pots with our giant imaginary spoons. During my fourth grade in school, I met the first of a long line of people who saw something promising in me. Someone who came inside my soul to help, guide, and inspire me. It was my teacher, Enrica. I had noticed her immediately for her radiant intensity. In our little village, Teacher Enrica was different: She was refined and intellectual, she had traveled, and she knew more. She was loving and conveyed the message to me that life was hard but could also be fun. She had the sophistication and coolness I craved and, like a person lost in the woods scanning a map for a path to safety, I studied her speech and dress for clues on how to be an evolved person. She took me under her wing and once she understood my struggles at home, often the topic of the gossip town for the laud fights among my parents and my father's violent abuse for which I was terrified. She asked my mom if I could spend a weekend at her house with her husband and her wonderful daughters. Teacher Enrica wanted to give me some joy I was not able to experience with my family. This kind of person, coming into our lives, especially at a young age, acts to confirm our dreams. She became the beacon, the uplifter, the fitness coach we need to stay strong. She is the kind of person we need to seek out, remember, and be grateful for throughout our lives. These types of people are like saints who have been mysteriously sent our way as we move between courage and doubt during our formative years and even beyond. I knew I had the inner strength and vision to guide myself along lines yet to be seen. I had the courage, the muscle, and the art of the invisible to endure and to wake up each day with hope and gratitude as fuel for my dreams. In every moment of despair, I could turn to the values rooted in my roots: faith, gratitude, and aspiration. Faith in a better future; aspiration to better oneself; gratitude for having health and food.

Some might say that my story is a fairy tale. If a fairy tale is full of magical beings and lands, then you can be sure I've pulled a few rabbits out of my hat over the years. But a good magician spends years honing her moves until they appear effortless in her acts, which is exactly what I did as I turned adversity into opportunity, loneliness into collaboration, and hunger into learning. Before I felt distressed by my poor economic condition, I was distressed by having a house without peace. In my small town, my parents' divorce—they finally separated when I was 10—was a real scandal. I was thankful that I hadn't been born in an underdeveloped country where even health and life are at risk and that I could eat a meal every day, but I must admit I often daydreamed of a distant family taking me away and transplanting me to an oasis of love and safety. It would give me encouragement, gifts, positive experiences, and the protection I craved. Yet, despite my desire for a happy family life away from my reality, I learned from misfortune. In my imagination, I would somehow escape the fate they had set for me. I learned to do more than run away in my imagination. I learned to sift through the mountains of my thoughts and wisely choose those with the most potential. I believe we all have this potential to think and act because we already embody the innate human trait of being able to imagine. It's like learning to walk by crawling until we reach our destination. Which means we will fall. Many times. We will be challenged to exercise skills we don't yet have. We will be called upon to build muscles we have not yet used. During the pursuit, it will take intense concentration, and it won't always be a fun ride. But over time, the muscle becomes stronger because we have trained it, hardened it, and pushed it to exhaustion.

You don't have to grow up in difficult circumstances to be determined to become a better human being, achieve goals, and fulfill dreams, you can build your focus and strength by choice. There are many, really many extraordinary people and great examples of humankind everywhere. Good people, maybe simple, who forge our species into the future remind us of our common thread, challenge us to be better, to express our light, which is available to each of us if only we choose to ignite it. These people are also close to us and in every corner of the planet, trying to make a difference in their lives, in their communities, and when possible, even in the world. Regardless of your background, you need to find your Core Strength as a key foundation of your being.

I have learned the nature of my core strength through experiences and long hours of self-examination and reflection—often, literally talking to myself, with Fedy. *Your Core Strength is the one within you that cannot be defeated or denied.* It is like an engine that propels the rocket up beyond the force of gravity. It is the force that refuses to let us be dragged down again, the one that saves us from crashing. When you find it, you too will rocket off to your unobvious mission to build your future. Have a good life and a safe journey!

One: Envision a Career
Human Pillar: Instinct

> *"We don't need magic to transform our world:*
> *we already carry within us all the power we need, we have the power*
> *to imagine things better than they are."*
> JK Rowling

Imagination is outside of logic. It is an ability to create on a sensory, emotional level. When you imagine, you enter another dimension, you go beyond all that is measurable and con- sequential, beyond what others present to you as obvious. I learned at a young age that my imagination had many answers and could coach me when to step forward, back, and to the side.

When we take time to imagine, our thoughts create crisp, powerful, energy-charged scenes, and project them onto the screen of the mind as if they were frames scrolling before our eyes. Imagining and seeing.

The "seeing" would invade my life.

My dreamy, scheming, capricious imagination would trigger intuition, feed the dialogue with myself, and nourish me with the greatness of thought: the conduit out of my difficult and poor reality.

A girl full of dreams

Why was I in such a hurry to scooch? Growing up in my tiny seaside Roman village, Santa Severa, was like walking around a replica movie set made up of miniature houses, only a few shops, and almost zero happenings. In no time at all, I could make my way past the liveliness of my Italian town center, a square surrounded by colorful flowers and pine trees, with the young boys running in the streets and the mothers with babies in their arms. I often find myself lurching around corners in search of a future in the same way a cat looks for mice on his way into the fields. *There is so much more to life than these few empty streets*, I always felt. Curious, like the cat sniffing for a mouse, my quest beyond my small surroundings involved fantasy, exaggeration, and something I call Dream-Plans.

There was a need to set unrealistic goals—to envision something that wasn't in my playbook. By magnifying each of my objectives, I was moving around inside the cells to see where change is born. And just as the cat may find a mouse here, there, or somewhere else, options presented themselves. This was crucial for me, a girl who, though living in a township surrounded by hard-working men and women rising at dawn to earn an hourly wage of what equaled US$2 back in the 1970s, was banging on the inside of an eggshell desperate to crack her way out. But I would need to stay clever and think outside the lines. My first Dream-Plan, a term synonymous with *strategic goal*, was to be a risk-taker. I didn't consciously choose that. I didn't tell myself, "You must take risks." No! I was compelled from the inside out. A life muscle was formed out of need.

Dream-Plan: To Be a Risk-Taker

My first risk was simply acting and thinking differently from the crowd. I would act from my gut and deal with the consequences later. Coming from nothing meant I had everything to win. Taking risks requires strength. For me, core strength was the first muscle I learned the name of. It was like my sympathetic nervous system, the part of the body that operates when we are under stress. It was at a constant high speed as I diligently worked to fight instead of running. Luckily, core strength turns out to be an invaluable tool throughout life, something that gives us perseverance to work hard; motivation to do better each time. And for me, it was something that drove me to roll the dice and ultimately learn that dreaming is the first step in planning.

My personal headquarters for Dream-Planning was at the seaside, next to the medieval Santa Severa Castle. It was a place I frequented year-round to escape the chaos and drift of my home into my imaginative world. In the summers the surrounding beaches are filled with the sounds of laughter and the excitement of people—primarily from Rome. Situated just 42 miles from the capital city, Santa Severa was a favorite getaway for the well-to-do and their families. For a few months every year, it seemed as if visitors from another country, richer and more advanced, had decided to settle among us. And then at the end of summer everything changed. I remember the distinct stillness of September feeling like a thief approaching my soul as our small seaside resort went dark. The tourists returned to Rome and Santa Severa was left as empty as an eaten box of popcorn tossed to the roadside after a carnival. I would walk the deserted streets in my little bubble in search of a summer memory, afraid of the hurt and loneliness the winter would bring. There were no activities to be found, no one in the shops, no one in the bar or on the sidewalks. The cinema, one of the only attractions besides the beach, closed, and everything remained shut down for nine months. Silence was the king of winter.

The one exception to the gloom of those winter months was my Castle by the Sea. Standing grandiose in all seasons, with its walls stretching high into the sky, the grand, antique foundation of the structure kissed the waves. To this day it is the true prize of a town built back in the 14th century, at a time of great cultural change and achievement called the Italian Renaissance. It was in this structure, ancient with wisdom, that I discovered a profound friend—one that could understand my dreams as I was born inside its walls I never passed. This friend would listen without judgment. This friend would teach me, as I overlooked the water, how to calculate my risks. With the sea echoing, as if it spoke with knowledge of the endless cycles of time, I had a strategic partner to help me chart my way forward. The robust and resilient castle, combined with the lapping sound of the water against the shore, allowed me to paint on a clean canvas and build my courage and confidence the way I believed it could be.

As I began discovering my core strength, I was always considering the things that drove me. What factors pushed me to achieve? Which risk did I need to take to reach my next dream? How much fortitude would it require to reach the mountaintop? Repeatedly I asked myself questions like these and many more. Over the years, this habit of taking a personal inventory turned out to be the foundation of becoming a leader and growing in leadership. But even as a child, I had the feeling that by knowing myself, I could walk a path full of resilience and go deeper into creating solutions for an alternative life. And so, I pushed back the pain with my mind like I was combing the knots out of my hair. Perhaps I would have been less ambitious in life if I hadn't been faced with some challenges I had as a child. Perhaps I would have settled into the traditions of my Santa Severa town and perhaps I would have been plentifully happy. Perhaps! However, I was different and didn't accept the cards I was dealt. I intuited there was a different game for me to play. With the Castle so close to my home, it was easy to get to and it became my sanctuary. It was a place where my thoughts appeared before me like an animated film—rich with colors, characters, and a storyline. As part of my invisibility act, I drew upon a fantastical heroine in my mind, Fedy.

Fedy was, and still is, curious, compassionate, and daring. She is the one who taught me self-love. She is the one with the quick step and fire in her belly. Like any authentic alien, Fedy appeared unfamiliar to others—dare I say foreign. She spoke in a language others couldn't understand, but like visionary leaders who have proved themselves many times over, she was never daunted by the negative opinions of others. Despite the limited means and poor background, she had great visions of her own. She was dreaming of her higher education, her travels to other cities, and how she, too, could be a leader one day. She was a big-city dweller living among small-town folk.

Although this was long ago, not a day passes that I cannot induce the smell of the Tyrrhenian Sea; feel empowered by the courageous spirits who guarded the soil of the castle many centuries before me; and remember my humble beginnings where I first began to envision. It was from there that I could see myself turning my seemingly impossible dreams into a tangible future alive with the bustle of a metropolis, the hustle of a working mom, and a life of being transformed from Underdog to Top Dog. As a willful girl growing up full of pride and curiosity, I was reshaping my life through the imagination of things. The walls of my Castle by the Sea shimmered with reflections from the water. To me they foretold a future when I would be speaking multiple languages, attending the opera, and giving back to those in need, all of which would require my constant Dream-Planning skills. There was much to do before I could start my journey out. I couldn't know for sure what all of this would mean. As I began to discover, gamble with, and trust Dream-Planning as a path to living a life of purpose, I needed to fly under the radar. Meanwhile, I would keep engaging with everyone in our community, choosing my close friends wisely. And above all, I would keep my mind and eyes open for every opportunity to take a step along the path toward a brilliantly *unobvious* future.

It was during my middle school years when I made my first business decision. I took a full-time summer job that required riding my bike three miles through rail and motorway to get to work, as my mom could not afford a babysitter to hang out with me at the beach when school was over. We lived in the Santa Severa North district, a countryside area closer to nature where we could buy our food from farmers and play in the beautiful wild green fields. Nobody helped me find the opportunity. I looked for it. I negotiated the package and organized my commute. Then, and only then, did I go to my mother to explain that I would be the shampoo girl at the beauty salon in Santa Severa near the historic Castle by the Sea. I discovered then that I have the guts of a gladiator, the will of a bull, and the seeing of an innovator.

The wheels of my bicycle crackled over sand and stone every workday as I made my way to start the job at 9 am to finish at 7 pm. I did not earn many *lira*, the Italian currency at that time, but I also did not pay for this experience which I respectfully refer to as my life "Executive Program." The owners of the salon treated me with the utmost respect and admiration as I was known for my academic excellence in town. Though I was considerably too young to work, my employers knew I was diligent and reliable, working long hours each day. They came to count on me during all middle school summer months. I greeted those mornings with an extra dose of exuberance as the sounds of the birds woke me up, the sun shone on my door and the beams cast bright lines along the walls of my bedroom. With the dark night behind me, thoughts of my day at the beauty salon catapulted me into what I expected would be wondrous intrigue. The shop was attended by prominent women from Rome. They thronged to our quaint town with their children in tow. Their husbands, far afield, worked as distinguished judges, lawyers, and bankers during the week, traveling back and forth to the seaside. Tony Perrottet—author, historian, and traveler—explains that the Roman Empire was the first civilization to enjoy the peace and prosperity that allowed people to take "vacations," literally vacating from their normal lives and work to get away for a while.

Much to my delight, the vacationing ladies at the salon engaged in comprehensive conversations about private schools, foreign languages, piano lessons, sports, and travels. My 20-minute trek across town to listen to their educated accents, broad ideas, and wily discussions was my greatest chance for adventure and a future that could wash off the shame that came from having a challenging situation at home. My bike rides to and from work were filled with the intensity of curiosity which was only matched by the profound smell of the wild lavender mixing with the summer sea. On the one hand, these women's lives seemed so far from mine; but on the other, they felt like a book I had read a thousand times. With my summer shampoo job, I was a sponge to the women's voices. I was a witness to their heartache, a pupil to their fashion, and an intern to their experiences.

Without their knowing, they taught me the finer sides of life—how to walk with confidence, how to ask with expectation, and how to act with leadership. Though they rarely spoke to me, I studied their every lesson on a mission to have the drive of a champion (something I would come to understand very well years later, when working at Ferrari). I firmly intended to make a success out of The Shampoo Girl, something these amazing ladies would most likely never see. I could stand in the corner and paint the extraordinary journeys of these ladies' children and grandchildren vividly in my mind's eye. With vigor, I began to color my life as well. There were the sweeping brushstrokes of French, the sketched classrooms of a top-world university, and the speckled skyline of New York City. I was connecting the dots; drawing my path with my imagination; building a future beyond the confines of my people and the safety of my Castle by the Sea. And I knew the needed ingredient to carry out my mission improbably. It would need to include formal education.

Dream-Plan: To Get a College Education

After a few summers washing hair and sweeping snippets into the trash, I found myself a job as a babysitter. It was the only acceptable position at my age. I needed better ROI (return on investment) to reach my education goals, and I wanted to exploit the summer by being outdoors, as my life was very much in nature when I was not studying. At fifteen, I spent my summer taking care of the child of a well-respected family. The father was a gentleman and the mother a gutsy sort. She was solid and smart and worked for a multinational company. I will never forget the time she looked at me and said, "You will become a strong woman. I can tell from the look of your hands. They're big and confident." I could not have been more embarrassed to be noticed for my hands. I disliked them greatly. They felt clumsy. Definitely too big in my opinion. They weren't feminine, at least not in the way I thought they should be. I have grown to see them differently though. In fact, just recently, while sitting at my desk, I sat gazing at the defined lines in my palms, the rounded shape of each of my fingers, and my short, manicured nails. Memories of that moment flooded back as I recalled her words: "You will become a strong woman. I can tell by the look of your hands." It is amazing how a seemingly mundane moment can stay with us for a lifetime. These hands certainly have shaped a few intangible ideas into being with the sheer brass of confidence.

The following summer I was old enough to work as a waitress at the Santa Severa Beach Club Café. There were a few cafés along the coast between the castle and the lighthouse. Two of them were owned by brothers. For four summers, I worked for one brother. A sweet teddy bear, and his wife, a firm British lady. They had no kids. I worked from the end of each school year to the beginning of the next one from 7 am till 7 pm. I loved interacting with new people, but even more, I loved that I was working toward my Dream-Plan to afford a college education by saving most of my earnings. During my free time, I was always studying even though it was summer and a time when most other kids roamed carefree. I became familiar with all the clients. They seemed impressed by my diligence, telling me how they wished their children were as focused as I was. I'd seen their sons and daughters around the club. They had big attitudes. Surely, they were not bad people, but they had a snobbish effect. In their wildest dreams, I am sure none of them could ever see me as a potential colleague at the university or at their jobs as future professionals. My youngest uncle, the only one among my relatives who believed in my promise, used to tell me that one day I could become a great manager like the one who ran the most prestigious Italian company, Fiat. To the boys and girls at the beach club, however, I was only a local worker, the daughter of low-class laborers who, moreover, were divorced! Even if many of these young adults liked me, I was still the girl from the bar and I could not be their friend, hanging out with them after hours.

My evenings were busy anyway, as I was dating a guy, Francesco, who was from a neighboring town, Santa Marinella. He didn't work during the summer. His family, wealthier, solid, and educated, wanted his commitment to be concentrated in studies during the school term and claimed that summer was for rest and recreation. I could not afford that luxury. I needed to build up my savings to guarantee that I could pay for university expenses. Being sensitive, I was often hurt by everyone's comments and actions, for example since I was not coming from a good and wealthy family, my boyfriend's mother didn't allow me to be in their home while my boyfriend was often in mine, but I used my core strength and didn't let anyone of them to win. I knew I had to prove myself to get to the top but did not feel I had to prove it directly to these people. I focused on my idols, people with big brains, deep souls, and considerable dreams. From Rita Levi di Montalcini to Gugliemo Marconi, Nobel Laureates were honored for their work. I have always felt strong and realistic in my thinking that even if you feel you are the best, there will always be someone better than you, smarter than you, richer than you, more educated, more attractive, more brilliant, and more sensitive than you. The most important thing to me was to get the best out of myself. Then, I knew I could reach a higher stage of becoming a person of substance. These feelings of strong drive and commitment to my future dreams fueled my happiness during the summers at the beach club as I was looking for my Itaca as Kavafis beautifully wrote in his poem.

The final summer after high school, I worked at the bigger beach club, belonging to the other brother. A family man, a very kind gentleman, hard worker. His wife, Valentina, was sweet and calm. They had two fun boys. One of them was my age and one a few years younger. They all had blue eyes like the color of the sea. During my shift, I had a one-hour break. Since my goal was to accelerate savings, I negotiated extra earnings by offering to make them lunch during that time. I had never before cooked in my life. My mother controlled the kitchen. But I had watched her enough to observe the basics and develop the skill when given a chance. I had just finished high school that summer and the local newspaper talked about my graduation exams as being worthy of a higher grade than the available 60/60. Everybody started talking about me, even the people from Rome. I was being considered as the best all-time student at my school. Finally, people were asking me questions about my future. I even became friend with a group of kids from the beach club through a sweet girl from Rome. They were all sons and daughters of lawyers, doctors, and managers. I finally was asked to go out with them in the evening after work. I was so happy and kept a low-key approach to anyone who talked to me. I could have been aloof with them, remembering all the mean ways in which others like them behaved to me in previous summers, but instead, I thought anger would just deplete my energy and rob me of the good feelings I was after in my life.

My work at the Beach Club Café—taking orders at the counter from the well-to-do kids, cleaning the tables thoroughly, mopping the floors at closing time—taught me a thing or two about core strength. It isn't something that is merely physical. Being strong permeated all parts of my being. I know I had emotional strength from dealing with the struggle in my family and the ridicule that came from my job. My mother taught me everything I needed to know about physical hard work. But I think there is this thing called ethereal strength. It is built from envisioning, and it gave me the endurance to succeed at school, earn at work, and eventually make friends in unexpected places. Shampoo Girl was more of an attitude than anything else. An outlook that drove me to search my soul, focus on positivity, and exercise my dreams into reality.

Dream-Plan: To Live a Meaningful Life

Another important part of life that touched my spirit from that young age was the act of caring. I couldn't give much but I wish always to help others. It all started when I was in high school. My boyfriend's mother was into philanthropy. Although she was unkind to me and didn't want her son to dating me, as I was not up to her standard by being poor and the daughter of divorced parents and raised by a single mom, she was helping people, and I admired her for teaching her sons to give back. Each birthday or Christmas, when offering them a gift of money, she gave the same amount to charity to set an example of giving. I started to contribute in my own way when she got involved with refugees en route to America. They were waiting for visas during their stop in Italy. These emigrants, mainly Russians, highly educated but poor, were looking to fulfill their own dreams—dreams of a brighter life in a new world. The impact on me was tremendous and I felt a calling to help. Although I could not give money as she could, I could devote time to volunteering and engage with them to lift their spirits. I was compelled to help provide them with the basics of food, clothing, toys for the kids, and shelter. In the moment of giving, I felt more a part of a whole and my envisioning capabilities expanded. I wasn't just thinking about my needs or my own personal pain. I was thinking outside myself. I liked the idea that I could ease someone's suffering, even if only with a small act. I found it quite inspiring to help people turn their dreams into plans as I was working so hard to do for myself.

My wonderful mother also taught me about having a big heart. Hers was bigger than a Queen's pocket! Without the means to give financially, she had to find creative ways to help. I remember one time she came upon a thief in our home. Instead of calling the police, she offered him something to eat. Can you imagine? Unworried about her safety, she thought it was an amazing lesson in humanity for me and my brother despite our deep concerns over her actions. It was mind-blowing to me. And so, I found myself staying very active in our local organizations, including at an animal rescue center where years later I went to volunteer and eventually adopted an abandoned dog. Giving back to others brought me joy, transported me away from my reality, and gave me something to focus on other than my personal aspirations. I thought that one day I would work for, and maybe even manage, a non-for-profit organization, and that in the meantime, I would find meaning in my daily life.

Taking care of my own health has always been a priority, too. Ever since my younger days, I have managed to fit in regular workouts at the gym, usually before dinner. And starting out very young, from the age of six, I competed as a sprint runner. During the summer months, our community organized festivals where people could sing, dance, and race. I participated in all three areas as they were the main form of entertainment in our lives. But running was my favorite because it was there that I could escape into my imagination and put the heaviness of my life aside. I even raced in Rome as a high school student until it interfered with my studies, and I had to revert back to running as a form of well-being. In every city I eventually traveled to for pleasure or for work, I made sure to run: New York, Sydney, Tokyo, Rio de Janeiro, Cape Town, London, Los Angeles, Paris, and more. I have also run official marathons in New York, San Francisco, and Kilimanjaro, and to this day, I am eager just to get outside for some fresh air and a jog.

Exercise, in general, revives me while at the same time it allows me to listen to music, my true source of emotional connection and a huge passion of mine. One of my favorite songs from 1988, just as I was finishing high school, was Tracy Chapman's "She's Got Her Ticket," from her self-titled debut album. For the longest time, I would expand my lungs on the treadmill and sing along to the famous anthem at the gym as I conceived the details of my university life:

She's got her ticket
I think she gonna use it
I think she's going to fly away

Luckily, since studying in Italy is strongly supported by the government, my savings, combined with my scholarships to attend La Sapienza University in

Rome, would get me through my college years. The only ticket I would need then was the one for the local train from small-town Santa Severa to the big-city college classroom. Just knowing that I had begun this stage of the journey, at last, filled me with the satisfaction of a job well done.

Super Shampoo Girl was on her way!

Making Clever Choices

I am sure that I would not have been able to save money after five years working at the Beach Club if I hadn't put it into a most purposeful place—my own little college fund. Of course, I could have spent a small amount of money at dance clubs and by hanging out with my friends, but my dreams were not ordinary nor were my circumstances. If I was to spend it on myself, I decided it would be to elevate myself in some way—for example, with a subscription to the theatre, which I got during my college years. That was something I could sink my cash into! Discipline with my earnings sustained me over time. Discipline was a huge part of my Dream-Plan gene, and it was mandatory for creating and maintaining a meaningful life. I was relentless in my pursuit of work and added tutoring younger children to supplement my income. While the kids napped, I would pull out my encyclopedia and cross-check the facts in my high school papers. I lugged around a second-hand backpack received from Mrs. Pandini, a lady who brought joy to me and my mother, especially when she gave us clothes and accessories, she was not using any longer: my first exposure to quality, fashion, and brands. What a joy! My beautiful second-hand backpack was my office. At any given moment, you might find me whipping out my pencil to work on my studies.

Learning of my extraordinary high school results, the Italian former President's sister, Mrs. Cossiga, who employed my mom as a maid in the family's summer home in Santa Severa, encouraged my mother to send me to university. I will always be grateful to her for this. I got to know her better years later when eventually I was attending university. My mother unfortunately had a car accident, and I had replaced her in her work to protect her post. Watching me washing her floors, Mrs. Cossiga admired me for having remained humble and often told me that education would give me the satisfaction I deserved.

Not all my mother's friends and relatives advised her to support my ambitions for higher education. Even my mom herself told me that I could be happy by becoming an employee at a local office, get married, and live my life in Santa Severa. That would have been a big accomplishment. She was afraid that higher success could make her life look poorer than ever by comparison. Luckily, she surrendered to my college plans and eventually provided me with everything from nourishment and a roof over my head to the monthly rail pass to Rome. I used every moment of the 52-minute ride to study. My mother sacrificed having the benefit of my income—a common tradition in our small town—and instead watched me go after my goals, defending our joint decision each and every time she was questioned. By the time I was a "fresh girl," (first year at college), I had the routine of getting up at 6 am, eating a quick breakfast before a shower, and starting my studies at 6:30. Then, there were my six hours focused on studying before a one-hour lunch break. My afternoon involved another six hours of reading, writing, and absorbing information. My mom saw how hard I had worked to earn scholarships and what I was willing to give up in my young age to stretch my destiny beyond the boundaries of home. The extra cash I earned through tutoring, though, enabled me to pay for my side of the deal: my desire to travel, my love of fashion, and my inclination to cultural activities. I knew I couldn't ask my mom for a ticket to the theatre or fancy clothes, but I could always count on her for the best lasagna!

I would become the first college-educated person in my family and among the extreme few in my hometown (besides the doctor and a teacher). I felt fortunate to be enrolled in one of the largest European universities and one of the oldest in history, founded in 1303. Sapienza, as it is generally referred to, means wisdom in English. For a poor girl like me, intellectually identified as I felt, living out my dream put me among alumni the likes of Nobel Laureates, heads of nations, notable religious figures, scientists, and even astronauts.

In Rome, I started to learn to care about the importance of manners—placing my silverware on the right-hand side of my plate and showing the ability to converse fairly by listening before speaking as I dove into meetings with people from different levels of society. Looking back on these years, I see that I was breaking from my tribe and meeting people across borders. I was venturing into new lands, seeking alternate experiences. In my youth, I often had spent hours envisioning attending an opera at La Scala, visiting the Pompidou Center Museum in Paris, or taking a stroll along Sydney Bay in Australia. For our geography classes in fourth-grade school, we had a big pull-down map of the world. I would get drawn into it so deeply that I could still see the layout of the countries when the map was scrolled up tightly around its wooden spindle. I had a Dream-Plan to explore that world.

Dream-Plan: To Explore the World

And now, as a university student, I was broadening my views, gaining independence, and beginning to live the dream that had sprung from that fourth-grade class. I didn't know back then why I was so attracted to visiting unobvious places like Auschwitz, Prague, and Israel. I had been making it all up as I went along—The Shampoo Girl; the Beach Café; Tutoring; an Education; Giving Back; Exploring the World—and it seemed to be working. To handle creativity with respect, I needed to surround myself with people and places that encouraged me. I wouldn't let myself be limited by my environment. I arrived at a place that was founded on self-trust. What I thought I had stumbled upon, I realized I had actively pursued. What I had wondered about as possibilities I found could be realized by remaining steadfast in my work. To envision, I couldn't veer away from my aspirations with fear or allow pressure to mount from the crowd. I needed to train the power of my notions and throw a line into the water to see what I could catch.

Sitting in my basement at home, sipping my morning cappuccino, I was mulling over topics for the last semester of my education. The thesis would be the crowning element of my master's-degree program in business administration, and it had to be more than good. I needed to find a job out of university that would pay the bills and give me the independence I so needed in my bones; never mind the fact it was something my mother taught me to seek. *Writing a standard paper isn't an option for me,* I thought. I wanted to find something interesting, substantial, and representative of a new industry, something fast-growing, so that it would be easier to get a job. I went on in my mind. *What is the next new big thing? An upcoming industry?* It occurred to me that the future, something I'd been chasing since a young age, would ultimately be about technology; and the best way for me to secure a position out of school was to go where few young women had gone: telecommunication. Mobility. At that time, in 1994, mobile phones were getting better and more popular while the wireless networks were growing and developing too. *That's it!* I declared with another taste of my espresso and steamed milk.

Better yet, by writing about the growth of mobile technology, I would be exploring a trend that was under-recognized at the time. Personal computers and the hard-wired Internet were being talked about as if they were the ultimate shape of the future. But the not-so-obvious mobile revolution was underway, too, and most people didn't realize how huge and important it could become. By 2014, the number of mobile phones in use would grow into billions. And back in 1994 when I made the unobvious choice to write about mobility, the first-generation (1G) mobile wireless networks were moving from analog to digital technology which allowed the beginning of text messaging, today's most-used form of communication. I had my finger on the pulse, and at just 20 years old I was making predictions that in hindsight surprised even me. This ingenuity permeated my research. I had found what I was looking for: A fast-growing industry that surely would need to employ people to keep pace with demand. I went to speak with the professor of the Industrial Economy Department, with whom I had chosen to work for my thesis, and with a convincing pitch, he approved my idea.

I tackled the industry's players to learn about each competitor's size—employees, global presence, and annual revenue. And naturally, I dove deep into their products like a loon into a fresh-water lake. Perhaps I wished that like those birds, I could fly. Fly to the base of all knowledge, sift through the papers of time, and soar up with the answers in hand. I was all in—a whirling dervish, a speedy marathon runner, a book on its last page. There was only one problem: a shortage of information about the subject. Because the industry was new, I could not find authoritative books. The technology magazine *Wired* had just been launched in the United States, but there was no Italian-language edition; *Wired Italia* would not appear until many years later.

What did I get myself into? I sat one day biting my lip thinking about how to tackle this roadblock. I had studied the economist John Maynard Keynes, and I recalled his theory of "animal spirits," in which he observed that our instincts and our "spontaneous urge to action rather than inaction" will often lead us in positive directions, more than logical calculations will. Something inside me convinced me that I was making the right choice with my thesis subject, despite the apparent obstacle. My drive to create a better life for myself was in line with Keynes' theory. Spinning forward, I was sure that nothing could stop me. I just needed a light bulb to switch on in my head to guide me to the next step. I already knew where I wanted to end up.

Newspapers! A door opened in my mind's eye. *Aha! For sure I can find information in the archived reports of recent history.* In terms of getting business information about a new industry, I thought of *Il Sole 24 Ore,* the Italian newspaper equivalent to *The Financial Times* in Europe or *The Wall Street Journal* in America. It was the perfect place to find relevant, fact-checked data. Indeed, the paper would have articles about the major players like Finland's Nokia, Sweden's Ericsson, and America's Motorola. And so, one day, bundled up in my camel-colored cashmere coat that I afforded myself after my junior year working as a tutor, I fearlessly went to the *Il Sole 24 Ore* offices in Rome. I remember standing outside the statuesque building looking up at its columns with hope in my heart. As a student, I was entitled to do this kind of research. But my actions were relatively unusual and bolder than what many students would do at that time. I opened the door, stepped inside the building, and felt the weight of information that filled the corridors. Looking around, my eyes found the sprawling marble reception desk with a lady working diligently behind it. *This is it,* I encouragingly prompted myself. *This is your next silver bullet. Go on up there and ask.* With my second-hand bag locked on my right shoulder, I walked up to the desk and said: "*Ciao. Il mio nome è* ... Hello. My name is Federica Marchionni. I am a student at La Sapienza in my final year. I am doing a research paper on the telecommunications mobility market and would be very interested to thumb through your archives to gather as much data as I can about the industry." To this day, I still think of the receptionist with gratitude for giving me access to the vaulted rooms where the papers lay.

As I dug into the papers, spending long hours in the archive rooms, I realized that all of the articles about the telecommunication business—on subjects from the manufacturing of networks to the service providers and mobile phone companies—were written by two journalists. With my fingers grazing the pages, I let out a *hmph* and a *ha!* I was trembling inside with delight but really trembling when it dawned on me to ask the receptionist if I could meet with the writers. As I started my walk back to the front desk, I could hear my thoughts racing: *This is going to be a much bigger ask than just reading the archives. Who do I think I am, to meet with such high-level and well-respected professionals?* Yet I knew I couldn't miss the opportunity to go straight to the source. I had an out-of-body experience while making my way down the long, winding wooden staircase. In a sense, it felt like I was plunging into the future. And an even stronger sensation was the feeling of being plucked from my past. As an observer of myself at that moment, I felt like I was an invention. I was creating myself just as an inventor makes an object. My focus, a laser force capable of piercing through barriers, was mine to use if I chose. And as I approached the woman at the front desk, I did. "*Ciao di nuovo* ... Hello again. May I trouble you for asking a favor? Do you think you could put me in touch with these two journalists" pointed out their names.

The lady, I guessed, appreciated my commitment, dedication, and curiosity. I was expressing a desire to get to the source of things—just like a good journalist does, instinctively. She said that she would speak to the one who was based in Rome and invited me to sit down to wait as she needed to make a phone call. *Sit down? I can't sit down;* I screamed with anticipation inside. And so, I paced. One foot in front of the other around the entranceway. Passing my hands along the grooves in the walls. Counting the seconds as they passed. Wanting to skip with glee. I was in the second round of my walking meditation when the receptionist returned with good news. She invited me to meet the journalist the following morning. I was to return to the same place, and she would escort me to our meeting room.

I sprinted back upstairs like a gazelle, gathered my papers, and bounced out of the building envisioning all the ways I would fit into the telecom

world months before I was due to graduate *summa cum laude* from La Sapienza University in 1995. The thesis was called "A Network of Billions" focusing on the companies that were making money by building networks in different markets (most often selling antennas, repeaters, cell towers, software,
etc.) to ensure good coverage for service providers. These companies, Nokia,
Ericsson, Motorola, Alcatel, etc., were selling network solutions to network
providers such as AT&T and Telecom Italia and both were selling mobile
phones to consumers with different go-to-market strategies for distribution.
The business was huge, and it was just at the beginning. All buildings would
eventually be used as cell towers and all the people would come to buy a
mobile phone. The demand would skyrocket. I couldn't have chosen a better
topic! It was fascinating to me and enough to keep me up at night, imbibing
as much information as I could gather. I could have stayed holed up in my
bedroom for weeks studying as I have a keen interest in digging for information. But I also have a solid foot on the ground and felt that meeting some
of the relevant companies out there could give me a much-needed touch of
reality for my paper. The American poet and educator Henry Wadsworth
Longfellow once said, "Youth comes but once in a lifetime." I do believe
that with youth comes naivety which can lead us to dare to do some of the
most unexpected things. Having had a successful first appointment with the
journalist Rendina, I decided to ask him if he could set up some meetings
for me. "I'd like to interview the CEOs of Nokia and Telecom Italia. Do you
think it is possible?"

What a memorable experience those interviews turned out to be. I prepared what I thought were relevant topics. Questions that could show my
interest and knowledge while at the same time could put them at ease speaking to such a young girl. I had it in my mind that there was significance in
them letting me interrupt their busy agendas for a student and her college
paper. I got up the morning of my interviews with the same daily regimen I
had during my college years. I felt like the brightest shining star in a sea of
constellations. Dressed in a professional white pantsuit, donning a colorful
scarf in elegant Italian style, I was in the bustle of people making their way
out of the train and into the importance of their duties in the city. I took my
nervous-nelly self to my meetings at Nokia and Telecom Italia with the kind
of click of my heels only a female can pull off. I was a professional that day
and did all I could to present myself as such. *Ready or not boys, here I come,* I
giggled to myself.

Betting on Envisioning

With my first two executive meetings complete, I was feeling sharp and more determined than ever. My Dream-Plan, to become a CEO, formed clearly before my eyes.

Dream-Plan: To Become a CEO

My amazing years in university were almost behind me and it was time to focus forward with ferocity. I could see that being an executive meant gaining knowledge not just about the market, but about the world and its people, cultures, and values. Having been thinking two steps ahead already, these things were a big part of my college life. There was national travel during our short breaks to the Uffizi in Florence, San Marco Square in Venice, and the Piazza del Campo in Siena, learning about Italy's rich historical landmarks, museum exhibits, and beauty on nearly every corner! And then there were the summers, oh, the glorious summer travel to foreign lands throughout Europe—adventures in Budapest, Prague, Munich, and Berlin for a start. When classes were in session, I took weekend jaunts into Rome where I fell in love with the arts: the incredible museums, opera, theater, and movies.

I eventually found a friend who had the same interests as me, Paolo. We each bought a student subscription to the Argentina Theater in Rome and became close friends. His family even offered me a place to sleep during weekday evenings at Paolo's grandmother's flat. They lived in a multi-family home in the city center. His parents made me feel comfortable as opposed to others who examined me as if I was doing a job interview. Those parents just needed to be reassured that their children were associating with the right people, but I felt like I was dying every time they started to ask about my background and family. I didn't want to talk about the father I hadn't seen in years, or my mom who worked cleaning other people's houses, or the brother wasn't going to any college. So, it felt wonderful to be in a place where instead I was accepted, and even nourished. Whether it was a quick bowl of pasta primavera before rushing to the theater or a nocciola gelato to wash down the show, Paolo's family's home was a thriving environment for me with his lively, kind, and fun grandmother at the helm. Also, there were no trains to Santa Severa after 8 pm on weekdays, not to mention how dangerous it was for a young girl to travel alone after sunset. And so it was, I found a home in Rome.

I was on track to finish college a semester early but with the travel bug in my veins, I decided to use that time to join the Erasmus Program, an international exchange program for students looking to widen their subject

knowledge and advance their language skills to eventually work internationally. No more sunny days of Rome and beautiful sunsets of Santa Severa
beach as my studies were in Lille, France, a place that baptized me into the
rainy, cold weather I would encounter later in my career when working in
Milan, New York, Beijing, and Copenhagen.

While waiting for the academic year to close, I learned to speak French
fluently during the six months of living in France. I made friends from all
sorts of backgrounds: Omar from Senegal who studied engineering, Gem-
ma from Barcelona, and Olivier from France. All great people with whom
I would spend much more time over the years ahead. I would recommend
a multicultural experience to anyone. There are many ways to get a chance
to live and work among people from a different culture than one's own. The
benefits include learning that it is possible to live in ways that you did not
expect—the *unobvious* is always around us! —and furthermore, being in different surroundings calls forth a state of high awareness. Everything is new,
even the language and words you use to express yourself. You begin to take
nothing for granted and move beyond the comfort zone into zones where life
is truly alive every day.

When I finally did graduate, I orchestrated one last hoorah before starting a secured internship at Saatchi & Saatchi, a global advertising agency. I
would take an overseas trip with two objectives: to learn English and to go
as far away as I could afford. The United States was far but too expensive to
stay for a month and a half, so I chose Australia, since I could pay my way
with a scholarship, I won from La Sapienza University. The amount was
equivalent to several thousand dollars today, enough to cover both airfare
and a backpacking trip with the Oz Experience bus. I flew to Sydney via
Bangkok. During the layover, I decided that I would add Thailand to the
trip back and visit it on my return to Italy.

Australia was liberating. Red earth crumbling beneath my feet; rock
formations talking like sisters in the afternoon; and white empty beaches
stretching for miles beyond view were all within reasonable miles from each
of the cities I visited. Once again, I encountered amazing young people. This
time, many were artists and freelancers. My dream to become an executive
was far from their realities, which was another lesson in relativity. Most of
them travelled for six months or even for years at a time. I, on the other hand,
was only there for a few weeks. More free-spirited than I might ever be, they
were in search of a very different dream than mine. My CEO Dream-Plan
piled responsibilities on my desk. My broadened horizons needed to be used
as professional skills. Speaking English and being more open-minded was,
for the corporate world, just a potential foot in the door. I felt it would give
me a competitive advantage over my peers. Whether this was true or not, it

kept me on schedule for the trip. Coming back to Italy wasn't easy, though. I was tempted to find a job in Australia and stay there, since the feeling of freedom was sitting well in my bones. However, I felt too far from the rest of the world as I wanted to start an international career.

Moving from student life to professional life was exhilarating. I approached it with fresh optimism and the quest to learn while savoring each moment to the last drop like peppermint candy. Saatchi & Saatchi, which later was named the Best and Bravest Agency on the Planet by *Contagious* magazine, was a great place to start straight from the gate. The internship there was invaluable to me. I learned that no matter how important one assignment seemed, others would appear on my desk in the thick of it all. I was faced with new personalities, taking on unfamiliar tasks, and stretching my thinking while putting forth confidence even in moments of doubt, of which there were plenty. Luca, the head of the division, gave me a good lesson about how a mundane task can be approached with a completely different set of eyes. Within his division was the woman to whom I reported directly, and she was not nice to young professionals, especially to younger women. She often gave me the dull job of photocopying piles of papers, and I felt insulted at times by the way she talked to me. Seeing the frustration on my face, Luca stopped me one day offering a significant tip. "Instead of simply making the copies, why not read the content of the pages and understand what is going on in the company? Ask yourself questions." *Brilliant*, I thought. It was a great way to turn my eagerness into practicality. After all, I was being presented with a real opportunity in this internship. I still didn't like the way my lady boss demanded her coffee and spoke to her subordinates, but I took it as a lesson in how not to act: *I will be a very different leader in the future.* I could be demanding without being unpleasant and unfair. Luca understood my wish to develop, and despite my humble position, he often invited me to big meetings on the pretext of taking notes. But I think we both knew he was looking out for me, to help me see how managers talk to each other and take decisions. He became the first example of an executive I wanted to become. *Open, objective, fair, inclusive, and confident,* I would recite to myself at the copy machine.

Learning the first tricks of the marketing trade was not enough, however, to guarantee me more than a short stint at the advertising firm. As my internship came to an end, I was faced with the unsettling reality of the economy in 1995 with a spiking unemployment rate of young people. I felt like my insides were drained out through my toes. *What a step backwards,* I thought. I had had expectations of entering the workforce with the same burst of speed I had displayed throughout my school days. *Staying out in front of the compe-*

tition, I would tell myself. But now, facing the specter of unemployment has brought panic like no other.

What rewards could I show for all the sacrifices I had made to reach graduation? Would I be able to give my mother some justification for all her efforts in understanding my yearning for a better life? Will her brother and sisters and all my other relatives say, "I told you so!"? How was it possible that with all the knowledge I had gained, I could not find a job? I had extra skills that others did not have—like using the PC and the latest software programs effectively, speaking multiple languages including English, and strong social awareness. Didn't any of that count?

I was approaching depression. Going from having distinct goals, many projects, and extremely busy days to having nothing to do at all made me feel like a high-flying hot-air balloon faltering from the sky. I was a huge piece of nylon lying crumpled up in a far-off field. *Would anyone find me here in the weeds? Was all my studying in vain? Have I missed out on some of the best years of my life?*

Thank goodness for my faith since this was a dark moment of my life. Still, I did what any determined warrior driven by the fear of failure would do. I mapped out my plan to stay two steps ahead. Like a good soldier, I made finding a job my job. I created an impressive *curriculum vitae* based on the guidelines and suggestions I looked up. I listed all the industries in which I could have an interest, then listed the most important companies in each where I could see a potential fit. I sent out resume after resume, reading announcements in papers and trade magazines while pounding the networking pavement the old-fashioned way, as the Internet wasn't yet the vast resource it is now. But at one place after another, *they want "experienced" people*, I grumbled to myself. Most of the companies did not even respond to my inquiries while others just sent letters saying, "We don't have a position for you." Desperation was close, though I never gave up. I thought about my dream of studying in the United States before start working and pushed myself to go after a scholarship there. I didn't even know where to start, how to apply, where to turn. And though I gave it a shot, unfortunately nothing budged there either. I rejected some work opportunities with big companies looking for newcomers to start on the sales floor as assistants. As much as I needed a job, I had done that work and wanted something I hadn't experienced yet but these corporations had standard procedures for hiring new talent and I didn't seem to fit into the boxes they had.

As the days kept passing with no job in sight, I began to see my two steps forward turning into steps back. I found myself looking into a dark tunnel. Light and safety seemed impossible to find. I questioned my decisions and thought I should have humbly accepted something. Yet, deep inside, I knew that accepting any of those roles would only leave me feeling disappointed. I had big dreams to tackle and people to report back to about my success. Believing in myself and in better opportunities, I kept searching. I found a part-time job with a company called Platinum. They were providing advertising jingles to Italian radio networks. It was not what I studied for and not what I wanted to do as my main profession, but I accepted the job to earn some money, knowing that it was left time to continue job-hunting in the afternoons. Plus, it was in Rome which kept me in the hustle of city life. Late one afternoon on my train ride back to Santa Severa, I thought of a summer trip I had taken through Europe on the Interrail. I was traveling solo in Salzburg, Austria, and just after arriving heard that Lou Reed was in town for a concert. Since he was one of my all-time favorites, I badly wanted to get in. Tickets were sold out, but I went to the concert arena anyway. I stood at the entrance and wished to find tickets on sale there, but no such luck. I stayed, listening from outside. The hills were alive with the sound of music. The outdoor setting was truly spectacular with the sound of rock and roll pumping through my veins. Just as I was settling in, I saw a man and woman walk out with a young girl not looking well. Mustering the confidence to approach them, I asked if they were leaving for the night. And just like that a chance presented itself. I got in. As I made my way to my spot, Lewis Allan Reed, American singer, musician, and songwriter, broke into one of his anthems. On the train to Santa Severa I was overcome with joy remembering this moment from university days and felt reinvigorated for the fight ahead. Knowing that life would not always work out precisely as planned, I sat in the train and found myself singing, once again, *Take a Walk on the Wild Side*—which I realized was exactly what I had been doing for all these years.

Ramping Up Skills

It was quite a few months after my internship at Saatchi & Saatchi, a Friday to be precise, when I got the call that changed my life. It was Samsung Electronics. They wanted me to write a summary of my thesis and come to the office the following week for an interview. I spent the entire weekend creating a presentation that documented my know-how in the best way possible. I was supposed to be enjoying a ski trip with friends, but while they were busy at the slopes, I was slaloming through the work of making transparencies. (That's right, transparencies, to be projected physically onto a screen. Have you heard of those? I didn't have any equipment for making a digital PowerPoint presentation.) Next thing I knew, I was seated in a tall-backed, black leather swivel chair in the boardroom of Samsung's Milan office. I was waiting like a secret ready to explode when a series of men filed into the room. They seemed stressed and impatient, especially the Korean one, who was in charge of the authority of Samsung's HQ in that country. He was the man who might become my boss.

I don't remember if I was even breathing, but I do know that I was prepared. I did not come from a big company like Panasonic with at least five years of experience, something they were looking for. Instead, these men had in front of them a girl recently out of college but who was talking with no hesitation about 3G broadband and the next strategic moves for the network providers and telecom companies—all of which I had studied with the resources and contacts that the financial newspaper *Il Sole 24 Ore* provided. I was curling my excitement into my toes as I went through my presentation. I could not know the effects of it for sure, as I watched a line of stoic faces giving me no sign of comprehension. But later that week I learned that I had my first corporate job as a manager in Samsung. *A Manager! In Samsung! Exactly what I needed!* It was 1996 and I saw mobility as my ticket to freedom and independence.

I was reporting directly to the star of the company, the Korean Mr. Pyo, who was head of the IT and Telecommunications Department. There were other Koreans heading TV or music departments, but Mr. Pyo was by far the overall leader of the company and its ambitions in innovation. He was the best boss I could possibly get, not because he was easy but, on the contrary, because he was the most challenging and demanding boss I've probably ever had. Yet he was a good person and a good leader. He had a family but wasn't able to spend much time with his wife and daughter, as he was working long hours and often on weekends. I began, then, to imagine myself at 40 and 50 years old, as I wanted to know the skills I needed to acquire and how to build my own pillars along the way. That was indeed my way of thinking: always ahead of time. Where I will be, who I want to be, how I want to be and with lots of exertion, creating a potential plan to reach the goals I had in mind. I didn't know which goals I could really achieve, but along with my degree, I now had an international job and the ability to live independently. Many of the big early steps in my Dream-Plans were either already accomplished or in progress. This made me feel that I could dream high and reach for the stars.

At work I dressed the part, aiming to present the highest possible version of myself. My mother had always done so. Even though she worked as a maid, when she went to clean the home of a wealthy family, she would arrive at the door looking clean and sharp in her own right. My goal was to arrive at the Samsung executive offices looking thoroughly executive. Suits with a touch of feminine style were and still are my favorites. Most of my colleagues were dressing casually. Everyone had his own style, as Italians do. The only ones wearing suits and ties were the higher executives (all men) and decided to dress as the new female manager on the rise. Feminine suits.

But looks can never be enough to make a good manager. As I learned in my internship, the right attitude and how you treat people are essential. Getting along with all departments at Samsung was easy for me because I took a positive and helpful approach. I could see that having any other attitude toward my colleagues would not help to get things done. I was kind and respectful, striving to give the best in any meeting, reports, or phone calls. This granted me support when I needed it. Indeed, I could ask almost anything of my colleagues or superiors, even at the last minute when truly necessary. They liked me and they knew I was passionate about the job.

My young, fresh approach to business also had me pushing for a change in their approach: *It seems to me that we need to be more consumer-oriented with our marketing strategy and less price-oriented. How about starting with developing better products, first becoming more product-oriented, to gain market share, and then consumer-oriented?* That was the essence of what I said one day in a meeting. The others understood that I was more strategic and able to sense the market. I couldn't discuss these strategic matters with the HQ in Seoul since that was my boss's responsibility. My only contact with the Korean HQ was to negotiate a purchasing plan and get more products (especially CD-ROM) faster than in other countries, in order to sell more. After the executives of various departments had observed me for a few months, I was invited to many more meetings to push mobility into people's homes and lives together with faster data and information into their businesses.

The Internet was expanding at such a pace that business communication was shifting from voice only to strings of voluminous emails in people's inboxes. And today, given how emails have transformed well beyond an internal tool for business messaging to a primary marketing medium, I could see that I was operating at the leading edge of the curve, inventing alongside industry leaders. I was working in roadshows, preparing all the tools to introduce new innovations that Samsung was offering in fax machines, CD-ROM, and cordless and mobile phones. I was developing and even performing presentations to male-dominated audiences—feeling the divide between us like a full eclipse of the moon on a cold wintry eve. I remember a trade-show conference at the Hotel Excelsior in Naples as one of the most successful and rewarding experiences. It was also a fun one.

Back in our spacious offices in Milan, the climate was instead very serious. The chief technology officer was a gentleman who was always busy helping anyone who needed it, while the controller, in charge of finance, took it upon himself to also control the workplace environment. Literally. He wasn't just making sure that financial statements were checked out. He would walk around the office checking on each of us most probably to see that we were focused on our PCs and our work, if we were being as efficient as possible with no distractions. I believe so since among his observations was having everyone touch-type with all 10 fingers on the computer keyboard. But ultimately, that was how I got to be faster in typing and learned to be grateful to him as well. Still, I saw a bigger picture. The hard-driving enthusiasm at Samsung was just the environment I had been envisioning for myself. Working with strong professionals and being able to make valuable decisions were some of my first successes worth celebrating. By 1997, my life-as-learning attitude won me an opportunity to work for a visionary man at Philips Consumer Communications, Guido Tuseo who was coming from the most successful corporation at the time, Nokia.

Philips Consumer Communications was itself a big deal: a new joint venture between the Dutch company Philips and the American company Lucent (owned by AT&T). I am proud to say that my continued perceptiveness secured me my second position out of school, as I stepped into a role with much more responsibility. It happened very organically. One day, passing by the Philip Consumer Communications stand at SMAU—Italy's most important trade show for innovation (similar to CES)—I spotted Guido there. I knew him as I had interviewed him when he was at Nokia, and I was writing my thesis. He said he was looking for people to create a new team in Rome and proposed to meet with me the following week. I felt honored to be invited by such an important person for me. After sharing his plan for the company and the role he wanted to offer me, he said he believed in women and wanted to empower me in reaching my potential and, of course, the company's goals. No one in Italy was really speaking that way in the late 1990s, especially to a young person.

When I presented my resignation to Mr. Pyo at Samsung, he tried to retain me and made a counteroffer by promising me a promotion. He knew that I needed and deserved a higher salary. To keep up with expenses, I was actually doing three jobs. I had managed to keep my part-time Platinum job on the side and was also teaching at a gym. Every evening, I received faxes with briefs from Platinum to create the copy text for new advertising messages, which I needed to deliver the next morning. That job only granted me a better shared apartment closer to the Samsung offices. From living with a tough lady who had me just for the money but with no intention of sharing her space, I moved into a larger apartment with two girls who were nice to be with: a very Mediterranean girl who dreamed of becoming an actress and an Ethiopian blue-collar who was very sweet. We couldn't have been more different in roots and dreams, but we respected each other. To afford the best gym where I wanted to train, I had applied to be a teacher to save the subscription fee and earn extra money which I could use for petrol to drive to the Milan city center more often.

A better salary would have allowed me to drop at least the Platinum job. As much as I appreciated the new offer, respected Mr. Pyo, and really enjoyed my days at Samsung, I observed that at that time in the executive team all across the global organization, there were very few women. I thought that the Dutch-and-American culture at Philips Consumer Communications would better allow a woman to step up and eventually lead, so I decided to give myself more chances elsewhere. But my departure wasn't really easy. The VP of sales who was instrumental from my hiring gifted me a business book and was almost in tears because he didn't want to see me leave. He had been my biggest sponsor from the day of my interview, and we had worked together closely both in the office and on the road, meeting sales agents and distributors. Although he was clearly moved by seeing me go, he didn't cry. I did, all through the six-hour drive back to Rome. In my Ford Fiesta filled with bags of clothing and appliances, I was leaving Milan, a dynamic city that had shown me the possibilities of becoming a future global executive and a strong professional. Thinking of all the friends I was leaving behind and the good experiences, I couldn't stop the tears from falling almost as if they were creating a bridge or a way to own my past and feel new for starting a new experience.

As the newly named Director of Marketing and Sales, I was launching Philips Consumer Communication, a first-ever mobile phone, besides selling fax machines and cordless phones for which Philips had truly the dominant position in the market. But the mobile phone was different, and it was equivalent to working for a startup company nowadays. One of my finest accomplishments at that stage was working with Americans for the first time—my US dream was forming before my Santa Severa-born eyes.

By 1997, what used to be one telecom provider per country was becoming three or four providers per country. A digital access divide was growing, with bandwidth becoming a greater necessity to compete. As third network providers were vying for space in the telecom market, so was I. By managing people, I was tapping into the world of leadership. By supporting the product development team, I saw the inevitable trial-and-error of the invention. And by working across cultures, I was stretching my thinking like glue until I made a connection. With good work experience on my resume, I was convinced that my dreamy view of the world was an asset I needed to cultivate further if I was going to continue to make non-obvious decisions that would positively impact my career and life. Working each day among a multicultural group of managers, and stepping into their meetings and being heard, were some early successes worth celebrating. The best moment was an international management meeting in which I was invited to participate. It was in Paris, and aside from me, only CEOs and CMOs (Chief Marketing Officers) from each country were invited. I was thrilled. It meant being in Paris and meeting the company's most important executives, from the Global CEO who was American to the COO, who was Dutch, and all the top country-level people. Supposedly I was attending just to assist and learn. But then when it was time for Guido to stand up and present the Italian business case, he said he didn't actually want to tell the story of our success because his team had done it—and he called me to the stage. Now, picture this: A young woman in front of not just local managers or small business owners as I had faced on the Samsung roadshows, but CEOs of entire country-wide operations. I needed to speak in English! And I had no prepared remarks, no slides, nothing planned! In a situation like that you can either survive and get stronger or die on the doorstep of opportunity. I used all the survival tools I was gifted with. I focused on three main areas of investment and told them the return we had in each one and I tried to be brief but precise. The presentation was a success, not only because I was able to very clearly explain why we were selling more phones but also because my boss was seen as a great leader. He didn't want the stage for himself; he was confident enough in his own power to step aside and give his team the chance to shine. Unfortunately, my direct supervisor didn't think the same way. He felt undermined, and I started to learn how politics worked in a corporation. Once we got back to our daily jobs, he started to treat me without respect—throwing catalogues at me to check them, saying that that kind of work was not interesting enough for him; discouraging me from taking any action; not approving any of my requests and so on. With Guido's trusted strategic long-range view of leaving the company after only a few months, I was juggling the ups and downs of professional life while making sure to still learn from the best, keep up with my professional development, and look for small wins to boost my endorphins. I had received calls for job interviews from two network service providers who were my clients, and from Ericsson, where Guido had gone. The network operators were very big, powerful, and definitely consumer-centric, paying high salaries and offering very interesting positions with great titles and budgets to operate. But both were mainly operating in the Italian market. Ericsson was building and selling software, infrastructures, mobile phones, and more, globally. On top of that, Guido really believed in empowering women which was truly rare at that time. My career couldn't have been as successful as it had become if he had not given me the opportunities he gave me at Philips, and then at Ericsson. At that time this was a huge difference-maker. Guido often introduced me as the "best man in the company," an expression I never liked, but I understood what he wanted to portray about me. I learned a lot by having such a strong man as leader and mentor. He told me in a few instances that I couldn't use his techniques and approach even if I could be as determined as he was; he wanted me to develop my own. Guido also wanted me not to make his mistake of taking every battle too personally but instead learn to pick the right battles and to let go when needed.

Dream-Plan: To Be a Modern Leader

In each company, I was observing the entire leadership team and understood the role that popularity played. For me, it was hard to be less instinctive and direct, but the risk of maintaining that approach was too high. If I was going to show a rebellious attitude with a clear mind and strong beliefs, I would be going nowhere. A woman was considered to be too complicated if she had unusual ideas or many opinions. Men can even have a temper and still have a great career, but that wasn't—and still isn't—the same for a woman. After so much hard work I had done, I couldn't afford to lose my chances by acting too spontaneously while speaking up. I started then to observe how I should react to disappointments, disagreements, unfairness, and pressure, and how to build a solid wall to protect myself. When people told me about the barriers you need to have in the workplace in order to move up, I never understood what they meant, and thought the barriers were just being mentioned as a way to keep other people from discouraging me. Instead, as I began moving up, I understood that building that barrier—protecting your feelings, being able to react with distance in challenging moments or under pressure—was essential to survive, get stronger, and keep going. It seems simple but when you are young you are very naïve and ingenious. The key was to observe. To see how people were acting in different situations and who was getting promoted and why. It wasn't only because of the performance. You needed more and that is what I couldn't learn by studying books but by experiencing many different situations, always with an observant eye and exercising new skills. For the first time I was learning about the "win-win" strategy, I had used it without knowing it. Being fair and building long-term partnerships was indeed the first foundation of my management style and all I wanted was to create win-win relationships. That was the key to my early success. A struggle I observed was people having difficulties in evolving, and I could also see how sad it was for tech companies not to keep their relevance when new products were launched by competitors. I thought that the best way to survive the obsolescence of the hardware was for companies to keep up with innovation, and for human beings to invest in their inner self, our software. We should not only grow in career getting more money and titles, but we shall also grow as human beings too. Living a life in chapters and making sure each one of them becomes a great experience can be an incredible way to evolve and update ourselves, personally and professionally. So that is what I decided to do, and I was proud making a change by following a Swedish company with a wonderful culture. *Ericsson, here I come!*

Some takeaways

Find your dream headquarters and speak to your alter ego. Imagine yourself in the future. Create your first Dream-Plans. Dream big with ambition but back dreams with a concrete plan.

After you get facts and necessary information, use your instinct to make clever choices. Observe the landscape, people around you, your idols, and understand their keys to success.

Don't overreact in disagreements and learn to self-control. Mature this skill as you grow. Work hard, be disciplined, and stay focused on your dreams but don't forget to enjoy life too! Be yourself and exercise the skills you lack while leveraging your strengths to move forward. Choose your values that will define you and your leadership.

Your future is not only made by your career but also by different experiences.

Keep evolving, living life in chapters.

Two: Envision Expansion
Human Pillar: Curiosity

"We keep moving forward—opening up new doors and doing new things—because we're curious. And curiosity keeps leading us down new paths."
—Walt Disney

Walt Disney was a man of powerful imagination. Fired by curiosity, this led him and his company to create ongoing streams of art and entertainment in new forms. Today Disney movies, Disney characters, the wonderful songs and music that go with them, and much more continue to inspire the imagination and curiosity of people everywhere.

Curiosity is a natural trait in each of us. It speaks to us in the inner voice of constant questions: What goes on inside that beautiful building, within those walls? Who is that person who looks so interesting? What would it be like to go to a place I've been hearing about? What would happen if I tried my hand at doing this—or that? The voice of curiosity is forever inviting us to *expand our lives*. To explore new terrain, to learn what we can do in a new realm, and to grow closer to our dreams or find greater ones.

Unfortunately, we may sometimes ignore or suppress that voice while dealing with the busyness of our daily routines. I would advise you to listen always and to follow the lead whenever it is OK to do so. Curiosity was a priceless companion to me as I grew into my adult years and beyond. Among other things, it led me into a new career, and into a life partnership, which were totally unexpected and unobvious.

Expanding Freedom

At Ericsson I stepped into my first truly managerial role, reporting to the Country Manager in Italy and to the VP of Global Marketing & Sales at the headquarters in Sweden. The VP, Stefan, was a Swiss guy with whom

I got along very well. We had a similar drive, which was needed, because at that time—between 1998 and 2001—the mobile industry was becoming increasingly competitive. I wasn't an engineer, so I couldn't create software or products, but I could dedicate myself to understanding consumer trends and the economics of the market. My challenge was to stay at the forefront of ideas. And while making great strides, I was also learning more about the prerequisites for success in life. Cutting-edge competence is necessary but not sufficient. Taking responsibility is important, and risk-taking tops it all. My former mentor at Samsung imparted a key insight to me about what that really meant: "It's not important that you made a mistake," he said. "It is important how quickly you correct yourself!"

Today I would say that my favorite success model is the one described in the book *Decisive* by the brothers Chip and Dan Heath. Their approach to decision-making is called "WRAP: Widen your options. Reality-test your assumptions. Attain distance before deciding. Prepare to be wrong." In our youth, we test ourselves and test the waters at every turn but with the right studies, examples and life experiences, we can build solid pillars. I have always felt an unstoppable determination in my career. The time had come for me to test my instincts for making decisions and trust them.

Together with fantastic Swedish colleagues and Guido's leadership, we made several successful launches gaining market share while driving marketing campaigns for new Ericsson phones. We launched the 888, obviously mainly conceived for the Chinese market (where 8 is for them a lucky number); the T68, a phone for young people, offered in different colors and with great value for the price; then the lightest phone in the world, launched with the extra-terrestrial ET reciting our slogan. The T28 was the first phone to use a lithium-ion battery, and it had a chat board and a connectible keypad to facilitate the use of SMS. We also introduced the first satellite service, which I tested while sailing with friends. And when the R380 appeared in 1999, it was the first touchscreen phone and the first to be marketed as a "smartphone," it used the Symbian operating system, an OS for first-generation touchscreen phones that resulted from a collaboration between Nokia, Sony, Ericsson, Motorola, and Psion in 1998, and that still attracts the attention of fans today. The R290, in addition to using the GSM digital network, for the first time in the history of communications also used the Globalstar satellite network. One could write a book about the evolution of these devices and how profoundly things have changed over time. Nokia and Ericsson were then in the forefront. Phones with web browsers and email were just being developed. Apple's iPhone, which popularized the design that is now standard—a flat shape entirely covered by a touchscreen—had not yet even been conceived: it wouldn't be launched until 2007. But when

I worked at Ericsson, around the turn of the millennium, the Scandinavian products were the ultimate products in futuristic technology. I realized that what I was learning was so unique, I couldn't help feeling on the moon for enthusiasm. Ericsson was also a large multinational company, where all processes and methods were clearly defined and structured. I was learning management with professionals at other levels, along with experiencing a different culture—the Swedish one, open, free, and fair, where I felt supported as a young person and as a woman. All the marketing and sales managers met quarterly, with the meetings rotating between different European cities. This was a great opportunity to learn more about the different cultures, customs, and habits of various countries, along with their ability to adapt to new products and services.

Flying

Because of my busy days, I had no time while I was on the ground to think and reflect, so I used the time on airline flights to do that. There, high in the sky, I could also read and get inspired. There I could connect to another dimension and feel at ease in thinking big, envisioning the unobvious and making clever choices. I learned by being trapped in an aircraft that I love to fly. I have always felt I was closer to the Gods and the angels up there. I was not afraid to talk to my inner me, Fedy, and I found ideas and projects. I strongly needed to have in mind a long-term plan for my life and update the plan as I was going through it. Back then, I was planning my life till I was over seventy—well, I was dreaming. Dreaming to become this and that, to do lots of things and more and much more. I was even deciding at what age it would make sense to have certain things happen. For each step on the way, I was giving myself enough time to make my dreams become reality. I knew that my goals and dreams were gigantically ambitious, considering that I was just a young woman with few years of experience, and I was coming from a background where none knew about things I wanted to experience. Thinking that probably no one could understand my dreams, or believe in them, I felt it was better to keep them quietly to myself and deal with them when I was above the clouds, literally.

I think it's very important to have a time and place where you can dream-plan. Ideally it will be a place where you can utterly disconnect from phones and email, from friends and family. For me, in my childhood days, it was outside the Castle by the Sea in Santa Severa. And then as a young professional woman, it was riding airliners above the clouds. It didn't matter if the cabin was filled with other passengers or even jammed into seats right next to mine, because usually those people were all strangers to me, and they were absorbed in their own thoughts and actions anyway. I could talk to them, which is always an opportunity to meet new people, but most of the time I chose to converse with my inner voice—and with the angels. They knew I was imagining my life and all the turns I needed to take. I was honest with myself. I never tried to think in ways that would push me into mere fantasy, beyond the ultimate limits of reality. But at the same time, I realized that within those limits there were boundless possibilities waiting to be envisioned, leading to many unobvious futures I could set my sights upon. As just one example, working for Ericsson brought me in contact with places in northern Europe that were new and dazzling to me. Not only Stockholm and Malmö, where the Swedish mobile company division was based, but also other Scandinavian cities. Copenhagen, the beautiful capital of Denmark, was a city where I would land before going to Malmö. Copenhagen was also a center of what I would call the modern Renaissance, splendidly combining state-of-the-art tech and culture with a long and storied history.

But in all such matters, I understood that timing is a key weapon, and I needed to build patience. I knew I would achieve everything I was deciding to achieve, and it was just a question of time. Already I had gone very far by making it through my college degree, into a life that once might have seemed unbelievable. For wealthy people, having a child without a degree is a disgrace to the family, but to me and most people who came from difficult environments, a degree was a huge achievement. On top of that I had achieved an international job and life, not yet at the top executive position but surely, I believed that would come with time. And of course, it would require the same commitment and preparation I had devoted to my studies and finding a job. So, in addition to expanding my ideas while flying, I was deciding my next actions and reading nonstop to expand my knowledge. In retrospect, I think that the frustration I had not to be at a higher level in my career was necessary to fuel my drive. Age is not a definition of smartness and capabilities, I knew I could do more, and I found obsolete the idea of only having older people in higher positions, but I must admit that experience brings a better and more mature approach to face certain pressure or challenges, let alone crises. Wisdom is a skill that I needed to master with time and experience. Among different books I was reading, a small one that made me reflect on my way of thinking was *Who Moved My Cheese?* by Spencer Johnson, which at that time was a bestseller in the USA. It's written in the form of a humorous fantasy story, about mice and "little people" looking for cheese in a maze, but it has a serious message: When the cheese in one place runs out, you have to go looking in new places and not be afraid of change. The feeling I had while reading that book was very strong as I had the same thoughts in my own mind! It felt like confirmation of what I always believed and reassured me that I was right in thinking differently and just needed to keep going. One day I was going to make it! But I was only able to share those thoughts with Fedy and imagine a life built on those principles, something I was used to do when I went to the Santa Severa Castle in my hometown. Even today I push myself to talk to my Fedy, dream new dreams, and think about which of my actions in the past right and which ones were wrong turns. Most importantly, I always try to update the specific steps and even the goals, since our desires change as we grow and mature. However, I do have the ability to see my long-term goals clearly, and I never abandon these central pillars of my dreams even if the steps to reach them are unknown.

An unexpected turn

On my own, I decided to go to Africa and learn more about Kenya after reading a book that was inspirational for me—more on a human level than on a business one—but still another confirmation of how crucial it is to think outside boxes and envision the non-obvious. The book was *I Dreamed of Africa* by Kuki Gallmann. Despite the name, she is an Italian woman who had moved to Kenya with her husband and son to live on a cattle ranch. There she built an extraordinary life filled with emotions and adventures, eventually becoming a citizen of Kenya and a leader in movements for conservation of the land and the interests of the Kenyan people. Life definitely gave her huge challenges but, in the end, she lived the life she was dreaming of. She could express herself, be herself, give what she wanted to give, and get what was important to her. When I went to Kenya, I met quite a few "Kuki." Indeed, whoever decided to move there from Europe or America was someone who wanted to try a very different life. These people had wilder souls than my dreams. I respected and admired them. But while to them, their wildlives were cool and mine seemed boring, I knew inside that I was going to build my own happiness in my own way. Life and work in Africa would eventually come but at a later stage, probably in the last chapter of my life. Not everybody is the same. I wasn't judging them for their choices and all I wanted was to have an exchange of thoughts and experiences to enrich my know-how of life. Connections can happen where there are some mutual interests and an open mindset, and with some of these people I established a nice friendship.

After returning to Italy my career took an unexpected turn. I remember the day very well. I had persuaded my tough boss to let me be the person who could entertain clients at the MTV Music Awards in Stockholm, since Ericsson was the main sponsor. Guido understood the need to entertain clients and prospecting for new but was always telling me to focus on more business-related stuff with them and not attending events. These were "things for others," he kept telling me. Just the year before, Ericsson hosted an amazing global event, a Caribbean cruise in which Ricky Martin, *the* megastar of that time, performed for the guests aboard. Of course, I was working on "serious stuff" and was discouraged from going. Although I was disappointed, it was the right call. In return, though, I negotiated that if I achieved the KPIs (key performance indicators) for the first two quarters of the coming year, the company could pay me a summer course in Cambridge to improve my English and offer to use my vacation time. I met the targets and Guido kept his word. So, on a hot August day in Rome, I packed for my Cambridge experience where I stayed with a mixed-nationality couple, a British lady employed at the BBC and a Jamaican man who loved to run. By attending the classes I could understand how much more English I needed to learn and how important it was to practice public speaking. After the summer we focused even more on our business goals at Ericsson: to beat our competitors, win market share, and enjoy good momentum. When the company created the slogan "Make your voice heard," consumers responded very positively, and sponsoring the MTV Music Awards seemed to be a perfect marketing idea. Knowing Guido's opinion about these occasions, I respected his guidance to a certain extent. However, I was working very hard, so I needed and wanted to enjoy life as well. This event was about one of my biggest passions, music—a source of inspiration, a gateway to dreams, joy, and shelter. In keeping with my personality, I had eclectic tastes in music, loving everything from opera to rock. Lyrics, meaning, and innovative sounds were my main criteria for choosing artists. David Bowie, Queen, and Sade were among my favorites. Because of my age, U2 were at the top of my list in 2000, and they were scheduled to open the Stockholm concert with REM to follow. I simply couldn't miss this. It was just too good, and I could go there easily if my boss approved me as an official ambassador to bring our key clients.

I went to his office with a plan. I would pay for my flights and hotel, all he needed to do was get me a ticket to THAT concert. Seeing me very determined and understanding that music and concerts were a passion of mine, he accepted. I had the ticket!! Still a lot needed to be done. The right flight, hotel, and outfits were key elements to perfect enjoyment of the opportunity. The event was only a week away, so after work that very evening I went to search for an appropriate outfit. I chose a beautiful light blue silk dress, chic and elegant. I needed matching shoes and a special touch, though. A friend who worked at a shoe showroom found me a light blue pump with an infusion of purple, which made it very interesting. I challenged myself to find something that would accentuate the color mix, I even found a scarf with the exact same combination of light blue and purple. Now I had the outfit I wanted, elegant but not conventional, chic but not boring, and needed to define the rest. The head of communication for Ericsson knew I was going to the concert and generously offered me a room in the hotel they had booked for clients: the same one where U2 were staying. I couldn't feel more excited, and of course privileged and grateful! Then I needed to book a flight and since my enthusiasm was very high, I decided to travel in business class although I was paying for it myself to keep my word to my boss. The ticket was almost equal to my entire monthly salary! So, I used some miles to still afford it as I was never overspending. On the contrary, since my young age, I have been saving to build my future. When packing my bag, I decided not to wear on the plane the Diesel jeans I was in love with but since I was sitting in business class, I thought it was more appropriate to wear a suit, a feminine unconventional one of course.

The flight I had chosen didn't go directly from Rome to Stockholm; there was a stopover in Milan. That seemed fine since it would allow time to work from the lounge and buy a gift for the colleague who had kindly reserved the hotel for me. When I boarded the plane in Rome, I was thrilled and pleased with myself all at once. At last, I was on my way to an adventure for which I had worked extra hard—going beyond the usual bounds of my job to make it possible in the first place, and then preparing for it with extreme care and thought, not to mention the considerable investment. I expected all the work and preparation to pay off. But I couldn't have predicted how spectacular they would. At the age of 29, I was dressed as the possible future CEO I was planning to be—appointed in a tailored black suit with a crisp, white-buttoned burgundy blouse matching my burgundy shoes and handbag. In the executive lounge at Milan airport, I was busy working on my laptop and two mobile phones when I stood up to take a break for a cup of coffee. I started talking to a young gentleman since I was struck by his unconventional style: a cashmere turtleneck under a sport blazer, styled with ripped jeans and elegant loafers. Who was dressing like that in 2000? I couldn't figure out if he was a businessman or not. He looked sharp but not formal and had been on the phone constantly with the air of someone who had important work to do. He told me that he too was booked on a flight to Stockholm. I was headed there on one of my frequent travels for Ericsson but this time was special for me. As we talked, another man, his "friend," joined us to say that the flight to Stockholm would be boarding soon. All three of us walked together to the carry-on area, preparing to say *arrivederci*, goodbye, once it was time to settle in our respective seats. But curious as I was, I needed to ask the men if they too were going to the MTV Music Awards. Their reaction was a bit

strange. They confirmed they were going there to "deliver" something....
Hmm! I thought maybe they were members of a new upcoming band I
didn't know yet about it?! To assure them that they weren't talking to a crazy fan but to a serious professional, I told them I was working for Ericsson
which was the main sponsor of the event and was going to incentivize our
key clients. And as we stood chatting at the escalator to the boarding gate,
we made our formal introductions. Federica Marchionni, meet Domenico
Dolce and Stefano Gabbana.

Dolce & Gabbana! I had no idea! The faces were not familiar even to
me, a lover of fashion, but the names? Of course, they were! They were in
the vanguard of design for the major fashion shows. They had designed the
costumes for Madonna's world concert tour a few years prior. Their company
was already an established brand with luxury buyers in Italy and abroad and
still growing. But, *ovviamente,* of course! To introduce myself I said "Well,
I am none, but I am your aspiring customer!" Indeed, the gift I had just
bought for my Ericsson colleague was a Dolce & Gabbana t-shirt (the only
thing I could afford to buy). In the exact moment, I shook their hands saying
to myself, "What if this encounter could change my life?" And indeed, it did.

Aboard the flight, I went to my assigned seat, in the first row on the right.
They were seated first row on the left. Another coincidence? Or was it fate
because I had bought a business class ticket? I was a bit nervous but wanted
to show I was super cool and calm. I decided to reopen my laptop and keep
working instead of initiating further talk with them. I didn't want to give
the impression that I was chasing after fame and VIPs, especially because
my real heroes were people like Maria Teresa di Calcutta and second because I have always respected people's privacy and space. Now that I knew
they were celebrities, I wanted them to feel comfortable. But this time, *they*
started talking to me. They were on their way to MTV in Stockholm to give
Madonna her award of the year. That was the delivery they had mentioned.
I was amazed at their humble approach. They appeared to be even shy. They
were also afraid of flying, so they were much more nervous than I felt, but
they were accepting the challenge in order to become more visible as people
and therefore build the company's brand awareness and recognition. The
businesswoman in me pushed me to ask them a sales question: "What kind
of phone are you using?"

"Motorola," they answered.

"Hmmm...," I thought.

I immediately saw an opportunity to turn them into Ericsson customers and
brand ambassadors, so I didn't lose the chance to present the full range of
Ericsson phones I had in my purse. I introduced the company, its competitive advantages, current and future developments, and gave them a sense of

the investments behind every launch. It was a perfect chance to get Ericsson products into their famous hands and the hands of whoever Dolce & Gabbana was dressing. "Why don't you try the new thinnest phone yet invented, the T28?" I suggested. "You'll be impressed by the beauty and the performance of the phone. It has a lithium battery so despite the size, it can last a long time. I will send each of you one at your office," I proposed. This was a common practice to create product placement. They had done it themselves with their clothes, so it was familiar practice for them. "Here is my business card. In case you have any technical issues, you can call me directly and I will make sure to get it fixed or send you a new phone right away." The telecom industry was indeed facing customer service issues for the many technical problems some product had, while the supply chain was quickly adapting to new product offerings in the race to keep customers from abandoning one company's brand for another. It was Nokia versus Motorola; Ericsson versus Nokia, Alcatel and Siemens; Samsung versus LG and Panasonic. The competition was high, and the speed of the market was higher. However, the industry was far from becoming global. Sensing that fashion, along with the entertainment industry, was leading the expansion in Western world trends, I wanted to place our phones in the hands of these fine men. I was also unwittingly putting forth my first vision to live abroad and be truly international. We left each other after the flight with a warm goodbye and I believe we all had a wonderful time in Stockholm.

I didn't see them again during my time in Stockholm. The city was magical and before getting ready for the event, I wanted to visit the places I admired the most there. The City Hall, where the great Nobel Prize banquet is held, was one of them. As I dreamed of talking to leading world figures who were awarded prizes there, from scientists to peace champions to literary writers, the visit reinforced my belief that my heroes were people who were making a difference in the world. I promised myself that one day, I would abandon my private career for a while to fully dedicate my time to something more meaningful than being just a successful executive. Inspired by that dream, energized by the encounter with the designers and about to enjoy a great show, I was exuding positive energy and offered my Ericsson clients an unforgettable experience.

Dominating Fears

A week later, Mr. Dolce and Mr. Gabbana, who probably saw in my presentation of the Ericsson company and products my professionalism, style, and passion for success, called me at work. I thought they were calling to discuss a partnership with Ericsson to create a co-branded phone, as I had suggested while we were talking on the flight. I asked for time to schedule a trip to Milan to see them. To my surprise, while I was confirming the meeting with a few colleagues they said, "Well, we are interested in you, not in Ericsson." It was a job offer! At first, I was shocked. Then I felt worried about having to explain to my colleagues that Dolce & Gabbana were not interested in the co-branding opportunity that I had been raving about. Of course, I was also flattered and excited at the prospect of taking a position with them. But when I shared the news with some of my mentors, they said I was crazy to even think of leaving a big multinational corporation, where at just the age of 29 I was working with respected executives and with a boss who wanted me to succeed. *How could you move to this small family-owned company run by two men? How about if they split? How about if one of them die as it happened to Versace?* Yet I was connecting the dots to the United States and global expansion. Dolce & Gabbana already had an office in New York, a place I was aspiring to be. I could move back to Milan, where the company was headquartered, and from there begin the leap overseas. I began to study the opportunity and the industry more closely. World textile and clothing trade had significantly increased in a few decades. I saw Dolce & Gabbana's talents, creativity, and willingness to grow into new markets—and my American dream perhaps moving closer. I was mapping out my own globalization and sought to risk it all for the opportunity to innovate and promote the Dolce & Gabbana brand on a worldwide scale.

I had the Christmas vacation to decide. During that time, as part of my desire to keep exploring the world, I took a trip to Africa again. And when I arrived, I was greeted by an unexpected host: fear. There had been previous times in Africa when maybe I "should" have been afraid, but I wasn't. For example, there was a time in Kenya when I went for a long run through terrain unknown to me—without any cell phone, as the systems were different, and I couldn't use mine. Here was a young blonde woman in short shorts, running past groups of Maasai—the region's traditional and sometimes fierce-looking people, about whom I knew little—in order to admire them. Yet I never really felt in danger from them and in fact I was not.

This time I had a different feeling. I was going to visit some friends I had met on my previous trip there. They were building a resort on an island which you needed to reach with an internal short-hop flight. But my international plane from Rome arrived too late for the day's only connection, so the airline put me up overnight in a hotel. Nearly all big cities have areas that are distressed and can therefore be dangerous because poverty can bring people down to hell and make them desperate to do anything for a few dollars. As a woman who often traveled alone, I had learned to recognize danger signs.

And on the ride from the airport to the hotel I could sense danger all around me. The hotel seemed to offer no promise of security at all. I found myself alone that night in a tiny room, behind a door that was so flimsy that just about anyone could barge through to get at me, my stuff, and my dreams. Panic set in. I knew I couldn't fall asleep feeling like that. So, I used music—my escape and source of strength—to entertain my fears. Alanis Morissette's "Thank U" and "Everything" were my favorite songs at the time.

> Thank you frailty
> Thank you consequence
> Thank you thank you silence

I danced by myself in that little hotel room until I got exhausted, and sleep was welcome. Nothing happened to me—fear was probably stronger than reality—and the next day I joined my new friends and lived with them the way they were living in Africa. Ever since that trip, I have continued to fall in love with the astonishing nature of Africa, which I have revisited several times. This was possible through recognizing my fears and learning to dominate them, not only by taking smart safety steps, but by learning how to deal with the inner churning of both rational and irrational fears which can eat us up if we let them. Indeed, that very skill would be needed when I returned from Christmas vacation to confront my career choice.

I resigned from Ericsson. And when I presented my resignation letter to Guido, he literally ripped it up in front of me. "You are playing Russian roulette with your career," he said. I told him I wasn't leaving him, and that I would miss his leadership and the company. I was taking the next step in becoming global and reaching my dreams. (He, by the way, became the best man at my wedding six years later as I managed to stay close to him and his family till these days.) Guido asked me to seriously think about my future, to take time and give him feedback after a more in-depth analysis versus an impromptu decision, because he knew I had too much to lose.

So, I gave the matter a deeper look. I asked for help from my mentors and found sensible advice from a McKinsey executive on how to proceed. He suggested I list the things that were important to me for staying with Ericsson in Rome, and the ones that could be relevant for moving to Dolce & Gabbana in Milan and then assign a numerical rating to each of them. The higher sum should give me an indication of what to do. I made that calculation several times, with different ratings given to various items. Although the sum each time pointed to staying in Rome, my instincts were stronger for going to Milan. One of my mentors, an executive from TIM, the biggest Italian network company, told me that fashion couldn't possibly be as fast-moving as technology, and I could get bored with the industry or not be stimulated enough by the challenges. Clearly, I had mixed feelings. I was living in Rome, a city close to my mother and a place where I had built a life again. My first adventures were the place where I lived, made new friends, turned youthful excitement into hands-on experience, and worked as a manager in the exploding technology field. In addition to that, Rome was where I had purchased my very first apartment. It was where I had finally banked enough money to feel a bit of security. As much as I'd like to think I am not the kind to be attached to material things, my own home was much more than a possession; it was living proof of my hard work and achievements to date.

The idea of leaving all of this brought some nervousness, and I had to focus on the instinct in my gut pushing me to take a leap of faith. "Walk On," a song from U2 with its beautiful lyrics, was my boost.

You've got to leave it behind
All that you fashion
All that you make

Listen to the crickets

After spending days reflecting on what to do, I followed my instincts and decided to take the risk. As I packed my belongings for the short one-hour flight to the fashion capital of Italy, I began dominating my fears. It was curiosity that had to lead me on my journey. The curiosity of surprise and all it could offer me would be one way to look at my venture. Or the curiosity of facing the things I did not yet know by moving to a whole new industry. These would have to be part of the habits I had practiced in Milan when I first arrived there with two small suitcases to work for Samsung just a few years earlier. And here I was again, with a few suitcases, this time at Paolo's apartment, staying with my old friend from university who hosted me again, now in his own place to give me time to find an apartment for myself. I cannot forget his generosity, or his willingness to overcome his shyness at having a blonde girl around his home late at night or early mornings in pajamas in the kitchen. After a few weeks of being a roommate, I finally found a one-bedroom very close to my future office. The rent was expensive for that time, and I had to pay my mortgage in Rome too. I was worried about not being able to make it. Back at Ericsson, I had a life contract (that is how the labor market worked in Italy then.) At Dolce & Gabbana my contract was for only two years with six months of probation. Since the work market was not as mobile as in the United States, making that change was a big proof of my audacity. But although the risk was high, I believed that being only 29 years old gave me a chance to start over again in case of failure. And most importantly, the opportunity to work for founders who were having a disruptive approach was the kind that wouldn't come along very often.

Fashion has always fascinated me. Beautiful garments and accessories can be like art you can wear and now I was curious to step behind the curtains of this industry and see how it functioned. I could learn to apply business skills in bringing the art of fashion to life, and there was no better way to learn than by working directly with the esteemed Designers (capital D!), Mr. Dolce and Mr. Gabbana. After starting the company in 1985 and winning extraordinary success through their creativity and craftsmanship, they now wanted to transform their family business into a leading global enterprise. I didn't know where this new venture would lead me, but I believed in the Designers and understood that I could be exposed to things and places I had dreamed about. Yes, I needed to pay a mortgage and a rent at the same time but if things were going well, I thought I could sell my apartment in Rome and buy one in Milan, which I eventually did. Finding different ways to look at things helped me to sleep at night and staying focused on my responsibilities was crucial to avoid feeling too overwhelmed by worries. Between 2001 and 2010, I was the Global Vice President of Dolce & Gabbana's Group. I led the Business Development Unit, which helped to grow up to 52% of the company's total revenues by the time I first left and which, throughout the course of my tenure, contributed substantially to the net profit and cash flow the company needed to sustain its overall growth. At the same time, I was expanding my knowledge, gaining new insights, and building my future with a view above the clouds. I was globetrotting to Japan, India, the United States, Europe, Russia, and the Middle East. I was attuned to where and how people were spending their money and devised the best plans for introducing Dolce & Gabbana to each country.

The very first week I started, the HQ offices in Milan were closed but not the ones in Legnano, a little village near Milan where the company had started and where part of the manufacturing was still done. I decided not to take a break but to be full in. I started to look at the industrial side of the company rather than the business side, to gain more knowledge of how everythings really worked on the back end of the operations. I was commuting for almost three hours every day, but by starting my venture this way, I saw the opportunity to get familiar with colleagues I would otherwise know only via email. I asked to meet the heads of the Supply Chain, Logistics, Finance, and Administration Departments, and everyone who could tell me about their experiences in the company, their roles and contributions. In short, I was doing the onboarding process by myself, which is a common practice nowadays but was very unusual in the early 2000s, especially in Italian companies. I didn't know how big of an impact I was making, but when the offices in Milan reopened, I was already known as a strong outsider with ideas and determination.

Again, curiosity came to help. I was curious to know how this company grew, who was doing what, and how they were organized. Curiosity was my friend from the beginning of my time in the fashion world. I probably looked like someone who appreciated style, but I needed to know more. I went back to study. I bought myself several books and studied the industry to be able to communicate in the same language with my colleagues and superiors, the Designers. I studied the fashion world from the creative perspective too. I wanted to know who the most respected designers were, why they had taken certain sources of inspiration from the past, how art and history were influencing their choices and more. I was perceived as a businessperson who came from the consumer side, therefore, some of my colleagues looked down on me. I did not come from the likes of Prada, Valentino or Dior. Others saw my determination to learn as a threat and depicted me as "the blonde ambition" girl. That was not a positive comment for a young woman who wanted to learn and advance in her career.

Luckily, the Designers and Ms. Ruella, who was called "General Manager of General Affairs" but who for me in practical terms was the overall CEO of the company, truly respected my observations. Later, when I spoke up about people's attitudes, they persuaded me to keep making my analyses and even sent me to different countries so I could come back with insights into how to keep building their empire. On those business trips, I essentially acted as a consultant to them. I analyzed the countries politically, economically, and culturally, giving them my findings on market trends and consumer habits with specific information on the luxury market. None had asked for such a thorough overview of the markets, but I knew I needed to exceed expectations to win their respect. When we restructured a few businesses, we also worked with actual major consulting firms such as Bain & Company, PWC, and Deloitte. The company was seriously committed to raising standards and becoming a global leader. And for me that was a tremendous gig!

Shortly after my arrival, we launched the Light Blue fragrance, and that was the prelude to a super-successful time in my career move. The Light Blue ad campaign was also cleverly built around the striking blue eyes of English fashion model David Gandy, and the brilliant blue of the sea at La Canzone del Mare beach club on the Isle of Capri. Riding my red bicycle in Milan in heels and suits, I often looked up at the sky feeling grateful for the opportunity to taste the beginning of a new life. The first fashion show I attended was a day I will never forget. I was dressed in a white pantsuit which I sparkled with an elegant gold shirt with matching shoes, handbag, earrings, and even sunglasses. I saw people taking pictures of me in the street, but I wanted to avoid that and ran faster to get inside the gate where the show was held. I didn't want to impress anyone but the designers. I wanted to make sure they knew I was understanding and appreciating their world, and that I was as passionate and committed as they were in building a global business.

I spent time in the summer traveling around the USA, from the East Coast to the West and then down into Central America. By studying our numbers, the country, and meeting businesspeople there, it was obvious that America was a market where we had more opportunities to grow. I needed to understand the status of the brand, the appetite for luxury, and what could be the ways to build a more solid business there. After returning from one of my most memorable business trips—which started in Arizona, visiting a distribution center where I was picked up in a long black limousine like I had only seen in movies, and ended on a yacht in the Florida Keys, owned by a business partner based in Miami—I met with the Designers to show them my findings and discuss a plan for expanding our American presence. The meeting was held at the very special library at the office where only designers worked and none from the business side had access. While sipping an exquisite espresso kindly offered by the Designers and brought by the house maid who smiled at me, making me feel less nervous, my plans were all approved.

After a few months of excitement, a tremendous tragedy none could possibly imagine came to play a role in everyone's life. The attacks on the World Trade Center in New York on September 11, 2001, were a shock to the entire world. I was sitting in Milan, on the phone with the CEO's executive assistant, when she suddenly said she needed to hang up because something terrible was happening. I had no idea why she was acting so strangely. But when I realized what she was watching, I could totally understand her panic. And I panicked, too. All of us did. Michela, a person on my team who had lived in New York previously, was devastated. As the news came flooding from every channel, we all felt devastated by the tragedy, for the people who lost their lives and for those who were mourning them. In the days that followed the event, we all felt a sense of emptiness and terror at the same time, which grew from day to day. As in many industries, the entire international fashion world came to a halt. Shows were canceled, travels were postponed, and sales were dropping faster than a hot potato. The market was already facing the onset of a recession. But the economic effects were, of course, only one part of a much larger story, which had to do with human and emotional impacts.

I was extremely sad, and it was not easy to regain any sort of enterprising spirit. I was young and not prepared to understand this gigantic human catastrophe. Fear, which had been sitting quietly in its corner hoping to be right, was now having a party in my heart and soul. I tapped into my rational thoughts and analytical approach, looking for ways to break through the dark and move into life again. Not only for myself but for all the people I and the company were impacting. I did the only thing I was able to do, working relentlessly to bring out a good spirit. However, the temper of the times remained strangely dark and uneasy. Certainly, Europe was no stranger to acts of terrorism and civic violence. There had been many incidents over the years, in many countries, due to sources that ranged from political tensions to organized crime. But 9/11 was different. The scale of the damages and the thousands of people killed were more like what a city might experience in wartime—yet this did not happen in the midst of any war. It seemed unreal, like a fictional scene from a horror movie, yet it was real. And though New York is geographically far from Milan, the city had always lived in people's minds as a center of excitement and positive energies, representing the best of what the world could produce. Now that sense was disrupted, and it felt as if the flow of civilization itself was disrupted.

We had learned a new, much bigger, and scarier fear. As human beings, we needed to face this new status, which had caught everyone unprepared. I couldn't control world peace or give back lives that were taken and feeling useless was hard. But I understood from others that being a positive force, helping others, and working harder in times of despair and uncertainty was giving some form of hope, for myself too as I was facing an unknown new future with terrorism. Little by little—despite the new war in Iraq and despite other terrorist attacks scattered around the planet—life gradually resumed. We were all learning to adjust somewhat to this new reality. Like actors on a set being reminded that "the show must go on," we resumed doing what we knew, even if with a different awareness. Although we were powerless to change things, being close to people gave us all a greater sense of purpose.

Connecting the Dots

As a child, when I was suffering from tensions at home, I prayed every day and often that somehow, somewhere, I was going to find love, safety and more. I stayed focused and followed the breadcrumbs with faith, certain that I would eventually find myself far from the stresses and in the haven of a whole new world. And in faith too I found a new family.

In my first tenure at Dolce & Gabbana, I kept expanding my knowledge, gaining new insights, and building my future while engaging new business partners, adding new product categories and reaching new target audiences. I stayed true to making unobvious choices for myself and the company. One observation I made while touring Japan turned into a breakthrough success for the company. On my very first trip, I noticed that many Japanese wore prescription eyeglasses, which they typically bought from a respected brand. This seemed like an easier entry point to the Japanese market than fashion clothing, which was much more expensive and more tied to individual tastes. Japan was also known for producing high-quality frames. I suggested that we ought to manufacture and mark our glasses as Made in Japan. And because the material needed to be top-notch, I pushed for authorizing the use of titanium, though we had never used it before. This turned out to be a little revolution for the company and a significant tool for adding new customers. After that project, Marcolin, the company producing and distributing our eyewear at that time, wanted me to go to more meetings. I visited them often at their HQ in Longarone, in the Italian Dolomites. I would drive there in the BMW car the company gave me as a benefit when I got promoted. I loved it, it felt rewarding, and I was truly grateful. The eyewear industry had annual meetings at the Mido fair in Milan, Silmo in Paris, and Vision Expo in the USA, along with the most important one, the Global Summit, which was normally held in remote places where people could focus on crafting new plans. At these meetings my role was to introduce Dolce & Gabbana's latest initiatives in retail and fashion and to emphasize our investments in building up manufacturing capabilities and brand awareness, in order to inspire manufacturers and distributors to do the same in their own businesses and countries. I was constantly challenging them to invest more to deliver better results. One of the Global Summits was held in Sardinia. When I arrived in the late afternoon, I had to multitask on different projects and tweak my PowerPoint presentation to strive for being excellent the next day. But I couldn't skip dinner, which might have been seen as impolite. So, I dressed up in a beautiful Dolce & Gabbana gown, went to eat something quickly, and left early to keep working and be prepared for the morning after. It was a beautiful evening, and I really wished I could just sit outside, enjoying the atmosphere and the interesting people attending. The next day, the couple from South Africa I had met at dinner came to congratulate me for my speech. To me, Karen and Lawrence were particularly curious and different from the rest of the crowd, so we spoke for quite some time during our stay. At the end of the Summit, they invited me to visit them in Cape Town when traveling to South Africa. I normally never mixed business with personal relationships, but the level of interaction was too good not to take the risk. I said to myself that if something felt wrong, I could find an excuse to move to a hotel where I could be more independent. Since the very first trip to their home, we have become so close that I introduce Karen and Lawrence as my "adopted parents" and they call me their "adopted daughter." No papers needed to be signed; we lived and still live as if we are family. I learned so much through them! I grew much more and much stronger with their love. All I needed and all I had missed were there: unconditional love, higher standards, and more. They also taught me the best possible manners and useful etiquette I could learn; I called them Queen and King for that. Most importantly, they show me a way of living and sharing moments that proved how mutual love can make us complete as human beings. They inspired me to keep dreaming impossible dreams and I found in them the best examples of humanity I could possibly find. For different reasons, I didn't convert to their religion, but I realized in a new light that spirituality is the key to being the peaceful global citizen I wanted to become. Up to the present, Karen and Lawrence are still my role models, my mentors, my shelter, and my inspiration. I feel absolutely blessed to have them in my life. As with everything, fulfilling this relationship took time, dedication, and belief. I always gave my "adopted parents" first-track priority even when we were only acquitting and casual friends. I throw my love to them as the Victoria Falls throw water and believe in our deep connection despite any physical distance.

Evolution and change

At Dolce & Gabbana later on, we decided to change our eyewear partner and began working with Luxottica instead of Marcolin. The split was very painful for everyone. Karen and Lawrence understood, telling me that "business is business, and one has to do what has to do." Luxottica was indeed the right new partner at that time to expand the eyewear business further, since they also owned a big part of the retail distribution network worldwide, including stores like Sunglass Hut, Pearle Vision, and more. Together with Luxottica and the many professionals I had the pleasure of working with, we built significant growth around the world.

We were growing at double-digit rates and reminded ourselves how important it was to look further and expand our leadership by taking examples from the best. I constantly analyzed and observed our competitors, knowing almost everything they were doing to grow their business and brands in each category, channel and market, bringing facts, numbers, pictures, insights, and more. Often, I was the voice of many executives and employees, since few had the courage to speak up and deliver inconvenient messages. Challenges were in my veins, but I never knew that and honestly only learned recently that they are part of my DNA. At the time, I was just seeing myself as one who had a different voice and point of view. The Designers' agenda leaned more toward being independent than being bigger, as their freedom to do what they wanted in the way that they liked was more important to them than anything else. I always thought they wanted to be known in the fashion history books as masters of creativity and craftsmanship. At times, I would sit in difficult meetings and think of how much easier it could be to work in places where the Designers were not the owners. Simplifying complexity became my mantra and simply used common sense to make even the hardest decisions. I wasn't a yes woman, and not because I had nothing to lose but because I was willing to risk!

People said that if I chose to work in politics, I would be the one who could negotiate peace amongst countries. Work never scared me. I loved that new business proposals were coming across my desk—from opening hotels, restaurants, and spas to dabbling in water, home furnishings, and cars. One business that didn't take off from the start was D&G timepiece. The creativity, the price point, and the communications were not resonating with consumers, so I was assigned to this business to fix it. I needed to attend in Venice a meeting with distributors of each country where we had entered the market: from Italy to Turkey, from the UK to Russia. Going there not as a tourist but as a professional gave me a wonderful feeling and experience. I was staying not at a B&B but in a beautiful hotel; I was not eating a sandwich but a meal in a great restaurant. The strongest memory I have from that time was not only my stupor at seeing the Excelsior Hotel, where the meeting was held, but the stupor of the distributors in meeting me. They saw a young woman who, in their eyes, knew nothing about their markets, industry, or products, representing a company that supposedly was offering to help them. They were expecting someone else for sure. But I was not intimidated by their expressions or comments and kept on introducing myself and the company's initiatives. I needed to earn their respect; it was never granted to me with a simple introduction. It was tiring at time to win over each and every single businessperson I was meeting. My young age, my look, being a woman, were barriers for many to trust in my abilities. But I was incredibly determined, and even if at times certain meetings were intimidating, I was confident enough to give it a try. The more I talked with them, asking the right questions and giving them examples of possible solutions to the issues they were facing, the more they reduced their barriers toward me. Radiant and happy as a movie star who has won the Golden Lion Award at the Venice Film Festival, I spent two wonderful days meeting with them and left with a clear understanding of what to do next. I returned to Milan and started preparing plans to discuss with the Designers and the CEO. Being driven by data, having a strong sense of business and the ability to connecting dots helped to manage both the creativity of the Designers and the commercial approach of the companies with whom we were working. Season after season we grew our market share and built an incredible solid successful business, globally. I met again the same people at different meetings and with some, it felt almost like seeing old friends.

If there were moments of doubt about my move to Milan from Rome, I was quickly reminded of what my Dolce & Gabbana boss said about me when I first joined the fashion company. "That girl has audacity!"

Growing

In 2006 I had an opportunity to leave Dolce & Gabbana to become the CEO of a smaller luxury fashion company specializing in cashmere goods along with other items. Being a CEO was of course attractive but whether to accept the job was a tough decision, in part because other things were going on. That same year, I was getting married. Two years before, during my sailing trips in the Mediterranean and the Pacific, I had met and dated a young man who was living in Rome and was willing to commute to Milan every weekend, waiting long hours to see me on a Friday evening. After meeting only while sailing, something that with music and running still give me a feeling of joy and freedom, we started dating and I had promised I would visit him in Rome twice a month, then once, but ended up not being able to travel at all on weekends as I was exhausted from business travels and my demanding work schedule. My goal was to build a career all the way to the top, traveling and living around the world, while his was apparently simpler: marry me. For him, it was love at first sight. He waited patiently to become first a good friend, then something more. For his dream, he too was determined and focused. He was not at all a successful man focused on his career, had different ambitious, and was not in any way the type of person I expected to see as a potential life partner. I had actually thought I didn't want to be married at all, as I wanted to be able to move and live anywhere. Antonio seemed like an unobvious match for me, to say the least.

But among the many people I met, he had the kindest heart and with me was generous with his little fortune. He was wise and confident. Antonio told me once that I had agreed to date him because I knew perfection didn't exist. I found that sentence very powerful. He knew he wasn't "perfect," at least not for me, yet he was confident enough not only to pursue me but to tell me that. Speaking of differences, my idea of an adventurous life was to live in New York and travel the world, meet and mingles with different cultures, explore nature and life for my own personal growth, while his adventure goal was to someday trek all around Asia—on foot. He believed to have a soul of a Buddhist monk. I felt I was in front of a different human being. A dreamer in a different way. All of my friends were astonished when I started dating Antonio. They thought I would only settle for a big executive or an entrepreneur guy. I saw in Antonio serenity, love, respect, support, and a wall to lean on. The type who could give me loyal devotion, a family, and an anchor to rescue anything that might happen. I believe my upbringing influenced my decisions as I felt the power of a protecting man for the first time. We decided to marry after dating for a year and a half. Being so different, we knew it was a risky decision, but we were going to give it a try in the name of love.

Meanwhile, when I spoke to the Designers about my new business opportunity, they immediately counter-offered me more money and responsibilities and assigned me to lead the new jewelry project on top of everything I had already. That project required me to study all the jewelry competitors, from Cartier to Tiffany, from Van Cleef & Arpels to Bulgari; and help to build the teams, production facility, sales procedures—which were different than in fashion—marketing tools, distribution channels, etc. It wasn't equal to a CEO position, a role I had been dreaming of from a young age, but I thought that I was still young and about to marry so it was better to be focused on one step at a time. Disrupting my life with two big decisions could have led me to fail in one without knowing which was the good choice and which was the cause of any failure. My brother, who knew me well, told me "Since you are so engaged with life and you live very passionately, opportunities will come again. Don't think it is the last chance." With doubts about whether I had made the right choice, I did pass on the CEO offer and filled with love and excitement, I married Antonio and got a promotion.

For the wedding, the Designers gifted me a stunning Dolce & Gabbana one-of-a-kind dress. They also advised me on the style with which I should wear it. I needed to be like Audrey Hepburn in *My Fair Lady*. This was a huge compliment from them, since all I cared about was not to be fashionable but elegant—just as Eliza Doolittle learned to be in the movie, a woman who, like me, rose from a poor upbringing. Mr. Dolce's brother suggested the setting, a restored abbey along the Portofino coast called La Cervara. I felt like a real princess that day; the poor young girls who came from the Santa Severa Castle couldn't feel happier. I invited people who had been important in my life through the years to attend the wedding from all over the world, and we had a wonderful celebration. A touching video made for us by a talented creative director showed the emotions of that day set to the notes of the song "You Are Beautiful" by James Blunt. I must say that Karen and Lawrence, my adopted parents, were instrumental in making that happen. Karen kept telling me that, as a woman, I couldn't feel complete only through work. I should marry and, most importantly, have the joy of becoming a mother, which is the best job in the world. But my true fear about getting married was not only that my career ambitions might be compromised. In my home as a child I had seen, from my real parents, how bad things can be when a marriage goes wrong, and I didn't want to suffer as my mom did. Seeing the deep love and devotion that Lawrence had for his family made me believe that it could be worthwhile to take risks in life too, not just at work. My amazing, "adopted parents" and Shaun, their bright son, were our court of honor. Unfortunately, their lovely daughter, Janine, couldn't travel to Italy but she was and is close to me as well as her talented husband Warren. Andrea, Shaun's wife, came bravely as she is, with her newborn baby Max who was only two months old. We may live in different places, but we know we to have each other's love, respect, and care.

For the long walk from the bride's preparation room to the abbey, which had three sections, I decided to walk with three men who had given me sources of love, encouragement and peace. They were Lawrence, the father I wished every human being could have; Guido, my former boss, who believed in my potential and gave me real opportunities, and Ardelio, my mom's new life partner, who brought peace and serenity to her and to my childhood home. But I also needed to pay tribute to my roots and decided with my mom to have a special wedding celebration in Santa Severa. My mother took care of everything: invitations, flowers, all the organizing and related costs. Her words in her greeting cards to me and Antonio and her generosity of spirit never ceased to amaze me. With my mother's relatives and Antonio's family, we were blessed by the priests at a church run by the *Francescani* (the Franciscans) and had a delicious lunch at "L'Isola" the beach club in front of the Castle by the sea.

New goals, new fears

After a beautiful honeymoon, I went back to work happier than ever. My hunger to stay curious and filled with hope was restored, as I attended every conference available to become a better manager and learn more about sales, marketing, finance, and best practices. I started to dream about studying at Harvard. In fact, Harvard Business School had an executive program that I was eager to take. Every year in my annual review I would ask the company to send me to the program in lieu of taking a salary increase. I still had my eye on working in the United States, and if it would be for Dolce & Gabbana, I knew that New York was a real possibility. The CEO told me that although they were not giving me the opportunity to study at Harvard, I would learn more than any executive course could possibly teach by being a project leader for all the new challenges they were giving me. In a way, it's true that experience is the best learning. The learning opportunities were especially strong for me because my main partners were leading companies like Procter & Gamble, Bain, and Luxottica, and my travels exposed me both to developed countries to emerging ones—which at that time included India and China, where I went for the first times in 2002 and 2003. But I always wanted to strive for more, and leadership can be shaped best by also learning from those who are exploring new insight and ideas beyond your specific field of work. So, while I was truly grateful for the opportunity to learn about the major players in fashion and beauty, and the industry standards, market requirements and consumers' needs, not being able to attend the Executive Programs, I started to read business magazines and newspapers on the weekends to relentlessly improve my knowledge: *Harvard Business Review, The Economist, Financial Times* and more.

Dolce & Gabbana wasn't yet in all the product lines that our competitors had entered, and after analyzing our strengths and the markets, we realized that we could stretch our brand into makeup, for example. A new set of skills was needed and here again I was learning from the ground up. We launched the makeup line with ads featuring the beautiful Scarlett Johansson as Marilyn Monroe and had a wonderful exhibit in Milan. Ms. Forte helped to organize it in collaboration with Anna Wintour, the famous Condé Nast executive, and the displays included remarkable work by the photographer Irving Penn. Many people attended from the entire industry, including international celebrities. I will never forget the moment I finished negotiating the budget to make that event, and the overall launch, possible.

At the time, it felt like an impossible challenge to manage. I had to run to the hospital for my newborn son. As with every gift in my life, I needed to earn this one with pain. I had learned after my fourth month of pregnancy that my child was going to be born with a malformation in his abdomen. He needed to be monitored through the entire pregnancy to see if he could make it and would surely need surgery as an infant. After my angel Gabriel was born, the doctors said the operation should be delayed until he was two months old to allow him to get stronger. A mother instinct pushed me to keep going to the doctors well before that date. Then, when I rushed with my son to the emergency room one day, they treated me at first as a mad woman in panic. Which I was, but for a real reason. Gabriel was not even a month old that day and I felt something was not right. It turned out that listening to my instincts literally saved his life. His doubled intestine was causing obstruction, and he could have died if it wasn't immediately addressed.

When the Designers learned of the issue, they stopped calling me constantly for business reasons and only tried to reach me to check on our status at the hospital. I don't know how I survived the moment I saw my son attached to all the machines in the recovery room after the operation. I was about to collapse. Antonio was there all the time. We spent this tough moment together and learned that, although we were different in many ways, we were going to be excellent parents.

Gabriel turned one year old, and I organized a great party since by then we could finally stop worrying and not need to take him in for all the exams and tests he'd been having for the past 12 months. We could finally celebrate his baptism as well. I chose the San Marco Church in Milan, which has an amazing baptismal area inside. A cool alternative priest, Father Luigi, celebrated the Mass and then we went to the Gold Restaurant in the Risorgimento square. We were all dressed elegantly, and the sun lightened up one of the most memorable days of my life. Gabriel, in his little tuxedo, was smiling beautifully at all the guests, as I had reunited people who were significant in my life, including the amazing nurses and doctors who took care of him.

Feeling blessed for their great service to the community, I used that party to raise money for the hospital, where I learned again that your own problems can be nothing compared with some others and that in life, all is really relative since at the hospital there were many more serious cases. Staying positive, enjoying each moment, and living as if we are grateful to be here is the right approach. But somehow, we take everything for granted, forget the blessings, and complicate our lives with unnecessary issues.

Now, at last, life could begin again, and I could continue exploring it by adding more experiences and learning. Not only as a businesswoman but also as a mom.

Some takeaways

Update your Dream-Plans as you go, you grow and the world changes.
Be curious and not afraid of changes, use them as an opportunity to keep learning.
Take a step at a time and be patient. Time is a great asset to build a future.
Chase opportunities and don't miss them for lack of knowledge, you can still learn.
Fears are inevitable even to audacious people, but you can deal and dominate them.
Look for patterns in your decision-making and choose your own winning approach.
Save money to build your future, do not overspend. Be wise in making and spending decisions.
Be a good negotiator, with a win-win approach.
Surround yourself with inspiring people who can add value to your life.
Build your career, and your life too. Your future is a 360° project.

Three: Envision the Race
Human Pillar: Courage

"If everything seems under control, you're not going fast enough"
—Mario Andretti

It's wonderful to work and live in a situation where you feel at home. But for a person with dreams, life is like a long-distance race against time. Can you make it to the next marker, and the next, all the way through, before your time runs out? If that is not possible in your current situation, it's time to step out of the comfort zone and get back in the race. That was what I thought. And courage was the superpower that enabled me to follow through. We all have it within us—more courage than we know. It is awakened at the very moment when we reject the compromise of buying comfort at the cost of our dreams. Then we need to learn how to fire up the courage to say goodbye to familiar friends and places and keep it aflame to run with the leaders of a new pack. Coding your Curiosity is the mother of expansion. Audacity is the midwife. As for the role that luck can play in business, or in life "Luck is what happens when preparation meets opportunity." The more you become proficient in what you are currently doing—just as I had become proficient in meeting people and marketing mobile phones—the better you can demonstrate that you're learning to lead and are ready for an expansive leap across cultures.

A New Competition

Dream-Plan: To win

After a life-threatening crisis, many different feelings can follow. We may feel drained and fragile. Or we may be reminded that life is precious and resolve to follow up on dreams that we have delayed. When I went back to work after passing the most challenging moments of my life with my son at the hospital, I was ready for a change. I updated my curriculum and went to the company CEO for a meeting. I told Ruella that I wanted to do something different, but before looking for opportunities outside, I wanted to give Dolce & Gabbana the chance to offer me something. I emphasized that my ultimate goal was to lead the American operations and be based in New York City, since I was attracted by the mix of diverse cultures there which made me feel at the center of the world.

Of course, living in New York had been one of my big Dream-Plans all along. I had joined Dolce & Gabbana in the first place on the premise of thinking that it could lead to that goal. Now, as a mother, I had a new way to look at my decision-making. I was thinking of the example I would set for Gabriel in his growing-up years. Would I be a mother who waits for her dreams to come to her? Or would I show him, on every occasion, the courage that each of us can summon to pursue what's good and right for us?

However, I did not see value in bringing up all of this to the CEO. Ruella's chief responsibility was to the company, not to me. I simply underlined my specific desire and my hope that in achieving it, I could be of even greater service to a company I had grown to love. The message was clear, and the meeting went well—except for the result. Although the top post in New York was open, unfilled for a long time, I received no offer to fill it.

Domenico—Mr. Dolce—often went to the same gym where I worked out. One night we met there very late, as we were both putting in long hours at the company. He told me that the reason they didn't offer me the US position was not for lack of trust in me. They believed in me, but they were just not ready yet to invest in building up again the US market, given the aftereffects of the Great Recession of 2007–2009: "The market is suffering. There are too many questions. It isn't the right time." I truly appreciated that he reaffirmed his respect for me and explained his position. However, I did not agree with the company's choice to leave the US subsidiary with no direct leadership.

I decided to speak to some headhunters. I felt I had been holding off my dreams to the extent that they seemed impossible, and the way to overcome that was to open my mind to something different. Indeed, a headhunter called me for a different company than I was expecting. It wasn't Gucci or Prada or Armani. It was a Ferrari. I told my husband I was flattered, as the company was a global icon, but I had no idea why they called me. I went to the meeting with no expectations and left with my heart racing like a Formula One car. Mr. Mario Mairano, the Chief of Human Capital at Ferrari, seemed to me the kind of boss you would want to have in any company. He said he was searching for talented leaders to work with. I didn't know if he liked me, but when I left that meeting, I started to pray that he would call me again—and he did. He arranged a meeting with the man who could become my actual boss, Mr. Luca Cordero di Montezemolo, the Chairman of Ferrari. This marked my introduction to the top ranks of Italian industry. The Chairman was known throughout the country. He had first won fame as the right-hand man of Mr. Giovanni Agnelli, Italy's most powerful business executive of the late 20th century. Now he was extending his own right hand to shake mine. I was being considered for the leadership of Ferrari's Brand Business Unit, in charge of all the merchandise and distribution for the Ferrari brand. Before we discussed an employment agreement, however, I was invited to a social gathering, which I later understood was probably a sort of test to see how I would mix with high-level people. This was a dinner in Turin, home of the Fiat Group (which at that time owned Ferrari) and also home of the legendary Agnelli family and the soccer team Juventus FC. When I arrived at the villa, I was directed to a table. I hadn't been told that I would be dining with Mr. Andrea Agnelli, the young President of Juventus, nephew of the late Giovanni, and the latest in a long line of Agnelli influencing Italy's business, politics, and sports.

My head was swirling among a half-dozen thoughts and feelings. I did not expect a dinner of this caliber, so I was nervous. I need to remember my etiquette. Above all, on each of these types of occasions, I couldn't stop flashing back to the little girl I had been in Santa Severa, riding my bike to summer jobs. Now, here I was, having dinner with one of the most prominent families in Italy in order to get a new job! Carrying yourself well at a function of this type takes courage. You want to exude confidence, not make any *faux pas*, be friendly with the people who are scrutinizing you—and do it all with an ease that feels natural. Fortunately, I had the courage I needed, because I had been learning and practicing for such a moment for a long time. I was able to stride to my appointed chair and be seated with a strong, yet elegant posture. This I had acquired from my mother, whose posture was exactly so. Confronted with a gleaming array of exotic-looking silverware, plates, and vessels on the table before me, I was able to use each item deftly for its proper eating or drinking function. These advanced table manners were beyond the kind that my mother knew, in our modest household. I had taken the trouble to learn them from Karen, my "adopted mom" and my "Queen."

When leaving the villa that evening, I understood both the level of pressure and the importance of the role I could expect to have at Ferrari. I chose to take that challenge and resign from Dolce & Gabbana Milan, the company that had seen me become an executive, a wife, and a mom. It was a very hard decision. During my long notice period, four months, I was careful to respect the interests of the people I was leaving and the ones I would be joining keeping this information for me and the Dolce & Gabbana board only and acting with everyday colleagues and partners as I was going to be there forever. But then I got a surprise. Dolce & Gabbana invited me to run the operation in China, move to Shanghai, and expand their brand there. "Shanghai is the new New York," they said. "You will love it. Take this long weekend to think about it. It's a great opportunity. We believe in you and want you to stay."

It was the end of October 2010, and a national holiday was approaching, giving us four days off. After facing a tough decision in thinking about leaving my current job, I felt that I had made the right choice for my future, suddenly I had *two* possible futures to consider. Both were from offers that came unexpectedly, from unobvious directions, with each one asking me to leave my comfort zone and leap into unknown territories. This was certainly a better predicament than having no good choices in sight. And in each case, leaping into the unknown would be the kind of challenge I love. But how does one compare the opportunities of a new company and industry to those of a new continent and culture? The manner of choosing, itself, wasn't obvious.

Lawrence, the man I call my "adopted father," was there to brainstorm with me as he always was (and still is) when life business decisions are needed. We looked at the pros and cons of each choice. Either way, the learning and growth that I could experience would be great, but quite different. Both could bring many possible outcomes and impacts, for me and for everyone involved. What finally drove my choice was envisioning the outcome nearest to my dreams. To go to Asia, the world's new frontier, in the early years of what was even being called the "Asian century"—that was an amazing opportunity. But it was not an opportunity that had to be chased right away. China is vast. Many doors to many futures would open in times ahead. The high-performance, high-speed automotive company had closer ties to New York City, the place I was craving to live.

The decision

I love the thrill of contests. I thrive on dares. Yet I couldn't have felt more out of control as I made the decision to pack up my home in Milan, say goodbye to my Dolce family and friends and move to Modena, a small city of less than 200,000 people known for its balsamic vinegar, for having been the birthplace of Pavarotti ... and for extremely fast Italian cars. I was living the words of the race car driver Mario Andretti: "If everything seems under control, you're not going fast enough." Just as race drivers are known to experience a wild mixture of feelings, from utter concentration to high and low states, euphoria and disappointment, it was as if the transition was indoctrinating me into the principles of that life.

I knew that, like an Andretti approaching his car, I could not let feelings of doubt enter my mind. But there they were. Was I making a mistake? What about Dolce & Gabbana and the incredible family I found in the company? And what about Milan? The fashion hub, where I spent nearly a decade; where I fell in love; got married and had Gabriel. Maybe Shanghai would be more exciting? I was leaving comfort, familiarity, doctors, culture, and favorite coffee houses behind. I was relinquishing an industry I absolutely was passionate about. And for what? To operate on some higher frequency. Engage with new curiosities and tackle them with extreme courage.

When I imagined the seat harness locking me into the cockpit of a Scuderia Ferrari F1 car, I could see Manhattan approaching and I could sense the Ferrari DNA in my veins—speedy, spicy, and risky. It would force me to adapt to changing circumstances the way any living organism adjusts to sudden changes in its environment: swiftly or die. Competition always felt right, as I was quite often at the front of the race. The question was how my drive to win would interact with the cutting-edge ideas in this new industry I was about to enter.

After the shocks of the Great Recession, all industries were feeling the pain and all companies needed to rethink. Who would survive? Who would go under? And, most relevant to my new post with the Brand Business Unit: How could any company use its brand and story to survive? Ferrari had been at the front of the pack for years. Innovation, precision, ready, set, go! That was the Ferrari brand. But for every carmaker, the only way to ensure survival was to reflect on what they stood for in moments of uncertainty such as these. It had to be a combination of heritage and invention. They must have seen these things in me. "Different! Yet familiar"—I could almost hear them say it.

Perhaps that was also how Ferrari would be for me. It was going to be different from marketing fashion but not from luxury. And technology, the field in which I first built my career? Well, it seemed my worlds were colliding, with Ferrari's need to exploit new channels like gaming, virtual reality, and mobile apps. The two elements of my experience, technology and luxury, came together. And with that, I was off to Modena, preparing myself for the race like Lightning McQueen, the protagonist from the movie Cars: "Focus. Speed. I am speed."

It turned out that one of my projects was working with Disney in the making of Cars 2. The entire learning experience at Ferrari fit with my need to be faster, in front of others, unafraid. The company was indeed embedded in the driver's race mentality: Okay, be afraid if you must, before or after the race, but not in the moment of competition. During the race it was like Nike's slogan: Just Do It. As Senior Vice President of Ferrari's Brand Business Unit, I was called upon to unwrap my imagination in terms of both design and technology. I was forced to push myself to my limits to keep up with the incredible people in charge of these innovations. Although I thought I had already operated with the pedal to the metal, I was adapting to a new environment and learning from the best.

Because my job was to create products such as games and clothing inspired by the actual cars, I had access to secret offices. I learned a bit about how the engineers worked and how cars were conceived and molded. The products I helped to make were extensions of luxury cars like the Ferrari FF, which upon its 2011 release was the world's fastest four-seat automobile. We were entirely focused on the future. Ferrari World, located in Abu Dhabi and Ferrari's first theme park, was giving visitors the look and feel of the company's innovations in virtual reality versus mechanical or traditional rides.

Ferrari produced profits and cash flow, which benefited the public company as it was a part of the Fiat Group. Ferrari itself was not yet listed on the stock exchange but needed to act almost as if it was, because that was the future goal. The executive team, which included me, had a great deal of pressure and very high targets. Quarter after quarter we kept making progress and scoring excellent results despite new obstacles. From the late 1990s into the early 2000s, Ferrari's racing team had enjoyed a spectacular run of dominance, powered by design improvements plus the mastery of lead driver Michael Schumacher. A champion everyone loved and a man we were all missing. Indeed, Schumacher retired from that role (prior to his incredibly unfortunate ski accident), and at almost the same time, the overall Formula One rules were changed which resulted in nullifying some of Ferrari's advantages. Then, not long after those events, the recession had deflated the economy generally. We needed to race into the future faster than potentially the past glorious days could be dissolved under our heels. Working at Ferrari could in fact stamp people with psycho-emotional and physical stresses similar to the ones that race drivers' experience. For my Business Unit, the challenge to license the Ferrari brand in new ways was higher than expected. And for me personally, as a newcomer to both the company and the industry, that challenge was even wider but, as always, I used my role as a form of liberation combined with a new kind of test.

The beauty of changing your environment is that it gives you the opportunity to present "a new you." Preconceptions that people formed about you in the past are left behind. When I joined Ferrari as a mature woman, a mom, and a Senior Vice President, my team and my superiors were going to see a different person than the "blonde ambition girl" I was once perceived to be in the fashion world. Any change of scene will allow you to reassess your leadership style and show up at your best, making adjustments on the basis of what you learned from prior experience. People at Ferrari were able to see the woman and the leader I had become. Their perceptions were not clouded by images of who I used to be. And now, going forward, they would be a mirror for showing me who I really was. If certain things that I thought I had improved upon were still limiting my leadership, then I would have a big call-out moment, which would mean a further chance to fix myself as a human being. It definitely takes courage to go on such a test drive and accept the results. To my great surprise, my team at Ferrari made me realize that in addition to the competence I had wanted to pass on to them, what they appreciated the most was my human touch. If that was going to be the stamp I would make, I wanted to make it from my own perspective—the perspective of a woman.

Not Only a Men's World

Ferrari was a powerful lesson in concentration, since I needed to bring out my female viewpoints in conference rooms among throngs of men. One study has shown that men normally dominated a conversation up to 75% of the time. Combining that with the fact that I chose grace as the means of making my mark, speaking up to address issues made double the challenge.

At my first executive committee meeting, I walked into the conference room only to hear the now-former Chairman sputter "Who is this woman?" My confidence sank into the carpet. I was still adapting to Modena's small-town feel and the faster-than-normal, off-to-the-race early-morning-gunshot start of every workday at Ferrari. This was hardly the way to make an entrance. However, I quickly understood that the Chairman must have forgotten about my starting date since we had only met four months prior during the hiring process and didn't speak with him again. And of course, it was strange to see a woman enter a room where only men would normally be.

During the course of work at Ferrari, I sometimes felt I was back in my old days in the telecommunication world where most or all of the executives were men. But, because I had gone through this already, I wasn't scared. *I had a history I could build on: A history of using my courage to establish myself in male environments.* This time I was also coming in at a different level, and as a Senior Vice President, and I was determined to make a stronger impact without overshadowing anyone. One of my goals was to work together with my male colleagues to help promote a diverse culture in the company. I intended to prove my values with the quality of my work and make my voice heard with the power of clarity, professionalism, and expertise. In meetings with my team, I made sure to give comments that could help win people over one at a time. Each person wants to feel engaged and valued. Good interaction along these lines is key to making sure there is a constructive dialogue.

Coupled with curiosity, my courage to jump into the unknown and gave me the fuel to learn rapidly about new fields. Using the methodology I had learned throughout my experiences, I was trying to set a fast pace in every meeting and gain trust amongst the boys. I knew it was harder as a woman to work in a men's environment, but I refused to take that as an excuse. Regardless of gender statistics, I used my creativity, my sensibility, and my empathy to propel me forward. It didn't take long before my voice got heard and my ideas started to resonate. A few short months into the job, I began to feel that I was not only accepted but also respected. This happened after I gave a big corporations' executive management a program for our B2B (Business to Business) partnership. By understanding their needs, I suggested a program including branded merchandise that could be useful to their teams and also be sold to consumers in their chains. Most importantly, I proved that creativity and quality could be achieved while respecting the budget and schedule. These are essentials for any program to succeed. It helped that I could draw on my work in the fashion world, where you can miss your target by missing deliveries for a season even if the product offering is great. But I always felt that my need for independence from a young age helped me even more in learning to conserve money and, therefore, respect budgets. Saving was very important for me. From my first summer job in middle school and onward, no matter how little I had made, part of my earnings, from scholarships to salaries, needed to be untouched to grow my personal savings. I have applied a *lot* of what I learned from my challenging upbringing in business. And because of my competitive approach to life, I was always giving myself higher targets than any boss could possibly give me. If the goal was to spend 100 as best goal scenario, I wanted to complete the job at no more than 95. If the best lead time for the production of something was eight weeks, I wanted to deliver in seven. One by one I kept earning partners' trust and respect, being for them a reliable source who could make things happen quickly and with high standards. Internally, my ideas were treated with more consideration and my presence came to be welcomed. Even the Chairman displayed a greater calm when I was around. Ferrari was the first place in my life where I saw, very evidently, the effects that a mature woman can have in a male environment: a soothing force in a driving room, an harmonious partner in an otherwise cut-throat negotiation, a breath between sentences, and a colorful hue amid a lineup of grey suits.

Being a woman slowly became a vapor slipping its way out of each room. I felt empowered and like just one of the other leaders, treated fairly and with respect. It couldn't be only a man's world after all. The only test that remained to be made was testing my ability to see things, and respond to them, as sometimes a woman in a boy's club is uniquely able to do. I learned that in a sea of men where it's raining aggression and ego, a woman can be like an umbrella that keeps the drench from staining shirts. If my skirt was the indication of a woman's touch, my courage would be the tone of a woman's accomplishments.

The Courage of Phenomenal Women

Not every woman has the desire or the good fortune that I had by working at Ferrari. Others will enter different environments and of course the results may differ, too. We don't live in a one-size-fits-all world. Everyone's life is a designer original. However, I would urge everyone to have more courage in whatever pursuit they have in mind.

Courage is indeed a superpower. It enables you to drive ahead, to go beyond your thought—while navigating through tricky turns among your fellow racers!—instead of just idling in place, wishing your dreams would come true. Far too many of us get stuck that way. Surely you, dear reader, know people who "hold themselves back" from being and doing all that they could. Due to fear of failure, or any of a hundred other fears, some of us shy away from even taking the first steps. We don't try out for the school play or the sports team. We settle too often for obvious careers and life choices instead of dreaming and planning as we really dream inside. Worse yet, we also hold back from seizing the on-the-fly opportunities that come and go in the flash of a moment. That friendly stranger you hesitated to speak to—might it have been someone who could change your life? Was there a time you had the chance to stand up for what you knew was right—and you didn't? None of us is perfect. We all miss some opportunities; we all have fears. But courage is more than a tool for overcoming or negating fear. Courage is a positive power within us, and once we get used to using it, we can feel what a "natural" superpower it is. *Courage comes from who we really are and expresses who we really can be.* This realization is especially important for women. Often since my Ferrari days, I have thought that I am just one of the MANY women out there who try every day to express the best of themselves. In search of change and progress, we all leave our mark on cities, countries, and worlds. And we learn endlessly. First, we learn from our families. Then we move on to learn from our teachers in school. Then, we move out—out of our homes and into universities, or jobs, where we learn from professors and managers. And, of course, we move up—up in our roles as we set our sights high to achieve and become role models for new generations.

When I think about the power and beauty of women, I cannot help but think of Maya Angelou's poem "Phenomenal Woman." Women are indeed phenomenal. Our radiance is energetic yet calming. Our endless search for fairness may bring us at any moment into a challenging fight, and our strength is compelling and comforting at the same time. In our workplaces, with our friends, and with our families, the world is filled with incredibly talented women. I have had a phenomenal woman in my life, my mother. A special lady in her kind.

Her surname, Arcangeletti, is a derivative of the English word archangel. She was more like a feline to me and showed me the living meaning of the expression *fight like a lion*. Yet she demonstrated generosity, fairness, and integrity every step of the way. My mother was indeed called *La Leonessa*, The Lioness, the great one amid the wilderness. To me she was the epitome of beauty: fine lines and a strong spine. When she put on her top-notch suit with makeup and hair just so, she wasn't being picked up by a chauffeur to be taken to the corner office. Instead, at a time when most women in Italy didn't even have a driving license, she would drive herself a few miles across town in her tiny old Fiat 500 Classic to arrive as the housekeeper at the family's home where she was employed. The Lioness, in all her pride, worked 10–12-hour days in rubber-soled shoes and a housecoat with a bucket of water and mop in hand. All the while, her hair was pinned perfectly, and her high heels waited quietly by the door anticipating the drive home. When prestigious people like the sisters of one esteemed Italian President came to town looking for staff, they always turned to the police for suggestions. My mother was at the top of the list as being honest, serious, respectful, and sophisticated. She had an elegant presence and spoke intelligently to her bosses, acting with the utmost discretion. She was as pristine as the water of the African Great Lakes and dressed to the nines like an acacia spreading her branches. She was much more than her social class; much more than her unfortunate relationships with men; and much more than her daily grind. In fact, as she is still living, I can say she has self-esteem, radiance, and an echoing roar from the cliffs of intention that go far beyond her circumstances. Mother was born in 1941 during World War II and was left to grow up in an orphanage at the age of four. There were no "The Sun Will Come Out Tomorrow" melodies lullabying her to sleep at night. The only candies she tasted were brought by Americans at the end of the war. She never attended college; in fact, she only made it through elementary school. But I never met anyone more willing to learn than her. Though she lacked formal education, she had the wisdom of proverbial expressions, and though I didn't understand their impact on me as a child, I have found myself using the very same colloquialisms at times with my son. She suffered from living in the same hazardous household as I did, she never missed a day of instilling honorable values in me. Growing up, I watched my mother work multiple jobs; act as the head of the family and manage the finances. When it became clear to her that my father wasn't making enough money as a bricklayer, she started selling her knitwear to boost our household income. And when that wasn't enough, she supplemented it with additional housecleaning and gardening. Word of her meticulous sweeping and tidying spread and she had a fully booked schedule, serving the affluent people of the village. Nobody can be sturdy as a stone without understanding themselves, their heritage, and the power of their actions, which it appears my mother did. Beauty is most certainly in the eye of the beholder, and mother was always splendid to me.

At Ferrari, I was privileged to bring about the positive effects that many other women believe in the possibility of having. Whenever I led visiting executives on tours of the Ferrari factory, walking around the big Maranello headquarters in my female suit and high heels, I was implicitly expressing my power. I never compromised my femininity, but I never abused it either to get a higher position. Men will test you sometimes to see who you really are. Sometimes they think they can approach you differently just because you are a woman. I was true to myself and kept the highest standards, first because I was confident of my abilities but, most importantly, because I always acted in life thinking that I had nothing to lose. My personal goal at that company was to be accepted by my male peers as a colleague they could trust and work with. I never went into meetings with a judgmental or challenging approach toward them. Instead, I went in feeling the same as the men: a human being with strengths and weaknesses, and a professional who wanted to achieve the best possible results for our company. I believe my way of acting and reacting was considered solid, mature, and serious. I think that having me around was as easy as being with other executives, and sometimes better. There were many times I could use my woman's viewpoint to shape a dialogue on how best to strategize and build business that was inclusive of Ferrari fans and owners and the people around them, mostly wives and kids. A step further would have been targeting women as potential buyers of the cars, but during my time, that was pioneer thinking. We started by creating better products for women and kids. One of the projects done was a new collection with the Tod's Group, where I met a passionate lady who knew everything about shoes. Marta was elegant and cool at the same time, wearing beautiful pearl earrings but of different colors: one with a golden yellow hue, one silvery grey. She taught me a lot about how shoes are constructed to be comfortable, and I think she enjoyed working with someone who could also bring a feminine touch to understanding the business of fashion.

Courage is contagious. I have learned to use my courage, in part, by watching my mother use hers. And courage is cumulative: I've been able to build a career in business thanks to the courageous work of women before me who broke down barriers. Which leads to another point we must grasp in building a full awareness of this superpower. Individual courage is not the only form. It is possible, in fact it is necessary, for organizations to act with collective courage as well and make an impact. Economic progress is driven by companies that have the courage to go beyond business as usual. Social progress is driven by groups and governments doing the same. Human progress on every front is led by those who use their courage.

Everything But the Car

Ferrari had the requirement of appealing to two major target groups. There were the lovers and collectors of Ferrari automobiles, who belonged to the luxury category. Then there were the Formula One fans, who, aside from being loyal followers of the race team, might purchase Ferrari-branded goods within a range of low to high price points. I was assigned to manage the worldwide product offerings—basically, everything but the cars themselves. My hands were in retail, wholesale, and online distribution, at every step from conceiving ideas to the manufacture of products; from the marketing proposals to the execution of advertisements; and from the go-to-market strategy to planning special events. My team and I needed to manage resources for promoting, positioning, and licensing the brand, always working to sustain growth with a constant analysis of profit and loss. I have signed significant agreements around the world, influencing stakeholders, from various companies such as Puma, Hublot, Vertu, Santander, and more. The breadth of channels I was covering stimulated my vision the way a kaleidoscope transforms light into myriad shifting shapes. Everything was an intense education in the agility and decisiveness needed to be a successful leader.

Somewhere in the thick of it all, I got caught in a fog, literally. This was during my trip to China to examine potential new supply chains and distribution channels. I went to meet the owner of a fashion company who had bought the rights to develop Ferrari merchandise in his territory. The meeting was held in his villa, which was located on an island outside Shanghai. I could see the ongoing development of China when I went to my hotel. It had an amazing lobby with the highest ceiling I have ever seen in a building other than an immense cathedral. The rooms were on the top floors, which should have offered a great view—but the grey density of the sky wouldn't let me see the landscape and panorama stretching in front of me. I wondered what people's sentiments could be like, living constantly in a place where you cannot see the blue of the sky. I wasn't sure if that atmosphere helped to develop an inner sense and strong imagination, or something else. The head of Ferrari China, a Frenchman who had been living there for a few years, told me the water was so polluted that he didn't use the shower. Instead, he filled the bathtub with mineral water. I understood from him that life there wasn't yet easy. Maybe it needed more time to become a nicer place to live.

It was interesting to witness the personal life of a wealthy Chinese citizen back then. His taste in interior design was impeccable and his leadership team was very professional, to my surprise, the Chief of Retail was the tallest Chinese woman I had met. She was skilled, elegant, and graceful. They have been working with Ferrari for a few years but have had some complaints about the partnership. I was there with the aim of renegotiating our deal and increasing Ferrari's market share and profits. However, I needed first to rebuild trust and mutual understanding and then improve our performance. The meeting went exceptionally well and throughout the entire time, with that trust and respect, we could keep challenging the Chinese team to deliver better product offerings, promotions, and point-of-sale support for the Ferrari products in his country.

Coherence

Elsewhere in the world, one of the most challenging partnerships to keep was the one with a sport brand. We had an important deal that helped to put the Ferrari brand and merchandise in their stores globally, while giving them the right to produce race drivers' uniforms with their brand affixed. I managed to renew the big, important deal with this company and strengthen the partnership by actively participating at each meeting, going to their headquarters in Europe and, most importantly, working closely with all the teams at different levels. I had learned from my previous time at Dolce & Gabbana that the success of any partnership depended not only on winning good terms in the negotiation process, but on how the execution from both parties was handled and how much commitment, resources, and focus were given to that particular business.

But at a meeting in which my boss wanted me to renew a deal that I did not think was right for the brand, I wasn't present. I didn't want to be. It was my way of distancing myself from something I didn't believe in. The Ferrari brand wasn't mine, and more than expressing my opinion and speaking out, I couldn't do anything. Or maybe I could. When my boss learned of my absence from that meeting, he called me on my cell phone and for the first time he was truly furious and disappointed. That evening, I thought he might fire me. But as I was removing my makeup in front of the mirror before going to sleep, I said to myself that even if that had happened, my son could have been proud of my choice. I simply could not act in conflict with my beliefs. That thought was enough to give me the stamina to maintain my stance and keep working hard. I was also very busy developing a high-end watch business for Ferrari fans through a partnership with Hublot. Their CEO was introduced to us by the Agnelli family. I was invited to a private lunch with them to learn more about the brand and potentially make a deal. While for certain things I was not in agreement with our Chairman, I have to say that he always included me in business decisions. That process was key to making me feel valued and truly empowered as I had never felt before. Guido had done the same earlier in my career, but the level of the people I was meeting during my time at Ferrari was much higher, and I never took any invitation for granted and always gave an enthusiastic approach to these opportunities. We signed an agreement for a special series of Hublot Ferrari watches, which we then introduced at the world's most important watch fair in Switzerland. I was learning the names of different cars and putting the design of the engine and wheels onto products like mugs, model cars, school bags, and even shoes. I was operating on what felt like pure adrenaline each day. With everything that was driving me to produce results at incredible levels of pressure, I felt incredibly under a lot of stress and unsafe driving myself to work under the unfamiliar thick fog on my way to the office and home. The highs and lows of the races I was running there every day could put me at risk of finishing my commute in a real-life crash. The stress was mounting and one way I could relieve some of that pressure was to have my husband bring me to the Ferrari headquarters. It became the habit that when he was home, he'd shuttle me back and forth to work, some days with scary moments for the lack or even absence of vision at where the car was going.

Close to the building where the Brand Business Unit was housed, we had an admired automotive salon called "Le Classiche." It displayed the most iconic Ferrari cars, which were used for special occasions by famous people and were collected by the company as well as by distinguished collectors around the world. I could not imagine how many different people were Ferrari fans, not for F1 but fans of the amazing sports cars, in which technology met the most advanced design. Everyone who passed by this hidden treasure had their jaw dropped twice, living an emotional experience just from being surrounded by so much history, design, and technology at the same time. Ferrari is an expression of art but in a different field. Instead of a showroom filled with dresses and accessories as it was at Dolce & Gabbana, I needed to pass this admired area each time I was summoned by the Chairman with whom I was working closely. I learned to appreciate our cars by seeing them with the eyes of the people I brought in. My favorite building was the one at the end of the factory, the most modern one where new cars were conceived. There I went as often as I could. My walk there was the longest from the building I was assigned to. Of course, I requested to be moved into my favorite one, since it represented the future and I wanted my team to be inspired by that, to stimulate their imagination and sense of envisioning. Maranello, on the outskirts of Modena, felt a bit like the Radiator Spring depicted in *Cars*. I watched that movie countless times with my son who was riding his first Ferrari bike at the time, dressed in Ferrari gear, and probably having the best food he had yet eaten. Life in Maranello was calm, affording the highest level of quality to raise a family with young children. While living this pleasant family life I was also programming performances for the future, since I had realized that was the only way to keep up with how the world was changing, faster than we could have imagined. For anyone leading an organization, programming personal and organizational performance is crucial. We need to consider how we can upgrade performance and embrace paradigm shifts to deliver innovations that will set new rules of the game.

Yes, I Am!

"Yes, I am" does not come without *No, I'm not*. Confidence doesn't exist without doubt or courage without cowardice. This truth can be traced back to the philosophy of Yin and Yang, which observes that black doesn't exist without white, or happiness without sadness.

It wasn't until Ferrari that I understood confidence on a whole new level. To begin with, there were very few people in the world whom I could trust. I was left to my own devices so often that as a child, a youth, and an up-and-coming woman of the world, I used tunnel vision to build the protective walls that I thought I needed to learn self-confidence. I was lucky that tenacity lived inside my toes; that faith walked along the labyrinth of my mind; and that curiosity pulsed in my dreams like a bomb ticking, ticking, and ticking without explosion. But my bold façade did not live without immense questioning.

In meeting with leaders, chairmen, and founders of high-caliber companies, I felt the same euphoria as a race driver approaching the paddock. It wasn't just being in their presence, exciting as that was. It was seeing that I could handle the conversations with them despite my nerves. It was learning that I was gaining respect because I understood business the way they were discussing it. As I was pulled into conversation after conversation, I became like a snowflake, able to swing in multiple directions. At Dolce & Gabbana, I had been a young woman in search of true confidence. I felt safe there. And what I know about confidence today is that when we feel safe, we can lose perspective. It is in raising new challenges that we get our hearts racing and that is how I became stronger. At Ferrari, I had real autonomy in heading up the branding and marketing efforts. I felt motivated by the description of the automobile as supreme, excellent, and legendary. I wanted to be all those things, and it was easy to get out of bed each morning and get my engine racing ... Or, at least it was easy until I began to feel that I missed living in a big city.

Five-star quality

Modena has a charm that appeals to many who have lived there for years. It does not offer many options of going to theatres or to concerts, or of having the wide variety of experiences that I have enjoyed in big cities. With all its beauty, traditions, and wonderful people, Modena at that time, while I wasn't even 40 years old, was feeling small as I was still dreaming of living in a big cosmopolitan city like New York. I started to sense that this stepping-stone I temporarily called home might turn me into a sculpture in the square and leave my New York City dream to drift into the mist of winding roads and disappear in the rearview mirror. I was having doubts.

On the other hand, I couldn't feel more spoiled than when I was living in Modena. My husband was happy. He likes small towns where he can move easily, have a slower rhythm, enjoy a stroll in the sunshine, and visit the local market. He interacts very little with people because he is shy and reserved but he liked everyone we were meeting at the shops and restaurants or on the street. On Sundays, we used to go for lunch at a restaurant just outside the city, where the quality of the food was worth 5 stars, but the price was for 2. During the week we had the help of our moms, giving us the freedom to leave the house at any moment with our son in their loving hands. My mother had been used to visiting my son Gabriel every other month. When she lost Ardelio, her amazing partner whom she met at the age of 55 and the only one who I loved too, I suggested that she wear a smile on her face and stay with us for a while, until she was healing and deciding how and where to live next. Our home in Modena was the largest I ever lived in. The beauty of the villa was astounding. The ceilings were painted as if in a church, the floor was antique mixed with parquet, and the spacious rooms all had green views of the trees. My whole family seemed to be having the greatest time. Faced with this grandeur of serenity, I began to ask myself difficult questions. *How long could I live without a big city life? Where would the self-belief come from, to get me to New York?* I had just sold my apartment in Milan, thinking that I would buy one in London to go there every weekend and have my son learn English from a young age, but while I was looking for it, I began to think I had made a huge mistake in moving to Modena. I loved big cities so much that a friend of mine once told me, "You are a city animal," and I never really understood him until I reached the point where I was feeling the lack of buildings and, most of all, the mix of cultures and variety of minds.

Moreover, there was no conversation with me about New York at Ferrari yet. That dream was made of posters in my mind, with the luscious green of Central Park abuzz in summer activity and the swarms of amazingly diverse people hustling into skyscrapers en route to the 52nd floor. In Modena, I wasn't feeling happier *per se* than when I was living and working in Milan. I had started work at Ferrari completely out of my comfort zone. Over the months, I was turning my core strength into genuine confidence, and it all happened as fast as a car notching up its speed from zero to 90 miles an hour. And just as I felt all the signs of becoming a champion, the missing of big-city life grew like the growling of a stomach after a full day without food. Happy at work but silent in my personal life.

One day I received a call from Stefano Gabbana. He asked, knowing me quite well: "How are you doing in Modena?" I told him about my constant travels and my executive management experiences but said nothing about my stomach pangs for city life. I resisted, despite my feelings to go back and do the same work he wanted me to do. I recall telling him, "When you became a successful designer of clothes and wanted to add other categories, what if someone had told you that since you are so good at making clothes, you shouldn't try? I simply need to try other things. And I want to get to New York one day, to do something different there." I don't know this as a fact, but I feel that those words and that call were significant for letting Mr. Gabbana understand that I was not wrong, and that my ambitions were not impossible or different from his. It wasn't long until Mr. Dolce stepped into the act, in a more romantic way than I could have expected. He contacted Antonio and asked for his support to give me a surprise. It was Valentine's Day. I received some beautiful flowers and Mr. Dolce's letter with a big red heart brushed on it, expressing his gratitude and love for me. Can you imagine how tempting it was to get back to him right away? I called to thank him for the beautiful message and touching surprise. I told him I would stop by to say hello on one of my many trips abroad, since I needed to take the international flights from Milan anyway. I also told him that one day I would come back to Dolce & Gabbana but the time was not now, and surely it would not be for doing the same job again. I think I was able to convince my former bosses that I was firm in my decision to move forward, not backward. And let me tell you, when I hung up the phone, I was about to cry from keeping inside the temptation to run back to my beautiful life in Milan!

After a few months, when my presentation on the 5-year strategic plan was completed, I was going to travel from Milan and only then I did stop at the Dolce & Gabbana offices to say hello to Ruella. While walking in, I looked at the pictures on the wall of beautiful dresses made over the years and felt a bit nostalgic. Ruella and I sat down in the black chairs, and I started the conversation by saying how much I had appreciated their offer to go to Asia.

"China is booming!" I exclaimed, having of course visited for Ferrari. "How is your person doing there?" I asked.

"Good, good. We've got our president there and we are on the lookout for the Chinese team. Everything is great."

"I'm very happy in my work," I said. "I think I am learning something I needed for getting to a new level."

Then, when I was least expecting it, Ruella caught me off guard: "The US post is still available. We decided to appoint a new President in New York office, and we want you to take the job."

In no time, my eyes filled with tears of emotion, and I was busy struggling to let them run down my cheeks. My mouth fell ajar as musical notes of joy pushed their way out and up into the air. Certainly, I would have zero negotiating power with that expression, but I didn't care.

"We've reconsidered the market," Ruella said, "and after strategic consideration, we understand the necessity of a new beginning for Dolce & Gabbana, with the D&G [a separately branded line] closing, the Haute Couture project coming and the first store ever on Fifth Avenue. Both our goals can be met. Will you rejoin us?"

I couldn't speak. It was all I could do to hold back the tears. I extended my open arms, as if for a group hug. This was exactly what I wanted and for which I had worked for such a long time. Ruella even told me that although she couldn't make the offer earlier, when I had asked for it, she admired my courage in leaving. She knew that with my additional experience at Ferrari, I would surely bring them the leadership they needed. They were ultra-kind in making out the terms of a contract and we were like a family in reunion. I felt my *Yes I am!* confidence bursting out of my cells as visions of New York blurred into a rollercoaster of joy.

The first person I called was of course my husband. I told him—probably screaming, crying, laughing, and letting loose every reaction that pure joy can give you—that we were finally going to move to New York. I needed to figure out my way of leaving Ferrari. And then, as we began speaking about how to organize ourselves for the move, we thought of the grandmas. We didn't think the move would be good news to them, since we would have to leave them in Italy. But when we broke it to them, they were super-happy for me and for us. They said that we were young, that we deserved to achieve our dreams and live our lives the way we wanted, which is what they had tried to do with theirs. We went to our favorite cozy restaurant outside the city to celebrate. That day, the owner didn't let us pay, despite knowing that we were not going to be repeat customers any longer. It was just a beautiful Italian touch we will never forget.

As much as I felt like the famous Ferrari driver at the time, Alonso, when he was winning a race, I needed to be like him when he was train-ing and focused on fixing the car for the *next* race. Indeed, I had many responsibilities, which I now needed and wanted to undertake. From how to leave my team, to how to leave the Ferrari partners, the Ferrari owners, and anyone who had given me the chance to feel like a confident business-woman—I owed all of them a proper handover and profound recognition. Mr. Mairano had said to me once, "Ferrari gives you the stars," and indeed I had earned them with the stripes of my hard work. We discussed at length when and how to communicate my decision to the team. Since I was always transparent, the people at Ferrari understood that I came in committed to them when I faced hard times adjusting to the company at the start. But Mr. Mairano warned me that I might get a strong counteroffer from the Chairman. I didn't believe that was even possible. When I met with him to inform him that I was going to leave in the fall, he told me that he truly appreciated me, my way of working and everything I had done so far. Hon-estly, I didn't expect that either.

When I spoke to the CEO, Mr. Felisa, a wonderful gentleman with whom I built a friendship that has lasted to these days, he explained that something I never knew: "at times, your opposite point of view to the Chairman was very needed in the company to create more harmonic choices. We will miss that, and the Chairman will miss you." While I was extremely happy that my dream was coming true, I felt bad for disappointing other people with my choice and hurting their feelings—including the team members who believed in my leadership. I sat with them and explained that I was going to pursue a longtime dream, which had come a little late and a little soon. I assured them that Ferrari was a great company; that I had an amazing experience, and that I was not leaving for any other reason than a personal one. Ferrari was great to me, and I wanted to be a point of reference for them anytime they needed me.

Before long, just as Mr. Mairaino had predicted, the Chairman called again to make sure there was nothing he could do to keep me. For a moment I thought that with such negotiating power, I could ask for anything. But a few thousand euros more in my bank account wouldn't make me happier. Antonio was in agreement, since money was not my criteria for making career choices. I sincerely thanked everyone at Ferrari but reconfirmed my resignation and decided to leave by October. In such a short time, my mark at Ferrari and Ferrari's in me had become as evident as all the victories of the seven-time world champion Shumacher. And every bit of it happened *fast*, as it did on a racecourse. While packing from Modena to head for New York City, I truly felt like a true champion!

Some takeaways

Doubting yourself is necessary to keep staying alert then test yourself with decision-making.
Configure your self-confidence from to trying new things and show the best side of yourself.
Challenge yourself to bring strong performance, keep deadlines, and stay on budgets.
Have a strong sense of responsibility while performing your job.
Create a sense of trust in you, your approach, skills, and abilities.
Balance your life to get into a healthy routing to reduce stress.
Get out of your comfort zone to keep growing. Don't look back to move forward.
Courage is a superpower, it's contagious and cumulative. Learn to use it.
Respect people you leave behind while you move ahead.
Be coherent with your values. Don't get into temptation doing something not to be proud of.

Four: Envision the American Dream
Human Pillar: Happiness

"This is the city of dreamers and time and time again it's the place where the greatest dream of all, the American dream, has been tested and has triumphed."
—Michael Bloomberg of New York City

What exactly is the American Dream? Simply that anyone, from any background, can have a shot at making their own dreams come true. It is grounded in the belief that when this occurs, everyone will benefit—as indeed the country has benefited from works of art, science, and industry created by dreamers ranging from the poorest citizens to immigrants. So, I invite you to flesh out your dream as follows.

Making dreams come true is not just about checking off achievements on your scorecard. It is about being fully human: enjoying what you achieve at every step along the way, while creating and sharing your happiness with others. And of course, making dreams come true requires hard work. But please let go of the notion that this is the "bad news." Indeed, it's good news. By working on your dream, you are living your dream. You are carrying out the plans that were born from your dream and making them real, every minute. What better life can there be?

We may be tempted to think of "joy jukebox" as a fuzzy concept, of little relevance to management or the bottom line. In fact joy is the greatest bottom-line return we humans can receive, and the way to reap the return is by investing joy up front.

Dreaming Is a Form of Planning

When I threw my American dream into the wind and jumped on board my flight to New York City, I was as present to my everyday as wet is to water. I saw a life-long dream manifesting before my eyes as I walked into the peak pages of my fairytale on a drug called happiness.

Many people have thought me crazy over the years, but no one watching closely could deny the workings of my grand imagination. And I most certainly could not, nor did I need to, hold back my exuberance with my move to America.

Dream-Plan: To Enjoy

Invention, as it turns out, is not something that happens through traditional strategic planning. We need to see the first step in strategy as what it really is, insight. Think of Leonardo da Vinci, centuries ago, painting fabulous pictures while in his notebooks, he sketched out designs for things that it wasn't yet possible to build, but which he was able to envision with amazing insight: helicopters, solar energy devices, and more! Traveling in your mind to more recent times, think of Maria Montessori with her ideas for a new kind of school, based on a new philosophy of education. Or think of Tim Berners-Lee with his concept of the World Wide Web. These creators knew their business and had plenty of knowledge to draw upon, but their great leaps began with a vision—they started with a dream. As I did. As Joy Mangano did with her invention of the self-wringing mop. As Coco Chanel did with the little black dress. They didn't start with strategy meetings to crunch numbers. Those things came after the insight; they grew out of the dream.

That's why, for me, dreaming is a form of planning. It is the preliminary stage in the process of bringing something into being. When I started envisioning myself living in New York City, as a teenager, I could smell the cold air of winter as it bounced off the yellow taxi cabs. I saw the feathers and glitter on the mannequins in the windows of the fancy department stores that I would one day stand in front of in awe. I felt myself waiting among the crowd in the elevator en route to my corner office and I heard my conversations on a Sunday brunch with friends over a good apple pie. With all my wild dreams, my expectations could not have been matched more perfectly than when I landed in New York City in October 2011 to begin my job as the President for Dolce & Gabbana, USA.

Central Park was brimming with leaves of bright orange, red, and yellow. The cold winds had not yet arrived and the sun's light reflected off the buildings creating rays in all directions as far up the avenue as I could see. My first working day was on Columbus Day—imagine the synchronicity I felt. My culture was honored with a New York City tradition, the Columbus Day Parade. A parade! The governor of New York State, New York City's mayor, and other dignitaries all seemed to be there to give *me* a warm welcome. People were in the streets celebrating my Italian heritage with our flag of green, white, and red waving proudly in the city it had come to regard as its home away from home. And there I was. The president of an Italian company, now living in New York. I felt like the happiest person on the planet. I couldn't contain my tremendous enthusiasm as my adrenaline left my body to run circles around the block. I felt stronger and healthier than any gold-medal athlete. There was a bounce in my exchanges with strangers inviting them to play. Everyone seemed to understand what I was going through without saying a word. People unknown to me, who felt like old friends, were embraced in my state of mind—love. For everyone and everything. I was radiating. In fact, containing my excitement was one of the most challenging tasks I had in those early days living in the United States. This brand-new experience—the sights, the sounds, my feelings—exceeded my long-standing visions. I wished everyone could experience the ultimate joy of a great achievement—the feeling of high satisfaction, of reaching a career milestone, a dream coming true. That was me. My smile was bigger than ever, fixed on my lips as if it were painted. My heart was dancing to the rhythm of my Alicia Keys song, "Empire State of Mind" as the lyrics were written for me.

And showing them my worth was exactly what I was about to do! That same day, I needed to fly to Dallas, Texas for a Dolce & Gabbana business meeting. Before taking the flight, I visited our New York retail locations to see our position in the stores. I was venturing to Bergdorf Goodman and Saks Fifth Avenue and as I approached Barneys on Madison Avenue, memories flooded my mind. Back in the days when I was traveling to New York as the Global VP of Business Development for the company, our offices were located right next to what was once an incredible store, which was once like a fashion museum inside a beautiful building. Our showroom was surrounded by a terrace, and you could even see Central Park. Years earlier that I imagined myself being seated in that office as the company's President. Though the Dolce & Gabbana office had since moved to a new location, my envisioning had come true! I thought it was unbelievable, but in fact it was what it had always been: My belief in my dreams that got me to each of my destinations.

Quite often when you realize a dream, it is easy to feel disappointed by it. The immagination is so vivid and perfect that the real world never lives up to the vision. I might go as far as to say that the dream is sometimes better than reality. But I have been fortunate to have lived my dreams nearly as clearly as I created them in my mind. Since I was a young girl living in Santa Severa, I have been looking outside boundaries to stimulate my creativity. On my way home after a long working day as the shampoo girl, my mind was the only thing spinning faster than the wheels of my bike. My ideas, rich with wonder, were the dreams I would learn to call insights. With this wandering of thought and mental freedom, I was plotting. My achievements started as dream seedlings from those days at the beauty salon and the Santa Severa Castle.

Hopes of these kinds do not come to fruition with the wink of an eye and the shake of two crossed arms, as they did for Barbara Eden's character in *I Dream of Jeannie*. Making dreams come true is about harnessing and honing the imagination. Even Clark Kent's quick transformation from glasses-wearing journalist to red-chested Superman should only be seen as a stimulus to awaken the real effort required to turn imagined heroes into real-world heroines. Many years before I got married, a wonderful woman reinforced my idea of imagining. She asked me if I ever thought about getting married and what I dreamed my wedding dress would look like. The truth was that I had never anticipated marriage which meant I had never outlined a dress in my mind. "I have other dreams. Bigger dreams," I said. She then gave me advice that still speaks to me through the years. As I recall, her words went like this:

> If you plan to achieve your big dreams, you need to picture every last detail of them in your mind. Fantasize and stay completely free in your creativity. Fabricate the dream with the biggest players of the day and the widest view in town. Then, the triumph and ecstasy of a successful finish will mark you forever as one who reached for the moon and landed on the stars.

She was right. You need to imagine the things that you want down to your shoes. You need to see yourself breaking through the ribbon the way a world-class runner is taught to do. Feel it, smell it, touch it, see it, and taste it. Ever since the woman and I had that conversation, I have added the poetry of her words to my pragmatism to build my life with intention. Each time I set out on a plan; I fill my hunger with the drawing of a dream. Dreams with vivid goals, distinct choices, and a commitment to the road forward. Since critical thinking takes know-how, control, and time, why not start with a bit of creativity? Think of a dream that comes out of sleep. When we have a vivid dream, we often wake up inspired. We remember the details of color, people, words, and feelings. However, if we pick up a pen to write it down, it seems to evaporate into the corners of the room. It's there, but not clear. And as the day passes, it dissipates like the heat from an un-sipped cup of hot chocolate. The deliciousness subsides. To put the dream into context and to give it a voice, we must go back to this notion of discipline. I believe that dreams come to us in simple terms. They aren't intricate math equations. They appeal to our emotions so we can aspire to great things. They are sweeping and powerful and believable. It is our job to learn how to shape them.

Lateral thinking

Typically, we don't think about imagination and strategy in the same sentence. Imagination has more curves while strategy feels more like a straight line. To be strategic, we do our research. We create a timeline; put expected milestones on it; have people in place to act; and expect it to happen pronto. Not necessarily so. In fact, when I got the job with Dolce & Gabbana in New York City, I had the major task of revamping the business and the brand after the financial crisis of 2008–2009, and a personal concern that worried me—my mother and my mother-in-law. With the contract signed and plans being readied for my family's move to the United States, you might think that we only needed to get on a plane heading there. But our moms were about to be left like two female canines without a family to be loyal to. Their daily contributions and interactions with me, my husband, and most importantly, their grandson—my son—had become the makeup of their lives. As I mentioned, they both had come to live with us during my days working in Modena. Having them close brought me peace of mind. They lovingly looked after Gabriel while I worked and constantly traveled. But bringing them to America with us was not a practical option. They would have difficulties getting long-term visas, getting medical insurance at their age, and more.

The move left me faced with a new conundrum—let our mothers go back to their individual lives and risk their feelings of isolation or invent a solution. I suggested that they stay together in our apartment in Rome to enjoy the community I envisioned for them. There, they could be close to their other children and a senior club that was around the corner from that home. Much to everyone's astonishment, my mother and mother-in-law lived together for almost 10 years, till Covid divided them. They enjoyed it, and I would not have been able to be as successful as I became in the United States without this peace of mind. If we look back to the Greeks in 850 BC, we learn that we can't always push our ideas through with force. We need imagination or something they called *metis*, which means craft. I used metis in my creative thinking with regard to our moms. Stuck in the mire of linear thinking, we lose the expansiveness that comes from letting the subconscious roam and find ideas. If we just pluck these colorful ideas out of the air, we can organize them into communication, action and ultimate strategy. This means that being envisionary can be at the forefront of our blueprints for life. Even now, I see this home-sharing as an answer to some of the social issues we face as humans live longer. Maybe we should rethink the way we live and also consider how to spend time with others we never thought of doing with a friend, a cousin, a grandson, a sister. I still ask myself how this vision I had for my son's grandmothers could be turned into a system to ward off the loneliness that can come either with old age, or with other circumstances. I was glad to hear that there is now a growing demand for residences where older people can share their lives and interests being singles. Not at all lonely souls, on the contrary, people with active social lives but with less ability to travel and move around. I envision this opportunity as a brighter future for many.

Being in New York City was surreal for me. Running in Central Park, working and dining in Soho, going to the Chelsea art galleries, attending the Metropolitan Opera, museums, and theaters—all of this was only a small part of why I was feeling on top of the world. I had successfully taken my "big idea" of moving out of my small town and into one of the grandest cities in the world and crafted it from dream to 3D reality. I was running a company. I was in America! I was about to interact with some of the world's most interesting minds, the most successful businesspeople, the biggest philanthropists ... the game changers. I reminded myself that this was an incredible feat. Not only for me, but also for my son, who could learn so much more in a city that is a melting pot of cultures, where all kinds of people live.

I was supremely happy—but this was not just the result of my circumstances. There are many stories of people who achieved all the success, fame, or wealth they could hope for, and yet they were not content. For true happiness to reign, it has to be something you bring with you. Be an architect of happiness. Bring your joy to the table, look for it in others. Scientists tell us that the source of joy lives behind our foreheads. It is the part of the brain called the prefrontal cortex, believed to be the center of personality, mood, and emotional memory. The workings of the brain are complex, and sometimes they get out of balance in ways that make it hard to generate feelings of joy in any situation. If you suspect this may be happening to you, it's very important to check in with an expert as mental health is essential. Medical or psychological care has put things back on track for lots of people. But it is also possible to increase our capacity for happiness by learning to cultivate this human pillar. There is a relatively new branch of psychology called positive psychology. It has emerged as a sort of complement to traditional approaches, which focus mostly on identifying and treating problems. Positive psychology focuses on the other side of the ledger, on what we can do to increase our enjoyment of life and find meaning in life. In that sense, it's like a science of happiness, and it was brought to the forefront over the past few decades by the work of Dr. Martin Seligman at the University of Pennsylvania. Indeed, some historians say that we humans have only come to see happiness *as a primary goal that should be instituted in our lives* over the last 250 years or so. The US Declaration of Independence, in 1776, listed "the pursuit of happiness" as a basic human right. More recently, since positive psychology got its legs, there has been an explosion of interest in the subject. We've seen movies like Italian filmmaker Roberto Benigni's *Life is Beautiful*, portraying an extraordinary feat of happiness under highly unlikely circumstances, and Will Smith's portrayal of a single father who finds himself homeless with no place to provide for his young son in the film *The Pursuit of Happiness*. These movies demonstrate that happiness is an exercise that requires discipline. The sole purpose of the 2011, multi-award-winning movie *Happy*, written and directed by Roko Belic, was to go out in search of the secrets of this great emotion. Gretchen Rubin's #1 bestselling book *The Happiness Project* and Pharrell Williams' virally successful song, "Happy," are just two more examples of the mainstream worldwide appeal of the topic. The little nation of Bhutan, in Asia, even has official government programs to measure and increase the country's "Gross National Happiness." I believe that Italy has a lot of potential to re-examine how much happier its inhabitants are, thanks to the great lifestyle and quality of life we grew up with. From a young age, I had wanted to live with a happy feeling about life. I understood then that most of the time, you cannot count on luck, but on your attitude and on your pursuit of your dreams.

I worked tremendously hard to get where I was, with almost 40 years of audacity, endurance, and resilience. I always maintained a positive attitude and a sense of total commitment. Yet I could not know, until the moment I stepped into my new life, how gratifying it would feel to see my faith have its day. Dreams really can come true if you have the courage to ignite them. Reaching a joyful state and achieving a dream is one thing, but it is another to train for dreaming, to make a vision authentic. To become a great seer, you must start with the knowledge that every thought you think shapes how you strategize. You may consider yourself to be a realist or to be a romantic; you may be spontaneous or structured. You may refer to yourself as someone who likes details or one who dwells on the big picture. You may like numbers, or you may like talking to people. Whoever you are, it is best that you know. And it is best that you gather. Gather your best traits and leverage them to help you focus on what you see. What you believe tomorrow may be different, and your ability to adapt to changing circumstances will define how you reach your dreams. Listen to what people say about you, too. I am not referring to small talk and useless critics but how reliable people (including those close to you) see you. What they say about you can be used to confirm your thoughts and visions. Look for the ways you repeat yourself. What are the things that keep coming back to you? Not silly thoughts and constant worries, but things you notice or insights you get, which reinforce a concept or idea you have? Grab onto those. Develop them. Be curious about what keeps showing up. Who are the scholars and experts on the subject? Who are the journalists who have written about it? Who are the leaders who employ your ideas? Talk about your dreams. Say them out loud to know if they are real for you. If they are, say them over and over. Write about them. Read about them. Be outrageous in your hunt for that thing. Then, be sure to bring it home to a place called love. Take the expanse of the dream and funnel it into generosity and purpose and something that others can relate to. Gain supporters to help you build a road to your non-obvious future. Take your broad aspiration and turn it into an outline. Then, you will begin to understand that it is not just a dream. It is indeed the first step in your plan.

Stars and Stripes

When I took over the President's role at the US company, which also included Canada, we had huge challenges to overcome. It wasn't just a question of improving the business, the margins, the profitability, and the cash flow. It was also to keep positioning the brand among its top competitors—Prada, Dior, Gucci, Valentino, and more—gaining a bigger voice, engaging with consumers and most importantly, budling a positive and distinct culture. I didn't know anyone in the United States who could be helpful in my new task. What excited me was that it was new. I needed to study, learn, and leverage my previous experiences, creating a team, leading them, understanding the contest, create solutions, drive growth, deliver results, and put the company at the forefront of the industry. Meeting the biggest wholesale clients, which at that time were the main department stores such as Saks, I could understand their frustrations over the limited line of communication with Dolce & Gabbana. No president had been in place in the United States for a long time. Those clients felt a bit neglected, and even though our company had a subsidiary to oversee US operations and more than 100 team members at the New York office, their top management wanted to know more about our top people's overall vision for the brand, the company's strategy and more. The local team wasn't necessarily equipped to give answers as these were big questions for the Designers themselves and the executives in Milan.

When I went to check the work in progress on the new to-come Fifth Avenue store, I received an impromptu visit from the landlord who was furious because the company didn't even tell him that a new president had arrived. He wanted to have a direct dialogue with the President, he didn't expect me. His Ferrari outside the door, with the engine running while it waited for him, was making less noise than his voice. He definitely had a tough approach, but the content of his complaints was no different from that of his rival and community friend who rented us our offices downtown. The media needed attention too. Although the company has always had strong connections with the editors-in-chief of the most important publications, the rest of their people were in need of clarity, information, and daily contact. At the office, some of the team members were enjoying not having close supervision. Wherever I looked there was a lot of work to be done. I felt a bit scared as I saw a huge gap between the perception in Milan and the reality in America. Not only in the New York office but at the one in Los Angeles and in stores around the country. The day I started, Mrs. Ruella sent me beautiful flowers with a note I would never forget. She said "Good luck. But I know you won't need it." Whenever I rode the subway from our offices on Lafayette Street to 96th street, tired of the heavy day and wondering how I could tackle all the issues, I would think of that note and get re-empowered.

Few colleagues were impressed that their President rode the 6 subway. They expected a driver and a black car but obviously, they didn't know my past. To me, that was a way to truly experience the real life of the city and to stay real. Besides, the commute was long and in rush hours the traffic was terrible, so I could continue to work while on the 45/60 minutes train ride. My apartment, which was chosen by someone who had different standards than mine, was far from making us feel we were in a charming home. I told my CEO that I was happy on my way to the office in the morning, but on my way home it was not the same feeling. I was at the 96th Street location because my son went to school just a few blocks away. I decided to take a longer commute for myself so that Gabriel could walk to school and know that he had shelter nearby if he felt lost. The transition was not easy for him either. He went from the loving arms of his grandmothers to a new environment where he didn't understand the language and couldn't communicate. School was a blessing. Not only were the teachers and staff members very caring, but everything was also bilingual, which gave him time to pick up his English while not missing his beloved "nonnes" too much. The school's principal, who looked a bit like my mom, once told me that I should be more worried about Gabriel losing his native Italian than not learning English properly, as she had witnessed many families in the same situation. Antonio and I decided to speak Italian at home and use the TV to give our son the right English accent to absorb. Since I had never lived in an English spoken language country until that time, my accent wasn't the best thing I could pass on him. The cartoons, which he refused to watch at first to express his disappointment, became a great asset for his first language skills. Meanwhile, his father was dealing with his own challenges and tensions at his work, and we began to argue about things in a very inappropriate way. Something serious with him wasn't working.

Very often I was away from home on business trips more than I used to be when I was traveling the world from Milan. I needed to meet all the wholesalers, the landlords, the people at the stores, and build the foundation to grow the business with new ideas to increase revenues. I also needed to spend time back in Milan. This was to make sure all departments there understood and conceived initiatives that could be localized to the US and, of course, to meet with the Designers, so they could feel inspired from the States and design collections that reflected the esthetics desired by American customers. More than ever, I questioned my role as a mom and a wife. After observing people who did similar jobs for other similar companies, I realized that I was one of the few (if not the only) women in charge. But those men were often away from home, too. How did they deal with their families? Looking at their agendas of early breakfast and business dinners besides the many daily meetings, and their intense travel schedules, I realized that they relied heavily on their wives and helpers to raise their kids, manage their homes, and arrange a social life. I thought my expectation should be to see my son on the weekends when he was not in school, and we could spend quality time together. If and when I could also see him during the week for dinner, it should be considered a gift. But there were two things I definitely wanted. One was to be present when Gabriel had a special day at school, such as a recital or celebration, and the other, most importantly, was to be there when he was sick or hurt and had to visit a doctor. At those times, I felt that my instincts were able to grasp what he really needed. But of course, I was in Toronto on the day when the school called to say my son needed to go to the hospital because he smashed his eyebrow while playing. I immediately phoned his father and asked an American colleague to kindly help him with the language and the insurance procedures since it was the first time we had such an experience. I was negotiating with a broker to take over a space Louis Vuitton was vacating, so we could open our first store in Canada, where we needed to set up a branch and I also needed to meet with a lawyer. The business trip was super-productive, but my sense of guilt ate up the joy of the great results. I had to learn how to live with that sense of guilt and win over it, with time. Do we, as working parents, have other choices? All people who work have responsibilities and commitments. None of us can simply call it a day or quit our jobs, as we have to provide for ourselves and our families. Understanding that this is the reality of the world, I started to develop a thicker skin in face of guilt and to enjoy my time with my family more fully. Each Friday, to reconnect after a tough and tiring week, we were going to enjoy sushi and watch a family movie. The weekend could start the next day with a more relaxed and reunited feeling.

Making things happen

At work, after listening to all the parties involved with our brand and company in the United States—which by the way, was the most important market for companies in almost every industry at that time—and knowing how the head office considered regional markets versus the wish of establishing a global approach, I had an interesting idea. I needed to put our business owners together at the same table with executives of the companies that we dealt with. Then our owners could understand the gaps that existed, and we could form strategies to close these gaps, by finding win-win solutions for each other. When I proposed to Ruella that I wanted to start by having the Neiman Marcus executives meet Mr. Dolce and Mr. Gabbana directly, she told me they had tried that type of thing in the past and it was better to avoid this discussion with the Designers again. Now, since I sensed that I had great chemistry with both the Designers and Neiman Marcus top management, do you think I stopped myself? I couldn't. I knew that I would be putting myself at risk of having my boss against me. Politics are played in companies more than in parliaments sometimes. But I was not political, especially when I was convinced that, in the best interest of the company, I needed to push delicate buttons to make things happen. Having a direct connection with the Designers and, most importantly, having their trust and respect, gave me an advantage no one in other regions could have, as I had worked with them for almost 10 years in the past. Just imagine my joy when I introduced the Neiman Marcus team to the Designers. Up to that time, Mr. Dolce and Mr. Gabbana had been meeting only with creative people and with the press. I felt extra joy in learning that, after that very successful meeting, they wanted to meet *all* of the biggest American clients. They did that only at the very early stage of their career when the organization was not big. I believe they liked to reconnect with that area of the business after so long. After meeting the American clients, they indeed decided to meet those of the entire world! A bi-annual luncheon meeting, during Fashion Week in Milan, was established which helped the Designers and the company to have closer connections with our main buyers, who in turn knew many of their customers. By doing so, we were strengthening our partnerships around the world and the connection between the "creative" side of the business and the market. This was one of the case studies I presented internally, as an example of how to move things forward. It came at a crucial time, since the company was closing the D&G line—a lower-priced but still luxury line of fashions, which then was making $500 million in revenue. The market wanted to know directly from the Designers what was prompting them to take this decision, what changes were happening at Dolce & Gabbana and in which direction the company was going. Of course, I knew all the answers and I was reinforcing the messages we were supposed to deliver to our customers, explaining and presenting the strategy. But it was far more effective for people to hear a few clear and impactful words from the Designers, with me chiming in when needed. I then started making plans with all of our clients to open many more shop-in-shops (that is, a dedicated Dolce & Gabbana "store" within a larger store that sells many products), and to renew a few old ones. This was something rare to achieve, especially in a relatively short time. As I traveled from Houston to San Jose, and from Westchester to Tampa, I was also learning the geography of the country. I visited every state of the US where we were distributing and parts of Canada as well. Meeting the teams at all levels, in areas from sales to store planning and from marketing to logistics, was my biggest passion. I knew they were thirsty for news and info that could motivate them to deliver better results at their local stores. And I spared no efforts in visiting the sales associates, along with the visual display and merchandising teams, to train them each time a new product or collection was launched.

The communication area was the most sensitive for the HQ. The more I talked with people in the industry, the more I understood the impact I could have in getting our brand top-of-mind with the right audiences. Whenever the press met me, as US President of Dolce & Gabbana, they wanted to give me the spotlight. But if I were to do that, I would lose the trust of the Designers who were the only two people the company was pushing to portray externally. I didn't care about being the public face of the company, as all I wanted was to do a great job and gain the respect of people I always admired. The more I tried not to appear prominently in public, the more I was getting noticed. It wasn't easy to manage my role, as the American mentality regarding personal publicity is totally different from what I had learned. Sharing and celebrating oneself is seen as positive and inspirational. One day, while I was having lunch with Deborah, an Editor in Chief of an important magazine, she said I reminded her of Arianna Huffington. I had never met Ms. Huffington before but admired her successful career. I also mentioned that I had heard an amazing speech she gave at the *Glamour* Woman of the Year award event and that I dreamed (of course) of dressing Ms. Huffington in Dolce & Gabbana. Without even asking, the next day I was introduced to Arianna via email. Now this is America! You don't believe it until it happens. The words Deborah used to introduce me almost made me cry. Arianna, in response (she responded immediately!) invited me to her home (her home!) since she was having a gathering of women to launch *Thrive*, her new book. A few days later we all met at a dinner for Tina Brown, the prominent journalist and media presence, where I also met other amazing professionals. I was getting closer to the people I considered real stars—the doers, the voices, the real deals. Never with a specific agenda but to establish connections. It's called "networking," and as I discovered it, I mastered it just by being myself. I had been doing it all of my life without knowing of its significance, as a personal and professional asset, in the United States. No wonder I felt at home in this country!

Creating the Customer

People from all over the world have looked at the United States for a multitude of reasons. They saw the country as their saving grace; their holy grail; their seat of higher learning—the list is as personal as each person who makes the trek and as long as a spool of thread in a factory. When we link happiness to customer experience, in Europe we see America as a great teacher. As their famous proverb says: *The customer is always right.* I was on a crusade to understand Dolce & Gabbana's next customer.

Knowing the power of influencers of successful people here, I decided to cultivate them to build a solid foundation for the company. For sure, celebrities like Hollywood stars were keys to attracting new customers, but to me they were not the only well-known people who could raise awareness of a global brand. I wanted to have other wonderful people too in many other areas wearing Dolce & Gabbana—from businesspeople and philanthropists to members of important institutions, lawyers, athletes, and more. I had one unshakable criteria, which was that brand ambassadors, celebrities, and behind-the-scenes contributors all needed to be respected in their fields. If they could afford the brand, I knew I had a chance to turn them into customers even if they hadn't yet realized that Dolce & Gabbana was the right brand for them yet. The company had never done business this way before, and I will never forget Stefano and Domenico's concerns when I insisted on having a strong American influencer, the likes of Melinda Gates, as host for the opening of our Fifth Avenue flagship store opening in 2012. When Mr. Giorgio Armani chose Mayor Michael Bloomberg for the opening of his flagship, just next to ours, he gave a $1 million donation to the New York public schools. In response, later on, the mayor declared an Armani day. While our Designers appreciated my search of possible philanthropist, and my innovative way of thinking, in keeping with their philosophy, they chose an Italian old-time friend of the house known by the New York fashion socialites.

The more I got to know Americans in many fields, the more I believed that the brand needed to expand into the world of business leaders and philanthropy. Finally, I convinced the Designers to let me attend *Fortune* magazine's Most Powerful Women (MPW) Summit. They were skeptical about these gatherings in general, but I knew that besides learning from other amazing business leaders at that Summit, the room would be filled with our company's most important audience: women! My gut told me that I needed to learn from them and understand what they cared about. Convincing Mr. Dolce and Mr. Gabbana gave some talk. I prepared a presentation giving them the results of my research on successful people in various fields and territories. America is full of brilliant people, everywhere. I brought with me a list of top CEOs published by *The Wall Street Journal* and showed them the many opportunities.

On the first day of the MPW Summit, each of the 500 female attendees stood one at the time to introduce themselves—we needed to mention our name, the company we worked for, and our title. There were prominent businesswomen who made it into the c-suite. My excitement made me feel like a little girl in a candy store. So much to savor. The moment I stood to speak, praying my ankles would not give out on me and my red pumps, I followed suit: Federica Marchionni, Dolce & Gabbana, and President. I still cannot believe what happened next. The room burst into applause as if I had just finished giving a rock concert. Trying not to look behind me to see if they were clapping for something else, I am sure my cheeks blushed as I instinctively stood a little prouder. The love in the room was astounding to me and my heart grew to another size. The affection emanated from the smiles of these important ladies, and it echoed off the walls as a hoot or two was added to the mix. I immediately thought of Mr. Dolce and Mr. Gabbana and how happy they would be when they learned of that moment because they were clapping to their brand! I have always acted with the belief that love is a guiding force. I cherished my every day in the United States, I was devoted to each component of my job at the office and when I received those accolades from the crowd, I was overtaken with emotion and delight. Interacting with these women, and networking with them in a very spontaneous and authentic way, helped me to further understand the spirit of America at that time, and for them it was a chance to see the world of fashion through my eyes. Stylish corporate women! By the way, with most of them, I have created a great friendship to these days! Sitting with Mr. Dolce discussing the upcoming fall Market Week, I recall telling him about my feelings for America and its culture. "You have totally confirmed my happiness and helped me to reach my American Dream, and for that I must thank you like the dry earth, thanks the falling rain. I am absolutely in love with the culture and my overall life here," I told him. I was indeed witnessing how closely love and happiness work together to create gratitude. I remember, one day while dodging the dogs, bicyclists, walkers, and other runners in the 10-mile Central Park loop, thinking back to the fifth grade when my mother transferred me to a protected school to keep me out of harm's way from my father who had kidnapped me twice before disappearing. It was a school for underprivileged kids where I learned also how tough life can be. Now, admiring the New York City skyscrapers surrounding Central Park as I ran, I remember feeling full of joy and gratitude.

A new branding strategy

As time went by in America, I observed that many companies were implementing a CRM (customer relationship management) software system to use customer data in shaping product offerings and marketing. But I wanted more information. I needed to stay savvy in my approach and remember the American motto that the customer is always right! *What could I learn about our customers that we didn't know? How could we tweak the fabrics, the designs, and the sizing according to their desires? How could I demonstrate even more that everything we do was not about us but rather about them?* Customers wanted to choose beautiful products but also from a company they admired. And what were we doing in that sense? In my opinion, the understated way the Designers had of giving back was not meaningful and inspiring for our American customers. Feeling inspired by the American approach to doing business and always wanting to do good business with positive impact, I began to tie the brand to special causes. While I was busy turning people into customers, and keeping them loyal, I was starting to raise social awareness on subjects such as health and culture, and I put in place partnerships between the company and philanthropic institutions. That was the beginning of a new approach at the company. Again, this was something no one had even dared to propose. The Designers' approach was to be understated when it came to philanthropy as they didn't like to use giving back to gain visibility. While I appreciate that was also due to cultural differences and admire the nature of true selfless giving, I also believe that giving examples of doing good things is not harmful, especially if it is authentic. I met a wonderful lady, who was the co-founder of the Melanoma Research Alliance, and knew about her personal struggles and her commitment to running a foundation to help prevent the illness which also had caused the death of the wife of the other co-founder. Their mission was clear, and their intent was admirable. We held an event at her house with lots of her friends and it was so successful that each year we kept doing it and even expanded it to other cities with friends based in Los Angeles, Miami, Aspen, and Chicago.

Dolce & Gabbana was always connected to the arts and artists, so I thought we should have something linked with a serious arts institution, but in an authentic way. From the very beginning of the company, each fashion show started with the Intermezzo of *Cavalleria Rusticana*, an opera composed by Pietro Mascagni. I knew opera was a passion of the Designers (as it is mine) and the Met in New York was in need of help to create subtitles for the Italian opera—in Italian, to go with the English translation. Lucia Pasqualini, Italy's Vice Consul in New York at the time, a passionate advocate of the Italian language, asked me to help her raise money for adding the Italian language at the Met. I knew the Designers could relate to that cause since it was the combination of many elements: art, opera, Italy, the world. With the help of a few other Italian families in New York, Lucia and I made that goal happen. I went to meet the director of the Metropolitan Opera and the head of partnerships and established great relationships. Kathryn, another lady who became a close friend to our fashion house, included us in a few events at the Met and I was dreaming of having the Alta Moda fashion show at the Metropolitan Opera House, which happens years later.

The sense of purpose in my life, keep raising my son strong, working closely with the team, choosing partners or social causes and more, kept me up at night. There were times when the future would visit me in my sleep, but more often it was in an awake state that my dreams flowed fastest. And so, I would lie down in the evening after an early dinner with business partners, preparing my visions for the next day's prime time. There were meetings with the Designers to be sure that we were cultivating our sourcing in a sustainable way. There were my talks with customer service people, to continue to grow them and their customer conversations in a loving way. And there were my efforts in inventory control with getting the right product mix to keep us focused.

I needed to achieve one more goal to expand the brand, the business, the company's perception, and its connection with local communities in American cities. Obviously, we needed to find brand ambassadors and influencers among those who could afford the brand, but I wanted more. A true and strong connection with their local community that would then be authentic and powerful. While I was in Los Angeles, a friend introduced me to a wonderful man who was dividing his life between LA and Boston. I had been going to Boston often for the opening of a new store, first to find a good location and then to supervise its buildout. One day he invited me to a friend's birthday party. The friend happened to be the principal owner of the Boston baseball team, who also bought a newspaper. He was married to a beautiful lady with Italian origins who looked almost like Monica Bellucci's sister. I immediately saw the connection. We kept in contact and met a few times, including for a beautiful lunch at the Rainbow Room in Rockefeller Center.

It became organic to ask them to be the hosts of our grand opening in Boston. They both came to the event beautifully dressed in Dolce & Gabbana. As I was opening new stores, I was challenged to find similar experience and connections in other cities, like Chicago and Aspen. In Toronto, even Mr. Dolce came for the beautiful dinner hosted by the Weston family.

In New York, attending a luncheon for women organized by *Marie Claire* magazine, I saw again a young lady who I had met other times but never had the chance to really speak with and know. She seemed to me like a strong, smart woman, not keen to waste any time and not interested in small talk. Not only in business have I always looked for challenges and connections; I look for them in my private life too. I thought she was someone I would be curious to know more about and maybe become friendly with. We had something in common, an only child, and they were the same age. We met again at another gathering and arranged to meet on a weekend for a play date with the kids. We went to the Metropolitan Museum and then toured Central Park. The kids became instantly best buddies; Desiree and I became best friends. Throughout the years, we have spent lots of Sundays and some vacations together in more relaxed settings than Manhattan, having Callum and Gabriel playing beautifully while we met in different parts of the world: Los Angeles, Miami, Italy, China, and more. Desiree is a busy woman, but she has always been there for me. Her business grew tremendously over the years, as our friendship did. I met often her whole family, including her husband Kyle who loves Italy, the food and the language I speak best. We have shared lots of fun moments together! They became our family in New York till they lived there, and I cherish their friendship every day, since, as the Little Prince says in the Antoine de Saint-Exupéry's famous book, *"The fox was only a fox like a hundred thousand other foxes. But I have made him my friend, and now he is unique in all the world."*

Team

From the time I arrived in New York, I wanted to inspire my team to be better, to raise their standards and to open their minds. I couldn't just *tell* them to do all of that, so I decided to lead by example. Every day, in every action, I was thinking of how to give them examples to follow when they might be in my shoes later on. Most importantly, in any interactions we had, I tried to stimulate their thinking, bring out their creativity, and empower them to work well together and believe in themselves. When they acted impulsively, I invited them to attain distance. If they were confrontational, I would suggest they soften their approach. If they weren't in agreement, I would suggest understanding the situation from the other side and pushing them to greater dialogue. I often saw my younger self in them, and I knew how valuable it was to gain other people's perspectives to help me advance in my career and evolve in wisdom. Whenever I attended conferences, from the *Forbes* to *The Economist* ones and from the DLD to TED, I always took time to tell them what I was learning. Sharing knowledge was definitely a key process. I was glad to be learning in a land that offered so much to learn from, but my biggest passion was to pass that knowledge to my team. One goal was opening their minds to acquire social intelligence, which could ultimately help us stay connected to the world and, of course, to our customers. Every now and then I brought in business books I had read, telling them briefly about the topics covered and then leaving the books available for any team member to read and pass along.

The books that I chose explored many aspects of business—and of thinking and working in general, from a broad perspective, not just things specific to the fashion industry. Fashion is a fast-moving business, and while creativity is of course essential, efficiency is a key to success. I felt strongly that the thought processes, the decision-making, and the operating methods needed to be more intelligently structured and formalized, and I was determined to implement that mindset. Meanwhile, I emphasized that as long as we kept passing useful knowledge to others, we could keep the teams engaged and challenged. Among the many books I gave them, these were among my favorites: *Good to Great* by Jim C. Collins; *Zero to One* by Peter Thiel, with Blake Masters; *Outliers* by Malcolm Gladwell; *Thinking, Fast and Slow* by Daniel Kahneman; *Start with Why* by Simon Sinek. I was inspired by these books, and inspiration was the feeling I wanted the team to have, to help strengthen their commitment. One positive note was that we already felt very connected.

Maybe it all started with a pumpkin. The day I arrived at the office I had wanted to give everybody a sign that someone was coming to look after them. It was October and Halloween was around the corner. I noticed a lot of stores selling pumpkins, something I had never experienced in my country. Antonio and I were feeling absolutely drained from our travel to New York, the jet lag and the move into a new home, where we had brought in our furniture and personal stuff and spent the entire weekend organizing a new life. But I wanted to do something special for the team. When I proposed to Antonio buying a small pumpkin to leave at each person's desk, he thought I was insane. We were so tired that adding another physical task seemed like it would push us beyond our limits. I insisted and convinced him. We went to a store, where I spent quite some time carefully choosing more than 100 pumpkins. They needed to be of equal or similar size and all in good condition. We packed them in two large boxes, hailed a taxi, and rode to the office. Then I personally walked around to each desk, placing each little token just right, to wish the whole team a Happy Halloween and to let them see how much I valued making a connection. I heard later that the unexpected gesture was very well received, and most people were eager to meet me and show their commitment. I rolled up my sleeves and spent time with each team member to understand their strengths and weaknesses, their goals and potential, and their areas for improvement to create a much stronger, more cohesive team. I didn't understand why a certain talented HR person hadn't been promoted and empowered as she deserved. I suspected that her not being a slim size could be seen as a limit in the fashion industry, but I didn't care! She was a great, super-committed professional who I thought could produce much more impact for the company if we gave her a chance to prove herself. I promoted her and she thrived during the entire 3.5 years I was president. On the contrary, a marketing person who wanted to lead the department was probably too good-looking and wasn't taken very seriously. I didn't care about her appearance, either; I thought she was brilliant in her work and promoted her too. A special one for me was Alysa, who excelled at her work with the highest levels of professionalism and integrity and a human touch as well. Due to a change in structure, HQ wanted her to report to someone in Milan who wanted to fire her. For no reason, maybe just ego. He was never working closely with her, so how could he really understand her job and value? I strongly defended her, and time proved us to be right. Ultimately, HQ fired the guy who was unprofessional and disseminating discontent only to please himself. Alysa instead went on to have an incredible career, including after I left.

As the business grew and we opened more stores, we doubled the workforce at the office, bringing in a larger team and higher standards. In 2012 I hired two gentlemen, one as head of PR and one as head of wholesale, who were super-talented but not experienced in managing large teams. They understood how difficult it was to gain support and respect from one's team members. Mentoring them in leadership took time but it was needed. And one I will never forget was the head of retail for the West Coast region. He previously held an amazing position in a competitor's house and was hard to attract. After a successful few years together, he revealed to me one day that he was able to save his marriage thanks to a discussion we had about life. To me, that was a much greater mark of success than the dresses he was selling to Celine Dion in Las Vegas. Today I am glad to know that all these people have had great careers, not only thriving while we worked together but going on to successful positions in other companies.

At the New York office, even though everyone always had something to gossip about—a practice I was determined to avoid and possibly eliminate—they were grateful for the challenges I gave them and the opportunities to learn. They could always count on me when they needed support or a sound board for making decisions. I didn't graduate from an Ivy League university, but they knew that I was constantly studying and always challenging myself, along with them, to set the curiosity bar high and keep performing at higher levels. At any possible occasion, I introduced new work methods and better procedures. The company was receptive to my approach of bringing more structure and rigor to the way we operated, assessed, and expanded the business. One day I received a letter from Harvard Kennedy School, the Graduate School of Public Policy and International Economics at Harvard University. They asked if I would be a panelist at a conference for MBA students focused on luxury, called "Europe 2.0." Other professionals invited to the panel included the CEOs of Jimmy Choo, Bang & Olufsen, and Montblanc. The distinguished Professor Stefan Thomke, an expert on innovation management, would be a moderator. Think about my beginnings and my many attempts to do an executive course at Harvard and then try to imagine what I was feeling when I received the invitation. When I saw the Harvard logo on the letter, I read the content over and over to confirm that they really wanted ME at the conference to talk about the impacts of luxury and fashion in the economy. I thought I was in a dream.

Company policy at that time wasn't in favor of managers speaking in public (it has changed a bit since then) but I was determined to ask for an exception. I think Ruella understood that if she didn't give me approval to attend, I would resign. I had never dared to dream of speaking at Harvard, only of studying there. While the United States is a country filled with many fine colleges and universities—enough to meet the needs and desires of all kinds of students—to me, an Italian who had looked toward America since childhood as a foreigner, the Harvard name represented the quality to which I aspired. I once even made an analysis which confirmed that many of the top Americans I admired were Harvard graduates. Can you believe the feeling of being called to be at the other side of the desk? Was that real? I wrote back to the person who sent the letter and asked to set up a call. I needed confirmation and clarification on my role there and to better understand what the conference was for, who the audience was, etc.

The day I went to Harvard, I brought my family: Gabriel, beautifully dressed in a cute little jacket and white shirt, and Antonio who was taking pictures during the whole time. I had chosen an elegant but bright suit to be appropriately dressed as an Executive, but with a touch of warmth to represent both me and my company. On the panel, at a long table in front of a room filled with MBA students, I was seated in the center, probably because I was the only woman. Happiness again, because dreams can really come true. The panel was great, and I met interesting people, including a Harvard Fellow, Nikos, whom I can now call a friend. The panel was about the implications of luxury for the economies of various countries. I had reached out to friends for some data I could use to prepare my speech. Of course, I also had the opportunity to represent the company, so I knew I was not there only to please myself. I was still representing the brand and told the students about the links between inspiration from Italian roots and the products the Designers created. I returned home inspired by the rest of the panelists and, last but not least, by the questions and curiosity of the students. They were international young men and women, eager to understand the fashion and luxury business, questioning how they could apply their studies in it, wondering if they could start companies in the industry and more.

Since I also wanted to create opportunities for the company, I asked the professors I met at Harvard to put me in contact with the Harvard Club in New York. There I visited a person in charge of programming. We connected immediately, met several times, and after some brainstorming on what we could do together for the Club, Dolce & Gabbana ended up being part of the yearly Gala held in November for the Foundation. I was proud to introduce the company to such a prestigious institution, to have my team working with a different kind of customers, and to have invited the Dolce family attending the event. We brought to the Harvard Club a touch of sophisticated elegance with our setup and a curated trunk-show focused on styles for the men and women in attendance: exquisite suits and tuxedos, beautiful cocktail dresses, and gala attire. All appropriate for their business and social life. It was such a success that the Club asked us to come back the next year. And of course, we were very happy!

Some takeaways

By working on a dream, you are living your dream. Don't be scared of the down moments.
To assess your dream-plans, speak to others and look for the ways you repeat yourself.
Be an architect of happiness. Bring your joy to the table, look for it in others.
Happiness can be found in different paths, not necessarily linear but lateral too.
For true happiness to reign, it has to be something you bring within you.
Work on your attitude to feel happier, not on external circumstances or luck.
You will have time for everything, just not for everything at the same time. Look for a longer span.
Network, nourish relationships and connect with communities, they bring happy exchanges.
Love and happiness work together to create gratitude. Love what you do and be grateful.
Turn people into customers in an authentic way, they will be happy and loyal.
Share your joy and knowledge back to people, it will make you feel extra fulfilled.

Five: Envision Disruption
Human Pillar: Excellence

*"Only those who risk going too far can possibly
find out how far we can go."*
—TS Eliot

Great creative leaps are made by people who have the guts to challenge the status quo. That is why, in fields from business to science, "disruptive" leaders and ideas are often celebrated. They disrupt old ways of thinking or doing things by introducing new and evolved ways. Modern information technology has utterly disrupted old ways of doing business and communicating. That is how progress is made!

But disruption is difficult. It's messy and unpredictable. During our modern high-tech age, countless startup companies and inventors have failed. Very often, the old order fights back, so disruption is risky. Yet in most cases, the risk of hanging onto the status quo can be greater. Especially in today's fast-moving world, a person who clings to a settled course of life or a company sticking with business as usual may be left in the dust.

Therefore, when there is a chance to pursue the non-obvious presents itself, it may be time for any of us to choose disruption. And the choice springs from a Human Pillar that any of us can build upon: the innate drive for *Excellence*. This may sound contrary. We tend to equate excellence with the perfect: spotless student who scores at the top of the scale on every standardized test, not with a messy ordeal like disruption. But in fact, excellence means *exceeding* the scale of expectations. When we excel, we break the standard and set a higher one. Always knowing we face risks that may require us to rethink and adjust. That was the risk I chose at a pivotal time in my life. Pursuing excellence does not make you immune to failure. It always involves trial and error, and sometimes heavy consequences. However, the ability to learn and move on, more capable than before, is a valuable—I would say almost essential—achievement. My pride is that, as much as I could, I made progress even though I did not finish a project to which I had devoted myself to. And it is the progress toward a better world that pushed me, and still pushes me, to look for new challenges.

We can't let the future just be something that happens to us—not in our personal lives, or in our organizations or in society. We must consciously envision and build the futures we want—futures that are unobvious at present, but discoverable if we expand our thinking into meta-thinking. Companies will need business models, and leaders will need mindsets that go beyond transformation to transcendence.

From Madison Avenue to Madison, Wisconsin

My New York experience with Dolce & Gabbana had me sitting on the ninth cloud in the sky: the cloud of happiness. Blue was all I could see around me and the earth's surface radiated support to me from miles below. I was stable. Or so I thought. I had taken America by storm and cast a spell on the land that made me feel comfortable being me. I felt a newfound "go getter and go giver" attitude while living as a dreamer, believer, and achiever with dynamism in my bones.

The Dolce & Gabbana Company was reaching further with each goal we set. I worked relentlessly to make sure everyone felt a part of this wonderful story—the US team, the one in Canada, and the one at headquarters in Milan. Even my family took part of it. My son was pampered by the staff when I was busy doing store checks with him on weekends, and his father had created a beautiful relationship with the Dolce family, so gatherings felt inclusive. Everything seemed perfect; we seemed perfect. Of course, nothing is, and everything wasn't at all easy as it seems. Because behind this very pretty appearance there is so much more people don't see. In fact, my American days were filled not only with passion, fulfillment, and celebrations but also with extra hard work, sleepless nights, and getting up at dawn. And then courage, sacrifices, the pressure, the stress, and the doubts. *Did I make the best decision yesterday? Will my courage be enough to meet the pressures of today?* I accepted these feelings, knowing that they went with my chosen career. To me personally, stresses and demands of this type were far preferable to the dullness of a life lived less fully.

I had paid little attention to headhunters contacting me about jobs at other fashion companies, because a sideways move made no sense. Why should I leave the company that had been so good to me, nurturing my dreams for over a dozen years, in order to do the same kind of work somewhere else? Only the promise of new terrain could catch my eye. With America being a land of opportunity, I was not worried that, in fact, opportunities would eventually come to stretch my mind and test my visionary capabilities in areas where I saw vast potential for the future. Two areas in particular seemed relevant to me.

One was digital technology, something not too far from where I had started years ago. Back in the 1980s and 1990s, I had envisioned that people everywhere would be linked by mobile phone technology, and I was part of the movement to make it happen. In 1984, Apple launched Macintosh, the first Mac created by Steve Jobs; in those years, if we wanted to record a film, we would have had to use a videotape, our files were stored on floppy disks, we still bought rolls of paper, we still had to use a computer and we were taking our photographs to be developed, since the first digital camera came on the market in 1981. While back then I was living that reality, I was sure that things would change soon, and that people would be connected everywhere by mobile phone technology. Now the next digital revolution was under way. As I watched the world from New York City, the new digital revolution was indeed in full swing. This time it was called e-commerce or online shopping. People were doing much more than talking and texting on their phones; they were buying and selling online in ways that fit in but also disrupted the usual forms of commerce. Where might these new methods of economic interaction lead? With the experience that I now have in fashion and retail, could I somehow play a lead role in shaping that future? This was me, being wired to the future and wanting to stay, if possible, ahead.

The other area relevant to me was one where I had long felt a desire to do more: corporate social responsibility. I always had the ambition to make a difference in the world while doing business and then beyond it. Indeed, I often thought that at some point I would dedicate more of my time to societal causes, maybe managing a non-for-profit organization. And while this was a Dream-Plan for years to come, I felt it was possible to start doing something more concrete currently. This need, for me, was a possibility I envisioned emerging more strongly in advanced societies.

Dream-Plan: To Lead with Purpose

Many companies were already trying to grow in responsible ways, while others had major initiatives to support creative work for the common good. Among fashion and luxury firms, one that stood out to me was Rolex. The watch company had an esteemed history of funding new work in science, sustainability, arts, and culture. One day, knowing that our designers at Dolce & Gabbana admired certain brands, I pointed out to the team that Louis Vuitton had chosen Bono and his wife Ali Hewson as spokespersons for their charitable campaigns. That time, LVMH even supported Ms. Hewson's own venture into fashion with a brand called Edun which featured ethically made garments "grown and sewn" in Africa. Dolce & Gabbana was known for the creation of beautiful garments that made all women feel empowered, almost like divas. Even if I understood why the duo-designers wanted to create clothes inspired by a concept of lightness of life that "is not superficiality," as Italo Calvino wrote in his American Lessons, "gliding over things from above, not having a heavy heart," I was still strongly attracted by these stories of taking care of the planet and the people—and a true icon for me was Stella McCartney for pioneering the vision of building a sustainable fashion house.

An iconic American company

When Lands' End sailed to my dock, three years after my arrival in New York, I thought I could be more incisive in making a difference. Lands' End was and still is an iconic company within the United States, known for quality, value, and customer service. Though not a fashion firm *per se*, Lands' End was in the garment industry, producing well-made, American mid-priced clothing for family members of all ages. My son's school uniforms came from Lands' End, so I was also a customer. And there were aspects of the company that aligned with the areas where I wanted to expand my visionary work. Lands' End was first conceived, in the 1960s, as a sailing supplier. It had a background of interest in the natural environment and philanthropic causes. The late founder, Gary Comer, had been an early voice calling attention to climate change, while personally funding social enterprises in education and health care.

Lands' End also appealed to me for its presence on the digital map. Originally a mail-order house, the company still mailed out catalogues but also had been a pioneer in online business, which at that point accounted for 85% of its sales while for the rest of the retailers' companies, it was almost in the infant phase. Here was an opportunity to explore and test new ideas in both the online world and face-to-face retail. Better yet, these opportunities were wrapped in a package that looked too hard to resist: CEO and Board Director, a position which was a longtime dream of mine!

Lands' End was seeking to build from past accomplishments into a promising future and I could execute it with the mission of leading visionary innovation and global expansion at a company recently listed on the NASDAQ stock exchange. As a platform for that venture, the company had a large base of loyal customers, but they were mostly middle-aged and older people who liked the brand's traditional styles and practical outdoor wear. A key goal was to keep those customers while also becoming a global brand for younger buyers. This would mean increased competitive pressure, because in addition to competing with similar companies such as LL Bean, there would be tough competition from the growing ranks of companies selling contemporary-styled clothes at moderate prices. At that time, foreign brands like H&M and Zara already had a strong reach. Most importantly, Amazon and many others were entering the field from the United States, including the Japanese Uniqlo.

Since I was operating with almost twenty years of innovation nicked in my belt, the Lands' End Board saw in me a potential answer. I would be an outsider bringing in new views and ideas, a classic disruptor, and disruption did not scare me. It was in my DNA. So, then, did all signs mean go for it? Not really. As I worked through interviews and meetings with the Board, my close family members raised some caution flags and so did my inner voice. For one thing, Land's End was not a company like Lego where in 80 years they had 4 CEO, the rotation was much higher since Sears bought them. Further, my career until that time had been in companies and industries where rapid innovation was a constant: telecom, with its continual move to next-generation phones and networks; fashion, with new collections for the shows and ready-to-wear lines twice a year, and Ferrari constantly updating the cars and the racing team. Lands' End was more a company built around different virtues: solid tradition and reliable offerings. When these factors merged in my mind, they formed images suggesting that I could be a fish in the wrong pond. But didn't the same factors point to reasons why the Board had approached me? To bring to the company a global perspective and some of that racing-team, move-fast-into-the-future spirit? To reassure myself, I ran a due-diligence checklist on the genesis and status of Lands' End.

First: I felt a strong connection with the philosophy of the deceased founder, Gary Comer. I was and am a supporter of the 3P approach (Profit, People, and Planet) and could add the P of Purpose. *Check.*

Second: The company had good cash flow. Sales were declining since a few years, but it was not losing money. This was a good starting point for my bottom-line-driven manager mentality. *Check.*

Third: Lands' End's strong online customer base looked like a definite advantage for leadership in the digital revolution. *Check.*

Fourth: While innovation and a new vision were needed, the company was widely respected for its quality, value, and service, all important points to leverage from. *Check.*

Fifth: The current foreign operations were only in three countries, but they were strong countries—the UK, Germany, Japan. Growth from these beachheads could be driven by the kind of international mindset that I had always had. *Check.*

Recap: I saw myself advocating for technology and sustainability with the support of the company. I felt I could team up with the hard-working people at Lands' End, and, together, we could make the company and their town relevant worldwide. The company was not broken, and I had the discipline to delight customers and employees while keeping the shareholders close in mind. *Check, check, check* and besides: although Lands' End might be an unobvious match for me in some respects, envisioning and pursuing the unobvious was at the core of my being. And didn't the company itself deserve credit for displaying the same quality? After all, looking at it from their side of the table, I must have seemed an unobvious choice for them too. Yet they were willing to make a courageous leap. Surely, we could then be compatible partners in disruption to create growth, couldn't we?

Still, I needed to keep facing my inner voice. It said things like: *Maybe the unobvious would turn on me. Maybe what seemed like a bold move would indeed be wrong and smack me from behind like a screen door snapping shut.* But for the first time, I didn't want to listen to those voices in my head and in my belly. I had my sirens, like the brave Odysseus, only I didn't let myself be tied to the mast so as not to give in and follow my journey, but instead I listened to the sweet sound of my dream of becoming a CEO of a listed company. And I followed that song. With that dream whispering sweeter tunes in my ear, I chose to focus on the positive possibilities that reinvention could bring, by leading a legacy company through cutting-edge transformation rather than the risks and the negative consequences. The Lands' End Board and I met many times before getting into contract negotiations. I spoke with the previous and (who later became) the new chairwoman about the vision and what was needed to be done, even giving printed material and a summary on how I saw the future of Lands' End. Each time we met I dressed in my own personal style, trying never to misrepresent who I was or what I believed. They liked what they were hearing and asked me to put my vision into a presentation. I prepared that presentation during the Christmas vacation of 2014, after having done plenty of research on the company, customers, competition, and more. The Board loved what they were seeing and decided to share it internally. Whenever doubts were raised by either side about my fit with the company, we found ways to dwell on the vision, the drive, and my track record of success. Those things framed me as the right candidate for the job, an expression of the future the company seemed to need. The Board and I reached an agreement on my base location, being New York City, where Lands' End also had an office since a few years prior my arrival that required my attention, but I would need to spend about half of my time in Dodgeville. The job would have me jump across great geographic differences and an equally great culture gap. Dodgeville is a US municipality located in Wisconsin, in Iowa County therefore I was headed for the Midwest. *How was I going to be considered over there?* My Jiminy cricket voice was questioning, but I quickly responded that previous big changes in my career had shown I had the flexibility to change industries and environments, so I was going to be well accepted. One of my fortes since childhood was being able to relate to people across boundaries. If I backed out now, I might always feel that I had let the fears of a similar challenge keep me from my brave dream of leading a significant company.

More complications arose before I could take the helm of that ship. Lands' End wanted me on board quickly. Certainly, two weeks' resignation notice to Dolce & Gabbana would be OK? Actually, it wasn't. The American quick-departure model did not match Dolce's Italian model, which called for notice periods lasting up to one month for each year worked. I knew I would disappoint the longtime employers who had embraced me, leaving them hard-pressed to find a replacement. But I was told that when a company is publicly traded in America, there are precise rules to follow that I could not abstain from. I had no choice but to accept to communicate everything in a short time. I tried to explain my difficulty many times to the Designers, but unfortunately, they didn't allow further contact after I left in that short period of notice. At that time, I was disrupting my family too. Because I specified, we would not move our home to Wisconsin, our son Gabriel could stay in his New York school and activities he just became accustomed, having just changed into a new fully American school from the Italian bilingual one. That was important as children need certainties and habits. But my husband Antonio and I grew increasingly apart after moving from Italy to New York, a distance as great as the ocean separating the two countries had been created between us. We believe that distance was always there, but the move made it show things we never realized we had to have and at that time they felt impossible to bear. We knew it was time to make some difficult decisions. However, we remained united on one thing, which was very important for both of us: We would have preserved our son from all the difficulties and suffering linked to our separation, seeking the best solutions for him and remaining present as we had always been supporting each other along the new way. Calling this a difficult step would be an understatement. Antonio and I loved one another dearly. What made us married was pure love, no rational thinking behind it, indeed, as I described earlier, we had married despite many differences in our personalities and life paths. Together we made the split as loving and as smooth as we could, having spoken many times about it. We prepared Gabriel for this life adjustment. His grandmothers, nevertheless, decided to continue living together and we could spend the most traditional holidays with them too, keeping being all together for these key moments. Separation happens and it is often inevitable, love changes shape, but I believe that this path can be faced with mutual solidarity, caring for each other and for the family. After meeting so many couples with difficult (at times impossible) relationships and some with horrible divorce stories, I really believe that me and Antonio can offer a great example of how to reach a happy and loving divorced parenthood to our beloved children being each other a real support, not only financially but emotionally. Kindness, gratitude, respect, and ultimately, acceptance are keys to overcome the mourning of the split. We are destinated to live several of them, however, as the Coldplay sing, I still believe in "Magic". But it is important to learn how to peacefully split and deal with separations to reduce the impact on the rest of our lives, including work. So, I informed Lands' End board chair, telling her that they should know about my personal life was about to change and I was giving them a chance to rescind their offer in case that was an issue. They did not. At the end of January 2015, I signed three very important papers: my resignation at Dolce & Gabbana, a new employment contract, and my divorce.

In the hours that followed those fateful days, I found myself walking through an unbelievable pile of disruption at my feet. The New York part of the globe was trembling beneath me. I had thrown a grenade into the safety and quality of life I had created. There would be no more taking my son to school every day; no more daily stops at Sant Ambroeus to get a cappuccino walking to the office; no more Milan fashion shows or backroom meetings with the women's network I had created; and no more familiarity with a hundred things, including what I had truly considered my "family" at Dolce & Gabbana. The chicken in me was loud-voiced and I quivered at the thought of leaving them. The sky was feeling grey and foggy in those early moments, with no lighthouse to guide me. Greater clarity dawned as the days ticked closer to February 17th, when I was scheduled to move my work address away from Madison Avenue to Madison, Wisconsin, the new place where I would spend much of my working time and focus. A special occasion on the 14th, Valentine's Day, helped to lift me over the top. In keeping with the American tradition to celebrate and praise new ventures, my dear friend Simone hosted a party in her beautiful home. We decided to have the house decorated with red roses and candies, a sign of the love we wanted everyone to feel. Throughout the crowd were many friendly faces who had been close to me during my fantastic first years in America. They were all extraordinary people in their own fields, from fashion to real estate, media, health, banking, and more. I took the opportunity to thank each one, while they surrounded me with best wishes for embarking on such a bold move. I was radiant; I was excited. I was ready to set sail and see infinite horizons where the earth seemed never to end.

The Alien

When I entered on my first day as CEO my enthusiasm was on par. The main office building at Lands' End headquarters is like a hidden treasure on the Midwestern plains. It is welcoming through extensive use of wood paneling and trim, with an airy atrium in its midst. Everyone had plenty of space, also my office was large with a view of the surrounding country-side, a long desk, and even a sofa. I arrived in my usual high heels but then changed into flats as I walked a lot between meeting rooms and several buildings. Connecting with the people at the company was my first goal. I wanted to stay humble and relate with them, learn their names, their stories, and help them to have a voice where needed. In meeting with the teams, I introduced myself by sharing not only my past work experiences, why I chose to take the job and what I thought we could achieve togeth-er, but also that I was a self-made woman, coming from a small country village not hugely different from Dodgeville. I told them that their town stirred up fond memories of Santa Severa. Until that moment, I had never spoken so openly about myself with strangers. In my judgment it was nec-essary. I knew that I looked and sounded different from most people there, or the people they were used to seeing—a petite young woman as CEO. Someone whose spurs were earned in the halls of high fashion, not the heartland. An immigrant with a foreign accent, who planned to descend from the sky in an aircraft every so often. It would be extremely easy to be seen as an *Alien*. I was feeling like the protagonist of the Sting's son, *"I'm an Alien. I'm a legal Alien"* and try to keep the words in mind from my "adopted mom" Karen uses to tell me (also in the Sting's song), *"be yourself no matter what they say."* So, I wanted these people to have a look behind the exterior at the fellow human inside.

While some team members gave me a warm reception, I perceived that other seemed worried about having a new CEO. Perhaps they were con-cerned about losing their jobs, or having their roles changed, or being affect-ed by new policies that could reduce their benefits. Their presence brought me face to face with the size and complexity of the organization I was charged with leading. Lands' End in early 2015 had about 5,000 employees, many of them local people working here at HQ. They worked for a company founded years prior but were very young as a public entity—pressured with high investors' expectations—and amid serious economic headwinds that were cutting down consumer spending especially on items like their goods. In my daily 50-minute rides from Madison to Dodgeville and back, I reflected on how I could bring positive energy to the company's people and get their commitment to a new course. If you go back to the news from 2015, almost every company in retail was laying off people. Observing the lack of opportunities in the Dodgeville area compared to big cities like New York, I decided that my plan was to take care of the employees first, just as the founder did, and that no one would fear losing their jobs. I did not have an extra budget to execute on my strategy—so the money to do it had to come from efficiencies—but the cost savings would have to come from areas other than human resources. That to me was the most concrete action to help the entire community. To assess the business, I asked all teams to prepare reports that I went through not just with the department heads but also with their team members. I specifically asked for that as I wanted to see who was doing the various jobs, while learning their skills, their potential and getting to know the culture too. After these meetings, I could see that the culture was strongly connected to the late founder, and I wanted to leverage that.

Having been a customer for my son's school uniforms, I knew I had the honor of serving a company important to many Americans, almost an institution for those who had grown up in their clothes. I took that role *very* seriously. Loyal customers had to be cared for and that should have been our main focus. But, at the same time, it was clear that just guarding the fortress would not be sufficient. Given recent declines in sales, plus a mandate to grow and expand, we needed a sense of urgency to innovate and to crank up the level of competition. We needed to develop with empathy new fits for different body types, from plus sizes to slim-fit. Looking at the situation in terms of existing customer base and product lines, the majority of our customers at the time were suburban men and women between 35 and 54. Many women bought for their children and sometimes for themselves. We'd want to give them more options without changing what they thought was great. Therefore, while keeping on check our core business and core customer base, we needed to add more product lines under which we could offer different styles—something which could not be done by tampering with the core product line, Lands' End. We needed to find different ways as other companies had boosted revenue with separate brands and lines added to the core: Ralph Lauren did it with Polo and Lauren; J. Crew had done it with the more casual and younger Madewell brand; Gap with the lower-priced and more family-oriented Old Navy line. This suggested a brand architecture strategy we could use to reinforce our core classics while expanding in new areas to attract new customers and shopping opportunities. We could revive an edgier-styled line that had been tried some years before, *Canvas by Lands' End*, as several employees suggested. It was aimed mainly at younger moms shopping for their kids and could be worth a more serious try this time around. For its appealing style, it ended up being very noticed—but contrary to what people thought and later commented on—it only accounted for a small percentage of our invested resources in terms of team involved, product development, inventory planning, and so on. The vast majority of our resources were indeed dedicated to the core line and customer base. To respond at the increasingly growing demand of new sports clothes—people started then to dress even at the office in comfy sweatpants, leggings, and sweatshirts—that's why we created a line called *Lands' End Sport*, that could spark more interest in the college students which used to be Lands' End customers in the old days of the founder. Last but not least, with the aim of growing sales in different channel than the existing Sears one, we needed to free the main line, Lands' End, to be positioned into storefronts at different malls such at Nordstrom, Target, or even Saks for example, therefore we conceived a lower tier brand, *Lighthouse by Lands' End*, as it could be sold exclusively at our shops inside Sears stores (the Sears corporation had bought and owned Lands' End for a while before spinning it back out in 2014). These different lines were going to form the "family of brands" and our website was architected in a way that enabled a customer to cross-shopping and choose from which line to shop more clearly depending on their needs. Execution would take a while, and substantial results would take longer with tweaking and course corrections needed along the way. But rethinking product lines and architecting a multiband product strategy, it is only one part of using innovation to recharge a company. Being a company that sold approximately $1B online, it seemed evident we could benefit from an upgrading of the entire technology infrastructure to be among the best-of-breed. This would also involve looking at how we *used* digital technology to drive marketing, supply and inventory control, speed to market, online presence, and decision-making. Our approaches to physical retail could stand for some fresh thinking, too. Meanwhile, in order to expand globally, we had to think in terms of planting flagship stores and creating a wonderful customer experience. Products for both the online sales platforms and the physical stores would have to be streamed in through flexible, state-of-the-art supply chains, for just as an advancing army cannot outrun its supply lines, neither can a growing company.

That breathless paragraph sounds like a lot. And it is, though it's only a brief overview of the work involved in transforming a company, while also assuring that it runs properly from day to day. No CEO could do all the work alone. Teamwork and unity would be essential. The above requires considering our uses of human talent—how to develop and lead the people we had, where to add new staff or contractors, how to avoid head-cutting—and everything would require finding efficiencies to reduce costs while protecting the employees for implementing these plans as just said. "Disruption" would come most strongly into play. Changing the way, a company is equipped, by putting in new machines or software, is tricky but doable. What is more difficult in *any* organization is changing mindsets.

Barriers to change

People think and act as they do for many reasons, depending on the individual. When they form into groups, they adopt shared patterns, which are reinforced with time. Within companies, they set up structures and procedures that support the existing ways, reinforcing them even more. Therefore, it is not entirely true that people "just don't like change," although some truly do not. The more accurate truth is that changing mindsets and direction among large numbers of people just does not come easy. Not everyone can look forward to results in the future; they mainly struggle with the toughness of today.

As I plunged into my CEO's work, I encountered instances of this so-called "path dependence." One example came in regard to the use of printed catalogues. Large quantities were still printed up and mailed out regularly, as in the mail-order days. The online aspect of the business kicked in when people consulted their catalogues and ordered over the web. I saw that if we would reduce the mailings, or send them out more selectively, it would lower our carbon footprint while saving money that could then be directed to newer, more targeted, and cost-effective methods of digital marketing. But resistance was both predictable and based on evidence from the past: *The more catalogues we send out, the more orders we get. Why do something that would give us now fewer orders?* I was envisioning a digital transformation that needed to start and eventually trigger the ambitious results we wanted. I was indeed asking: "If we keep sending catalogues to the same customer base spending there most of our marketing money, how can we reach the new?" To me, customer acquisition and reaching new generations were important goals as well as keeping the core. Of course, I could agree to keep sending the same number of catalogues if I was thinking of short-term goals and personal success. But I was more committed to a long-lasting future for the company than my own. The same happened with promotions. *The more you run it, the more dollars you bring in.* If I was thinking of the quarter in front of me, I was putting my feet on this pedal and run as many promotions as I could to increase consumption, but my compass was always directed at building the future with healthier margins and pushed to change the status quo of heavy promotional approach.

People are not simple-minded. They are able to consider the reasons for new ways of doing things and to think about cost-benefit numbers like the amount of sales that come in versus the money spent to get the sales, and eventually they can change. But this can take time and effort because the tendency is to keep doing what has been done before. And if you multiply these brief examples by many more encountered across the company, you can begin to form a picture of the obstacles that confront a change agent. Especially if she looks like an *Alien*! Indeed, as the business consultant Gary Hamel put it in his book *Humanocracy*, most big companies are bureaucratic and "bureaucracies are also innovation-phobic." Therefore, says Hamel, "being a maverick is a high-risk occupation." But I persisted along with many of my new colleagues.

After giving the Board a 30/60/90-day action plan early in the game, I decided to present a strategic three-year plan once I had a better grasp of the business and could try a few initiatives to test the company's capabilities. My thinking was ambitious. I stayed audacious in pushing the company to think bigger, seeing no reasons we could not build the kind of international network that Japan-based Uniqlo eventually did. At the April 2015 board meeting, I laid out a sound plan, which took tremendous teamwork, and had it accepted. To enable ongoing innovation, methods like *Scrum* were key drivers—not the rugby term, but the fast-moving approach borrowed from agile software development, which promises getting twice the work done in half the time was fascinating (and you can learn about it in the book of that title, *Scrum)*. One key message was the need to move fast but be patient in expecting results. That is why investors in high-tech startup companies play both a speed game and a long game. They want their companies to act quickly to develop, test, and refine new ideas—which can be a lot of work in itself—with the expectation that a few years later, once a good idea has taken hold across the market, big payoffs will come in. Overnight hits are extremely rare, just think of Amazon, the company took years to reach consistent profits. For the Lands' End Board, I used case studies of successful transformation in clothing firms, noting key drivers of success and risks that could lead to not making it. The first long-run strategic objective—in which I strongly believed in—was for us to move from being an iconic legacy company to a "meaningful global lifestyle brand." I insisted that we used the word "meaningful" despite some push backs. Indeed, for many Millennials and the newer generations in the pipeline after them, Gen Z, it wasn't enough to present a pretty face or have a recognized logo anymore. These thoughtful younger people were starting to care about how people everywhere lived and worked, and many older people were caring equally if not more. Whether it was advocating for girl's education with Malala Yousafzai or converting cof-

fee grounds into biofuel with Arthur Kay's bio-bean company, they liked to
see sincere commitment to equitable, sustainable practices. And they favored
buying from companies that exhibit such commitment authentically.

Meanwhile, I concentrated strongly on efficiencies, which were and are
my North Star. My philosophy, rooted in the cash-poor upbringing that I
have described, has always been to "look behind the numbers" and find ways
of doing more with less. I was delighted to see teams at Lands' End respond-
ing to challenges to do likewise, as they quickly learned that "no" was not an
acceptable answer for me for at least three times. Through 2015, for example, we in fact spent less on marketing than the previous year while doing so
much more with that budget (and people who later said the opposite were
just not well informed, as the numbers of the balance sheets are clear). Another key element, which required upfront investment, was installing new
technologies for optimizing all parts of a company's operations, which in
turn can lead to positive gains in company-wide efficiency.

There was urgency pressing hard upon us. The stock market was stut-
tering and falling. Almost every fashion retailer, from high-end to low, was
reporting any or all of the following: job cuts, sales reductions, tremendous
margin pressure, and store closures. On top of the many articles written
at the time on this stall momentum in 2015, all public disclosure earnings
calls will confirm this reality, and everyone can verify these facts. During
sleepless nights and weekend jogging back in Central Park, I was constantly
analyzing every detail to figure out what to do best, how to do it, when further business decisions needed to be made. I continue to focus on excellence
- building brand equity, business capabilities and skills. We were working
hard, and the only real weapon was T I M E. You can't change the course of
a big ship with a magic wand; you have to persevere while having confidence
in the overall endeavor. And, in the *Alien*.

Leading in the 21st Century

A fundamental asset to infusing innovation, designing new collections, rein-
vigorating existing ones, and revitalizing the organization are the people—
the human capital. Human capital is the set of skills, knowledge, emotions,
and abilities that a person acquires during his or her life and that are aimed
at achieving social and economic objectives, both individual and collective.
The logic should always be that of sustainability. Human capital has been
the subject of numerous studies and analyses, in particular by economist
Gary Becker, who was awarded the Nobel Prize in 1992. The future development of our societies cannot do without it. In the first nine months at

Lands' End, I spent half of my time with the team in Wisconsin to cultivate internal talent (not just a week a month as per my contract). To build new talent, I spent time in the New York office too, where we transformed the existing space into a Lab with very little spending, so we could attract more innovators to gain the experience that I thought was missing. One of the new talents, Scott, a long-time manager of an established American brand, was in charge of the supply chain to improve product quality and sourcing. He, like the other key hires at that time, could integrate very well with the rest of the organization. I needed to build a bridge between the old and the new and adding "aliens" wouldn't work. While hiring new talent was important, promoting internal ones and continuing to cultivate know-how was also a priority. I empowered teams and pushed for promotions at Dodgeville. One of the first promotions was Becky, a talented resource who had left and come back wishing to become an executive vice president, and I was happy to help her break into the "C" suite. After her, many other internal talented people were promoted, and nothing was making me happier than seeing them thriving!

In the area of digital technology, which is crucial for competing in the future, we launched many initiatives. We began by improving the technology infrastructure and order fulfillment. One of the first contracts I signed in my early months at the company was for an ERP program. (Enterprise Resource Planning is a category of business management software that companies use to collect, manage, interpret, and store data.) The goal was to be better positioned for e-commerce expansion in an omni-channel mode and the ERP was a key tool to dramatically improve efficiency across many functions: merchandising, operations, finance, accounting, and more. Shortly after, we signed an agreement with another company to help with change management, as it is not possible to transform the digital platform without the support of the people. From a customer perspective, in my opinion, it was mandatory to improve the shopping experience by making it easier for people to find attractive products and buy them. Therefore, we needed to upgrade the operational efficiency, algorithms, and search functionality of the website since the way people were shopping had been increasingly influenced by evaluations, comments, suggestions on buying behavior, and so on. I often took screenshots from competitors' websites and sent them as examples to my team. Improvement requires an innovative approach and *analyzing* to *learn* is key. How were other leaders in e-retail doing it? Who was setting the standards? Why didn't we have them yet? How could we integrate them? What could we bring to the customer to improve the KPIs (Key Performance Indicators)? These were the types of questions I often asked the teams. They seemed surprised at how much I had been able to observe, both internally and from our competitors, which then led me to push them to understand the need to try new things. The company's main technology players rapidly bought into upgrading our digital infrastructure and customer experience. I was focused on improving exactly that for both core and new customers and just three months after my arrival, we successfully debuted a more modern web presence with a microsite that gave an idea of the innovation I wanted to bring. We tested products with selected audience segments on that microsite which also served as a springboard to launch a multi-brand architectural site six months later to introduce the cross-selling of the various product lines and categories we were creating. In addition, the website had strong editorial content to stimulate sales and attract new consumers. We were constantly updating the entire site to offer a better merchandise assortment and to streamline the checkout process. Finally, we restored the creation of a digital catalog we had launched in the fall to spur the company's digitization.

My so-called "digital revolution" ultimately involved creating a mobile app to make the shopping experience as consistent as possible from all touch points. And I hoped to introduce video streaming at our stores and call centers, so customers could have immediate interaction with the extraordinary people in them.

#IamLandsfriendly

While executing the strategy and restructuring the operations, I was also launching initiatives in the area of corporate social responsibility. And we showed that CSR could go hand in hand with building the business. One of our first projects was a focus on sustainability. It had the social purpose of promoting and supporting sustainable practices, while positioning Lands' End as a leader on an issue of great interest to the younger-generation customers we wanted to attract, too. Because of the company name, I called the overall project #IamLandsfriendly and presented it on Earth Day, with a series of activities that were about taking care of our land and where the land ends. The timing of the launch had extra significance for us. In my research, I had learned that the person who initiated the first Earth Day in 1970 was US Senator Gaylord Nelson of Wisconsin. Just as that Earth Day went international from Lands' End's home state, the company could aspire to do the same following this footprint since we could do it while supporting the same principles that Senator Nelson had hoped to see adopted everywhere.

For most people and organizations, in 2015, this was truly advanced thinking. Just consider that six years later, in February of 2021, and even after the pandemic, the newsletter *CEO Daily* remarked on the number of companies starting to do social projects were still questioned whether this was just an attempt to make the companies look good or if it made business sense as well. Alan Murray, the former CEO of Fortune Media, concluded that: "The business focus on social goals is not a passing political play. It's a fundamental business trend. And all signs suggest it will continue to grow." So, you can probably imagine that since I was already understanding this trend several years before, I began to draw some attention for being in the vanguard. My focus was on sustainability, which wasn't yet so very common among fashion companies except for some leading players. At a New York conference called "Woman in the World," I was honored to be an invited speaker, among leading women from many fields, to discuss sustainability. A video still available on YouTube, will confirm my bold vision for our initiatives at that time which spanned a broad range of projects, including the Zero Landfill Project aimed at creating a landfill-free world. As individuals and corporate members alike, I felt urged to reduce the carbon footprint and strongly wanted to set a goal of planting one million trees to help restore natural resources, which we did in 2015 with the National Forest Foundation. In line with the digitization project, we sought to reduce the company's use of printed materials. To become really sustainable, we needed to study a better way to recycle clothing and tell the world that Lands' End products were "forever"—that is, extremely long-lasting—so that buying them would be a conscious choice. The following year, along with planting one million trees, we encouraged our customers to "Take the Pledge to Plant," and on April 22 (Earth Day) gave a free tree "grow kit" with every direct or online purchase. For every tree that customers planted and registered at ForestNation.com/LandsEnd, the company planted a tree in a developing nation through Forest Nation. To create team spirit and keep our community-building approach, we also participated to the "clean the lake" campaign and, together with other colleagues and our children, we went literally to our close lake to clean it from waste. It was one of the fond memories I have while working at the company.

We had many initiatives in place to drive customer acquisition. One I had in mind, which fit the vision of building a meaningful lifestyle brand, was to elevate the customer experience not only online but also offline. A way to reinforce the message was to have a few flagship stores but to be more efficient, we decided to open first some pop-up stores in big cities. The pop-up concept at that time was not very common or widespread in retail as it become after. It was used mainly by businesses that sold seasonal merchandise, such as for Halloween, so they could have a short-term sales presence without leasing a storefront year-round. But it could also be seen as a way to break new ground, and to learn from experimentation. A pop-up that is well-designed and placed could expose the company to new customers, give them memorable in-store experience, and allow trial-and-error testing of the company's capabilities along with new approaches to retail. After an intense summer focused on trying to impact existing projects while creating new ones, I thought our company was ready for such experimentation in a few major cities where we could get traction to being later the international expansion, such as New York and Boston. While gaining great visibility and relevance overall, we could acquire new domestic customers and finally test foreign customers' appetite for the brand. We wanted to showcase the best selection of products the company offered and could potentially sell to many more people in addition to our loyal customers who engaged in the catalogues, growing the customer acquisition. With time I developed a good relationship with my previous landlord of Fifth Avenue while I was at DG, and he happened to have a free space so I proposed to rent it temporarily for a much lower rate so I could get an amazing deal to use over 9,000 square feet on a highly trafficked corner to make an idea become a reality. The pop-up would be open throughout the busy holiday shopping season, from around Thanksgiving of 2015, through Christmas and into the New Year when the city teemed with people—while a similar pop-up also opened in Boston. In line with the overall strategy, we wanted the opening of the pop-up store to sync with a meaningful event. I chose November 11th, Veterans' Day. We invited veterans to the ribbon cutting and agreed to donate a per-centage of sales to a veterans' foundation (something we later repeated for Memorial Day weekend).

This new store gave all of us the opportunity to work more closely in building something new and test new abilities. It was the result of an ex-traordinary teamwork—from the merchandising, to the logistics, to the IT, the marketing and, of course, the retail teams that we ended up having beau-tiful, innovative pop-up stores that gave a wonderful customer experience as we envisioned—in a very new efficient way. The concept store was modeled after a ski chalet concept and designed to be a fun-filled destination. Cus-tomers were able to experience the brand and products first-hand, and we reached millions of media impressions as well. For the innovative way the store was conceived, we had media coverage both locally and nationally, in outlets from NY1 who came to the store to interview me and the team, to Bloomberg TV where I went to give an interview for the early morning pro-gram, to a full-page article in The New York Times and more. They were impressed by the way the store was merchandised, with comfortable and appealing products for men, women, kids, and the home. In the adorable kids' section, we had an area for them to play while parents were shopping.

There was a section for home products and one dedicated to pets, and adorable stuffed animals were all around. The atmosphere was truly warm, thanks not only to the overall set-up and decorations, but for the attention to every single detail from the place and the people. I had passionately suggested having a video screen on the big street-side window to show a beautiful video called "We Believe in You," which featured an ode to an extensive family reunion full of joy, love, care, and everything that is great about America. Everyone could feel like a customer while watching it. I still get chills when I view it today! Inside the store, images on the walls captured the same family reunion. We even printed a few books with these new images. At the front of the book was a young girl with a globe in her hands, looking at it with questions filling her mind; in the end was an old woman with the same globe but with a great smile on her face, as if she had lived and learned a lot in life. That was the essence of the video: a life worth living. I recommended we use a gigantic globe as our iconic setup piece and of course made from recyclable material! You could hear the beautiful "I Believe" song ("*for every drop of rain that falls a flower grows*") over the sound system while shopping—and delighted customers with comfortable chairs and a digitally generated fireplace to warm up the atmosphere of the holidays.

For being "just" a pop-up, the best surprise to me was the impeccable, efficient service we were able to offer, as everyone was well trained in how to win a customer's connection to the brand. I had learned the value of that from my previous experience: training, training, and more training! Throughout the store, we added special touches that customers could enjoy. There was a station for monogramming scarves, totes, gloves, and other products with initials of the customer's choice, and hot chocolate was offered at the cocoa bar we created. My very favorite area was—of course—the one that featured innovation. At a conference in San Francisco, I had met the CEO of a company working in virtual reality. So, I asked if we could make an agreement to showcase their products in our pop-up. Working together with his company's team and mine, we brought a new dimension to the store. By wearing VR glasses, you could explore new lands around the world, something great for entertaining our customers! Also, in speaking with a talented friend and founder of an innovative retail business, she told me about a company that had a machine for making selfies (we couldn't yet do it with our phones). The pictures could be printed out right there or shared virtually. I thought this could be great for engaging younger visitors and, indeed, it was. That year, Black Friday and Cyber Monday set sales records for Lands' End. Since I had been with the company for only three quarters, it was still too soon to be showing overall revenue and profit growth, which didn't yet kick in, but I felt confident that the growth mode would come. And for the time being, I was glad to celebrate with my team and spend holiday time with my New

York family and friends. I felt incredibly grateful and expressed all my sense of gratitude.

Non-obvious lessons

As innovation at Lands' End gained momentum, I was invited to speak to a class on innovation and the power of story at Stanford's Graduate School of Business, taught by the behavioral scientist and professor Dr. Jennifer Aaker. They were particularly attracted by my approach and the "design with empathy." To set the stage for the discussion, they created a case study called "The Innovation Playbook", to which they added the title of my presentation and work "Envisioning the non-obvious." The case delved into my strategy for creating growth, profitability, and adaptability, with a focus on the first period of my time at the company in which meaningful projects were indeed a priority.

These projects branched into multiple areas, as we were engaging in partnerships to do initiatives around sustainability, historic preservation, education, and family health. In the classroom setting at Stanford, I discussed how these efforts aligned with our overall vision and strategy to build a stronger foundation for Lands' End, enhance our existing strengths, and evolving the company. The case also sparked a deeper discussion of how Lands' End could potentially turn the young generation into new customers. On a personal level, as I watched the students, I reflected on how cool it must have felt to be in their position, where learning is the main objective and recommended that they would keep a lifelong learning mindset in their jobs. As they were envisioning their lives, I spoke of how my experiences had shaped a thirst for constant improvement. And I shared a few key principles I strongly believe in.

- *Cultivate a 360-degree Mindset.* I always encouraged my teams to conceive projects with a 360-degree mindset. It is a mindset that allows you to think across all categories, markets, targets, functions, and channels. I have also encouraged the teams to apply the same thinking to create holistic projects that integrate all touch points and maximize our messaging and results embracing the entire value chain, not only the most evident external point of contact. If you broaden your horizons (drawing on the Human Pillar of Curiosity), you have more chances to amplify the outcome of anything you do.
- *Excellence Supersedes Perfection.* Many leaders focus on perfection, using that as a bar to judge employees and projects. The problem with this mindset is that it eventually breeds a culture of fear—the fear of failing.

Focusing on excellence means continually raising the bar for the team to improve performance. Excellence doesn't mean you should not make mistakes, but you should keep trying new things and quickly learn from mistakes. Before acting, you must gain the best possible knowledge of things, assessing the risks and striving for the best possible outcome. But then take risks and then learn from the results on how you can still raise the bar next time. I encourage employees to engage in lifelong study, gather knowledge, act swiftly, and use an analytical, research-driven approach to achieve excellence.

- *Change and Adapt.* I suspect that one reason why changing, and adapting has worked for me—and what I continue to cultivate even now—is what Carol Dweck calls the "growth mindset," in which you are open to changes, and look at challenges as opportunities to learn. With that, you can do much more in your career and in your life. The more you learn how to adapt to change, the bigger the range of opportunities in front of you can be. As it has been said in a summary of Darwin's thoughts, "It is not the most intelligent or strongest of the species that survive, but the one that is most adaptable to change."
- *Be Nimble and Exercise Skills.* To win competitively nowadays it is crucial to be fast and nimble. Along with speed, I motivate my teams to achieve greater efficiency with our resources. The reality is that you can get twice as far in half the time if you have a dual focus on speed and efficiency. As for skills: We are all born with aptitudes for excelling "naturally" in certain ways, but there are others in which we struggle. In environments that reward being nimble and adaptive, it is important to find ways to not just execute on your strengths, but also to improve on your weaknesses. In this way, you can both reach your short-term objectives and build new skills for winning in opportunities to come.
- *Lead with Purpose.* True leadership always has a purpose. Whether it's fostering a sense of unity in a team, keeping in mind the greater cause behind executing strategies, or ultimately feeling a sense of fulfillment in our work, we must have a purpose. As a CEO, one of my purposes in leading Lands' End was to ensure that in doing good business, the company would also make a difference as being a great citizen of the world.

I will tell you in a moment how hard it was for me to perform at Stanford that day-not only because I was in a place where people dream of going to college and in front of an audience that knew a lot about being different and innovative, but mostly because I was dealing with an unexpected and traumatizing issue.

Legends

During my first year as CEO, I received several calls about opportunities to leave the company and take bigger roles in much larger corporations. The calls and opportunities were definitely flattering. But from my point of view, they were coming at the wrong time. One in particular, as in the movie *Sliding Doors*, could have probably changed my life for the better. But I was truly committed to everyone in and outside the company to accomplish something greater, so I felt I should leave that golden door closed for the time being. Indeed, I needed more time; I was fully convinced of that. I did not know that life was about to show me another turn and send me an unimaginable challenge, which unfortunately would make that gold door completely inaccessible for the future.

A key reason I had joined Lands' End was, in my understanding, my alignment with the DNA of the company's founder. Gary Comer had the heart of a sailor, with a passion for the land, and he loved to give back. While transforming a legacy company and increasing financial performances, I made corporate social responsibility and sustainability our priorities, and that was why I proposed the word "meaningful" in building a global lifestyle brand. Another thing the founder and I had in common was the passion to create visually stunning material, enriched by great content and storytelling. He was a champion. When he created the company, he made sure to have great editors and creative talents following him. They were called the "founding fathers." I spent a lot of time searching for the company archives on his work and fell in love with his ability to create such work. The visuals were striking, either for the beauty of the pictures or the irony they conveyed, and the words were simply elevated. Many times, I wished I could have met this founder, a visionary man for sure! Gary Comer was a pioneer in the concept of making product catalogues almost like magazines, with stories and essays that made you excited to read them, and the advertisements were that way too. Subjects ranged from the company's chinos to the colorful sport line, to his travels around the world and to the "First Person Singular" cover dedicated to working women. Many of his past catalogue issues inspired me to create new ones.

And so, after facing the daunting tasks of streamline operations, reducing the inventory level, increase margins, and building new capabilities, I wanted to elevate the storytelling of our main promotional materials and suggested to create a new program for the catalogue called the *Legends Series*. In each issue, we would feature an interview of someone who could be broadly identified as a "legend." Each would be an inspirational leader or high achiever in some way and would serve as a sort of ambassador with whom customers could relate while reading the catalogue. We thought of including men and women, from young to old, all of them people with wide acceptance and coming from different fields—from business leaders like Jack Welch, to sports stars like Derek Jeter, to entertainment and media legends like Oprah Winfrey and more. Since we saw this as an editorial piece and not a paid commercial, we would contribute to the legends' favorite charities if they would agree to participate. We had a long list of prospective legends in mind and were trying to meet some of them to determine their interest.

First up? Something meaningful for me to talk about editorially was women's equality. I was thinking of someone who could be considered a leading, "legendary" advocate, and could be interviewed on how she saw women continuing their mission to advance equality. The goal was to engage with customers and give them another reason to read the catalogue and possibly shop with more excitement. So, at the beginning of 2016, I was glad to present Ms. Gloria Steinem as a featured legend in our catalogue. My interview focused on how she intended to contribute to closing the gaps that still exist between women and men. She agreed to be photographed with our Lands' End look—a pair of jeans, a T-shirt, a nice scarf, and a cardigan— and as a return she asked that for each "ERA" monogram that customers chose to put on garments bought that month, Lands' End would donate $3 to a foundation she supported.

Growing up in Italy, I had never heard of ERA before I met the president of that organization. *"What does it mean?"* I asked. "Equal Rights Amendment," she told me and explained. Sounded interesting and needed! Now, leading a company that has many kinds of customers, I needed to make sure it was something with broad acceptance. *Is this a bipartisan project?* I asked and checked. I got the confirmation that this issue was broadly supported by women and men across the spectrum in America with a proof of an interesting article in which two major women from the opposite political parties were indeed asking for this Amendment with their signatures. Then, I was convinced—although perhaps only in my ingenuous dreams could certain topics transcend partisan politics. Before we printed that issue of the catalogue, in order to be reassured once again, I sent the interview with Ms. Steinem to some internally who I thought could give me the right guidance. They were enthusiastic about the result of the shooting and interview, and we went ahead with the printing of the catalogue the next day which was mailed out in February of 2016.

Different opinions

The reaction of customers was like a powerful lightning storm, shouting down and blacking out every other light.

> *OMG! What is happening?!!?* I kept asking myself.

Many customers were furious. They reacted to the interview with vengeance on social media. Emails flooded our inboxes with accusations of supporting abortion. *What?!* It was never mentioned in the interview! That was not the subject of our dialogue and the initiative! *Really?* Who thought that in 2016 the abortion law was being questioned?! I only really saw the full extent of things later. In Italy the law on reproductive rights with specific restrictions was made in 1978, so probably my mother fought for it. I learned that in the United States, it was decided in court even earlier, in 1973. The issue of abortion was not on my radar at all since women of my age took that right for granted. For me, the current issue for women to fight for was equality, closing the gender gap, especially in the workplace! I was able to be a businesswoman thanks to many women who had paved the way, as indeed the legendary woman I interviewed did by creating the first magazine dedicated to women causes, and equality was what we were discussing in the editorial piece of the catalogue. Yet many wrote to us in a heated and resentful way. There was rage and contempt, and disappointment all wound up like panties in a bunch. It seemed that everyone got hurt. Indeed, Lands' End issued an apology for having offended some of customer's beliefs but then other customers, who instead liked the interview and the overall initiative, scolded us. *Oh my.... What on earth is going on?* We were left like a camper out of gas on a cross-country trip—high and dry. When I signed up for retail disruption, this is certainly not what I had in mind. I was distraught. There I was ... the unlikely character ... whose striving for excellence was being criticized ... whose fair and inclusive nature was being put to the test ... whose strength was being challenged. *What lesson is this?* I asked myself.

I knew that perfection did not exist and that mistakes had to be part of the game. *But this?* In a very naïve way, I had touched a nerve none, and me of course, had realized was so sensitive. Still, I could not give in to fear, not with my background, my sacrifices, and my life! I had to take a step forward and fight with excellence in my hands. To fight every battle, every action, every obstacle in front of me with strength and will to do good. I was born with that outlook on life. I had a hunger inside me that pushed me to dominate my fears. This simple ability allowed me to envision the non-obvious. The young girl from a small village outside Rome, now faced with the indignation of the American public, needed to recall the criticisms from her childhood and her art of quietly persisting by drawing on strengths invisible to others. She needed to face the truth with the same courage and humility. All I could rely on, were my Human Pillars—especially Courage. I needed the courage to rise above confusion and fears. Above all, I needed the courage to do what I could for whoever might be helped by it.

The day the PR crisis erupted should have been a wonderful day. I was at Stanford, preparing to speak to the students. Before taping videos of my principles which I described before and giving the lecture, my phone was burning with calls and emails from all over: from my team, from customers, from our HR department, the PR agency, the board. I couldn't cancel the session, although my mood was not what you need for performing in front of a room filled with enthusiastic students who want to learn from you. *What lessons can I give them?* I used stamina I didn't know I had left, after a year of running against the wind. I did okay. The content of my message at the university was something I strongly believed, so I stayed on course and kept going. The evening after the class at Stanford, I went to a book presentation at an important venue in Palo Alto which I had committed to attend. I was glad to speak with a graceful lady who was stronger than I expected after the loss of her son, the host's husband. She truly impressed me with her wisdom and brought me a sense of relativity. But being there wasn't the place I wanted to be and couldn't really think of mingling with anyone. I went outside the big room to speak with the Lands' End board chair on the phone and told her I was going to leave that night, taking a red eye to be in the office the next morning. I wanted—and needed—to be with my team. I landed around 5 a.m. and drove to the headquarters to arrive before anyone. Above all, I wanted to meet with the customer service people as they got a lot of phone complaints calls. They saw my human side in a way they probably hadn't seen before. That vulnerable moment was our hook, and we became much closer, feeling like being together to face the issue.

While I bonded more with most of that team, it seemed very clear that some executives and directors were disappointed by my choice to run that interview. Reflecting later on what happened, I concluded it was surely true that I wasn't aware of certain social and political divisions in the country, but also that the *timing* of the interview's release was a key trigger point. 2016 was indeed an election year and most importantly, everything was used to divide, and these divisions were taking on sharper edges. Most likely, our initiative—which could have been just one of many in celebration of women, and for which I had chosen a *true legend*—was seen differently than it might have been at another time. The cultural shifts of division in 2016 were stronger than expected. In my opinion, this was the biggest obstacle that I and others hadn't foreseen when we decided to go ahead with the initiative.

And now all eyes were on me! I was feeling that my head was WANTED. I was tempted to stop and leave at that moment, but I did not have the luxury to do so. In addition to my responsibility for my family, I couldn't abandon the people I had brought in or the many who had worked so hard on the projects we had in the pipeline, and which were about to take shape. I swallowed my pride and decided to move on with launching those projects. I was focused on mustering up the strength to do better. As perfection is something that cannot be attained, I knew that my rule of excellence would be a realistic value to stick to, as I needed to stay stronger than the critics. With some necessary fortitude—the kind made up of family, faith, and a fair work ethic—I thought I could meet the challenges of my role head on. My search for excellence comes with a clear and outspoken point of view, and I gave my guts, soul, and creativity to my stewardship of the company. I did sense that although I was an attractive choice at first for being different, my difference was probably not so attractive anymore. Still, I was committed to bringing the company up in the world, with the same intensity as if it were a child placed in my care. The projects I had worked on, my quest for excellence and my work ethic would have to be proof of my commitment.

Since the start of my journey at Lands' End I knew that it would take time to turn around the business, especially considering the tough retail environment we were facing. Revenue growth was not yet coming, and the board was becoming impatient. Most probably, the company realized that they didn't need to change after all, and if that was the case, then I was not the right person anymore. While we were planning the following fiscal year in September 2016 the board and I agreed to part ways. I agreed that it was better to let someone else lead the company in the future. Indeed, at that point, we had made much progress which was enough to trigger much success. Despite all the boulders that had to be moved in shifting to a company of 5,000 people, I believed I had infused innovation at all levels. And I learned a lot too. We definitely enriched each other and came to understand our skills more deeply. Furthermore, after many years, the company was again in the public eye. Not only due to the catalogue incident but also due to many positive steps that ranged from a better shopping experience, customer-centric focus, sustainability initiatives to the pop-up stores and much more, Lands' End was being noticed and seen as relevant by the media, the investors, the influencers, ... and above all, by the people!

It is quite normal that disruptive people do not enjoy the results of their work during their time. I would often say that I was working for the next CEOs. I had inherited a company in which direct (online) net revenue was decreased by 8.2% compared to the previous year I joined and the net revenue from retail stores was down by 15.5%, compared to the previous year's perimeter. Exactly two years later, a few months after I stepped down and a new CEO was appointed, net revenue in the direct segment showed just a 1.7% decrease and retail net revenue had *increased* 2.1%, on a same-store basis. The company I left was indeed at the cusp of the positive trend we had worked hard for, which in fact kicked in from the second quarter of 2017. I had given all I could to make a remarkable change and in my short time at the helm of the company we had done a lot. On Friday when I met the Board to face my tough new reality, I texted Antonio, my biggest supporter, and the person I could always rely on, asking him to be home for me that evening. I felt the meeting I was going to attend could have been a tough one. And it was. Indeed, we discussed my end at that land. I spent the weekend working on necessary documents and a press release which was sent out the following Monday. To avoid any potential leak, I stayed home the whole weekend and canceled an evening commitment with one of our partners who had invited me and my colleague Khadija to see Adele in concert. She had just released a fabulous new album. The song "Hello" felt like it was written for me:

"...Hello from the outside. At least I can say that I've tried."

Some takeaways

Perusing excellence doesn't make you immune from failures. You learn more from mistakes. Innovate, transform, and improve operation excellence challenging status quo. Be a maverick. Keep an open mindset to grow. Understand the context not only company culture.

True leadership always has a purpose. Choose yours wisely. Fact checks even best advisors.

Focus on growth, profitability, and agility. Find efficiencies, looking behind the numbers. Build capabilities, improve your offer and services a step at the time. Allow time to adjust. Drive always customer acquisition, delight your customers.

Win competition by knowing them well and creating your adding value proposition.

In each profession what is always key is great training and team empowerment.

Be a team player, stay close to them especially in tough moments. It creates a unique bond. Visionary people take higher risks for long-term success. Prepare to see others taking credits.

If your decisions were wrong, don't give it to fears. Give it all you can to correct and learn. When pioneering, remember to listen to your inner voice and distinguish challenges from mission impossible.

Six: Envision Leadership
Human Pillar: Compassion

*"Out of suffering have emerged
the strongest souls; the most massive
characters are seared with scars."*
—Khalil Gibran

Two vital qualities serve as foundations for being a great leader. One is the ability (and willingness) to constantly learn, evolve, and grow. This is important because leaders are constantly *tested*. Unexpected challenges come up; some ventures don't work out; conditions change. To lead innovatively, it is necessary to innovate who you are: ever learning from the past while evolving and enriching oneself for the future. The other quality has to do with being a so-called "people person." This is necessary in the sense of seeing and treating others as fellow human beings, who have qualities of their own that can be cultivated. The best leaders relate to people positively. They look for goodness and strength in others. They know that each of us can have hard times and sorrows; their goal is to help people move from today's lower or darker states into tomorrow's fullness and light. This particular quality becomes as superpower if it is elevated to *compassion*. It goes indeed a step further than empathy. We find it in great spiritual leaders, and you may have seen it in leaders who've made a difference in your life: great teachers, coaches, supervisors, or people in your family or neighborhood. Maybe sometimes they were tough on you, but you knew they cared for you. *That's* what inspired you to follow their lead and become who you are today.

However, we are left with a perplexing question. If a leader is somebody who cares for others, then who cares for the leader? Once again, the arrow points inward, to where everything starts. Leaders become even more caring and compassionate by showing care and compassion for themselves. Compassion then becomes a currency you can invest in others. Everything you learn will make you more ready, and eager, to invent a future worthy of humanity's vast potential.

The Hurricane

The human brain is incredible. It stores everything, even what we no longer think about, that we forget. At the right time, like a magic box that knows what artifice to present to you, thoughts, images, and sentences re-emerge and manifest themselves on the stage of the mind. In my stormy days, those in which I crossed rough seas no longer knowing what course I would follow, I thought back to a poem. In Elizabeth Barrett Browning's Sonnet 43, she wrote: "How do I love thee? Let me count the ways." And to that I add, "How do I feel for you? Let me count the ways." Compassion is the thread of gold. Forget money. Forget fame. If you really want either of these things it starts with empathy. And not just for others. If we don't have empathy, I would say here, compassion for ourselves, we can never have it for others.

In the days that followed my departure from Lands' End, on mornings without an office to run to, I found myself looking into a stark abyss. Where would I refocus my sense of purpose and my energetic mind? I soon learned that I would need to reach back into time and remember my solid companion. Self-love, self-esteem, and self-determination were skills I mastered as a child. I would need to turn to them as the feelings of loss set in. I found myself standing in front of the mirror looking at myself. Every day. And each day I looked deeper to see who I was. There, I reminded myself of what I was capable of doing, who I knew I was and who I could be moving forward. I had to squint to bring myself into focus, so that the image of myself would become clear and I could find myself again. The headlines started to appear. Thank God my mother could not understand English, I thought, as they were brutal and hard to accept. "CEO Marchionni Out After Failing to Take Brand Upscale." *Failing? Upscale?!* Now wait a minute! Building company skills and capabilities through innovation is not a failure, especially in such a retail environment! And improving the esthetic of the products did not mean increasing prices across the board, we didn't do that as we only added a small percentage of new products under a new name to offering something different. And again, "Controversial CEO Quits Lands' End After She Tried to Boost the Company's Image with Gloria Steinem Ads." *Really?* We did so much more and now they pick *that* story for the headlines. As mentioned, something that could have been seen as an edgy, meaningful marketing campaign for women empowerment, became an opportunity to point out the other potential message behind it and, inevitably, divide people. Today it's all very clear but at the time it wasn't at all.

Christopher Vogler, in his famous book The Hero's Journey, which actually relate to all of us, shows how, at a certain point, a human being finds himself in what he calls the "abyss," the lowest point of the journey, when all seems lost and only defeat appears on the horizon. *There, dear Vogler, I was right there: That point exists for real, if you wanted practical proof, here I am; it happens not only in literature but also in real life.* Like Vogler's hero: I had left the ordinary world; found the courage to cross the threshold to live the dream; mentors and role models had shown me the way; a group of peers, colleagues and team, had supported me from time to time; and then here I was looking for myself. Where was I? Who was I? I was talking to myself as I continued the road into the future, and it certainly wouldn't stop where I was. When we need to connect with our values, we must not forget to always look beyond where the future beckons with what we can still live and create, with what we still have to give. We should learn to feel the electrifying thrill of what tomorrow still holds in store for those who do not give up but continue to do so. The path to the hero who in the dark begins to feel the walls to see where the way out is. But perhaps Vogler's hero lived a little easier because at least the headlines didn't mention him. During these days headlines continued on TV, online, and in local and industry news.

I was heartbroken.

No one seemed to notice, or care, that they were giving me all the responsibility for a work arrangement that didn't work out fast. None had the patience to wait longer. And I felt like the target, as I certainly was an easy one. For my appearance, for my approach, for my differences. This moment was especially hard because I had never experienced anything like it. I had only ever known success as we all normally call it. When success has been the name of your game, and when flying high is the feeling you're used to waking up to, it stings to be written off publicly as a failure. It stings like a wasp stuck to skin. However, my mind has always had the ability to analyze situations and, not finding examples to appeal to in my personal history, it began to look around, to look outside. I remembered, for example, Henry Ford: In the attempt to succeed in making the first car model—the Model A—he was even ousted from the automobile industry: How did he feel? Like me, I guess. It felt like the beautiful REM song where *"Everybody hurts .... Sometimes everything is wrong..."* So, as the song continues, I needed to *"HOLD ON, HOLD ON."* I was even reminded of a movie, Batman Begins, from which I remembered a line: *"Do you know why we fall, Bruce? To learn how to get back on our feet."*

We fall to learn how to get back on our feet.

Long ago I had formulated the idea that I could achieve everything I set my mind to. I was an excellent student in school. My thesis landed me an extraordinary job after college. In every position since then, six up to this last one, my hard work was always rewarded, and my visions were either realized or on track. I was seen as so valuable to the business that whenever *I wanted* to move on, they tried to keep me and called me back. Everyone did. More-over, in every job along the way—from shampoo girl to President of Dolce & Gabbana—I was accustomed to being greatly liked as a person. I sincerely valued my employers and colleagues as human beings, which led to the warm feelings being reciprocated. I was used to walking into places where people were glad to see me, and vice versa. I was accustomed to navigating through life on waves of mutual human warmth. Now, I felt as if those life-sustaining bonds were completely shattered. It was hurting, deeply.

Back to the roots

In addition to facing public criticism, there were practical consequences to face. As the breadwinner of the house, I was worried for our future. I was very fortunate to have a financial cushion to carry me for a forced break from work while looking for my next career step. But what would the next step be? Retail was spiraling, from department stores like Macy's to upscale brands like Neiman Marcus. Finding a new opportunity would be hard, particularly for a "high-profile failure." People only recall your last act not the entire path which brought you there. Plus, women normally don't get second chances. I take the opportunity to underline that this is where we need to improve tre-mendously as a society! We need to raise that issue and make sure we have a level playfield, and I hope someone will be a pioneer in seeing opportunities where others see differently, giving and taking second chances.

Knowing that my road to the future was blocked, I knew I had a prob-lem. To face a problem, you need to know the cause. If I had indeed failed, then how and where, exactly? I began analyzing each decision I had made at Lands' End, including the initial decision to take the CEO's job, and how I executed on each one with the team, the partners, the customers, and all the stakeholders. As the gusts continued to shatter my security, I had only one choice: To reflect on what had really happened and return to my roots, waiting humbly as the flurry of the wind passed. And in my roots, I re-es-tablished care for myself as the compassion I would need to cross the dark caves and rocky waters that awaited. The outsider hired to bring innovation was me. And I was thinking back to those meetings, to the reasons for the choice of both and the much work done. The icy wind of the media cam-paign kept blowing against my confidence and state of mind. I couldn't stop but feel angry, disappointed, misunderstood. That's how I strongly felt, mis-understood. But there was still a place where I knew I could return, where I would find comfort and refuge. Imagining that I was in front of "my Castle by the sea," there I would have found the care for myself and that compas-sion that, like a shield, had been a part of my life of protection, which would allow me to cross those dark sensors. Vogler's hero emerges from the abyss as he shifts his attention to himself, finds a glimmer of confidence that grows and allows him to rise again.

The time had also come to talk to my son, I needed to tell him that mommy had no more job and assure him we were going to be fine because of my good cushion. I chose to surprise him and go to his school to pick him up after I was done dealing with the legal paperwork and press reactions. I was planning to explain everything to him on our walk back home. Gabriel (who was eight years old at that time) was sad and worried about me, as he knew I loved my work so much that he even made a painter of a lighthouse for me a few days prior, but he wasn't surprised. My walks with him crossing Central Park from west to east around the nineties became beautiful moments I will never forget. His understanding and sensitivity were heart-lifting. A boy beyond his age was giving me his wisdom. And I chose Central Park as a place to reflect. I went there during his school time for long runs and training for a marathon I had decided to run. It was the best opportunity to reflect. *"It's quiet uptown."* The famous song from the *Hamilton* musical, performed beautifully by Kelly Clarkson, rang in my ears over and over while I was jogging, with tears falling faster than the pace of my feet.

"Forgiveness ... can you imagine?"

I had indeed needed to forgive myself for having taken too much of a risk in going to lead a legacy company. And forgiveness was the right approach for everyone involved in this peculiar journey, from the early skeptical to the strong opponents and hard judges. Most of them didn't understand the consequences or simply didn't know better and, while I learned how to win prejudices in my past, I didn't know how to deal with that level of opposition (something I learned well from this particular experience).

I read constantly about leadership and transformation. I kept talking with my mentors and others who graciously offered me support. All the people who expressed their wisdom to me while I was searching for reasons, mistakes, and learning, were an incentive for me to reflect and learn deeper. One subject of reflection was how I had conducted myself as a leader. Through good times and bad, I went into each day with a mission to serve, support, and uplift my team. I always told them, "I work for you, you work for the company." Despite the challenges I gave them, they knew I truly cared about all the people, and I was listening to them and their perspectives. I wanted to be helpful to them and make things happen—quickly, of course. Leading by example is often the single most powerful form of leadership. But this time it was not sufficient. For disruption and innovation to happen and flourish, there needs to be an entire ecosystem geared to it. I was always trying new ways to move forward and expected other people to do the same. I was trained in change and agile approaches and wished the team could learn by doing. What could I have done to build the desired ecosystem and culture? Was I missing some tricks, or did the process just need more time? Furthermore, leaders' thoughts and feelings are not considered as important. But why? Why not? Many questions piled up one on top of the other until I fell off into sleep each night. Finally, one day I awoke and came to a very obvious conclusion everyone says but one can only understand when you live it through it. Leaders sit in a solitary chair. They are often left to their own battles, doubts, and convictions. The only person who can be counted on to offer up appreciation and empowerment to a leader is the leader herself.

Life gives us challenges and opportunities to learn in ways that we sometimes don't immediately understand. Perhaps everything had happened to give me the opportunity to strengthen my leadership. When I spoke to my friend Alysa, a longtime former colleague who knew me well, she had these words about my departure from the CEO's job: "Please, think that this could be a blessing, you were working too hard. That was not a challenge but a mission impossible."

I was determined to find any business lessons that I could learn for leadership. Ticking through nearly every strategic decision and initiative and how I executed them, I asked: *Was this wrong thing to focus on?* Strengthening the core business by becoming an omni-channel? Leveraging quality with a Quality Time Campaign? Not changing the leadership team at the beginning as some suggested me doing? Cutting back on printed promotional material to be more digitally oriented? Improving the merchandising plan and carrying less inventory, while still meeting customer demands? Trying to improve the full-price sell-through by reducing the use of discounts? Promoting a can-do attitude? Refusing their first pushbacks? Proving we weren't perfect but could achieve excellence? Teaming up with other retailers to push sales nationally and eventually globally? Creating a multi-line brand architecture to offer different styles? Attracting young customers? Finding a way to get out of the existing shop-in-shop retail footprint without losing the business that it provided? Being too available and accessible? Being direct? Speaking the truth? Not accepting a "no" as the first three answers? Strongly supporting CSR? For sure, at that time, I did not have enough experience in mid-west corporate America and knew too little of the political division that was starting to invade businesses. I spoke with several business leaders to get their views on these topics. They all steered me to the same conclusions. While any decision can be debated from multiple angles and each decision could have been executed differently by different leaders, my difficulties at

Lands' End seemed to be due mostly to timing and partially a mismatch. I am sure that today, for how the world and myself have evolved, the story could have had a different "end." It was indeed also a matter of being too fast and forward thinker, combined with the short-term approach of the publicly traded company—topped with an overall retail negative momentum. I needed to accept that truth. I should have known that the short-term approach is not in line with disruption and change, since those things take time—and reflect now, I realized that I actually *did* know it before joining the company. My gut and my instincts were telling me so. I had been too fascinated by how the opportunity looked on paper, by the offer, the title, and by all the reasons which were the shining ones, but not necessarily the right ones. One day I read "by chance" in a magazine a phrase by Heraclitus, an ancient Greek philosopher: *"You will never find the truth, if you're not willing to accept even what you didn't expect to find."* Could it be that the words of a man who lived 500 years before Christ were addressed to me? Looking at it that way, patience was again the key. I should have been more patient in making changes and waiting for a more appropriate CEO offer. Up to that moment, I had always displayed patience with my Dream-Plans. But CEO opportunities for women don't come very often, so I had taken a chance even if it was too risky. As someone whose career decision-making had been one of her best assets, I should now accept the failure of having made a choice that didn't work out. And because of it, many people were disappointed: The team members who believed in me and were now left without their leader; the outside supporters who wanted me to succeed and tell a story of success; and other stakeholders who were liking what I was doing.

My mother, who always showed me her wisdom, told me to remember that I had reached my Dream-Plan in becoming a CEO without taking any shortcuts but, in reality, did quite the opposite as I venture in new a new country, the most competitive one! Given from where I came from, it was not at all obvious that I would ever even get near achieving such a thing: The first Italian woman CEO in history leading an American publicly traded company. But of course, for over-achievers that wasn't enough as I wanted to have a different end to this story. Back then I didn't think of this experience as a chapter in my life. A dear friend, Kathleen, gave me a useful message in her own words and style. She said I should feel proud of my choice for having tried something hard, and now to try face the next challenge I needed to "Toughen up and move on, girl". And that's so true! I needed to change focus, build resilience and look at the future but it's very hard to even think so in those moments!

Another friend offered me some advice that I chose not to follow. Since everyone was writing in the media about me *except* myself, she insisted that

I shouldn't accept how my story was being told. *"Go on social media and write it."* But this approach was not for me, I would be acting as someone I was not. I have always seen a leader as someone who takes the high road and who lets her deeds speak most of all. I needed first to understand, for my own good, what had happened and who I was in the process of becoming. To do so I pointed the arrow inward. My runs, my reading, my meetings and phone calls with mentors, my travels and my son, my family: These were all essential tools for my learning. There was so much to rehash while I began to rebuild my core strength and resilience. My determination, unwavering, along with a good dose of kindness, was the cappuccino I consumed on my way up and out of the rubble. Although I thought I was a good person before the Lands' End experience, after having gone through what I consider to be "grief," I feel I am more compassionate today. I'm softer and I have learned that the greatest chief to be is the "Chief of Me."

Cycles of Change

Dream-Plan: To Evolve

After going from the top dog at a company to what felt like a lost dog, stranded in the wide expanse of an empty desert, I saw a new phase I never experienced. I wanted to see how this phase could possibly be for the good and help my development. So, I picked up the Kubler-Ross Change Curve and started reading. In the typical working hours, when I would normally be engrossed in the details of financial budgets, team or board meetings, sales plans, and more, I found myself immersed in an important lesson: my change. Change, as the Kubler-Ross model explains, is an inevitable part and truth of life. Being that I am drawn to truth, I asked myself not why, but what. What was inside the membrane of that particular change that was necessary for me to digest? A failure truth? That everything happens for a reason? Elisabeth Kubler-Ross first came up with her model when writing a book called *On Death and Dying*. She was a psychiatrist who worked with people facing the most profound truth and the ultimate change in life: that they were not immortal, that they would die before long. She saw that in order for them to live out their lives in the best possible way, they had to move through a series of stages in mindset and emotion. The stages go basically as follows. Upon learning the bad news, it is natural to react with shock, denial, and anger. Then, after this first period of high agitation, it is also quite common to descend into a valley of deep depression. The key is not to stay there, at the bottom of the curve. By moving to a stage of acceptance—accepting the truth that life has changed and is about to change more—one can climb up out of the depths, learning to live at peace in the new reality, even finding high notes of joy and fulfillment. The Kubler-Ross model has been adopted for use in other realms of personal experience, as well as in business. Any time that one is confronted with a loss or an unwelcome change, it can be helpful to recognize the stages and keep moving through the curve. I could certainly see how this applied to me. The knowledge helped me digest the bitter pill I had to swallow, starting with the recognition that I was still in the early stages of grief agitated. My thoughts were all over the place. I couldn't pin down one of them. Soon, however, the world began pulling me back into focus.

As the CEO at Lands' End, I had made commitments to speak or participate in some events that were still on my schedule, so I wrote kind emails saying that I could no longer attend them because my situation had changed. To my surprise, people wanted me to come independently of me not being in the job. Although I was no longer a CEO, I felt respected by the people who mattered to me. I was beginning to see how a title would never define me. At the first formal event of this type, I was received as an Honoree by the Columbus Citizens Foundation, a New York group that supports persons of Italian heritage for doing valued work in American society. My speech was the first I had given without a company to represent or a title to prop me up, other than being the newly appointed "Chief of Me." I was very nervous! Indeed, I did not have the positive energy sparkling out for the joy, I was sad inside. But I didn't want anyone to see that and tried my best to perform onstage with a strong speech. Delivering the content of my speech helped me to start the process of change. At one point I stopped reading my scripted remarks to say something from my heart. *There is a difference between our countries. In Italy I was ashamed to say I was self-made. Here, I am so proud to say that I am self-made.*" I felt that my future needed to begin from there, from pushing more into that spirit. In a subsequent commitment, also as former CEO, I attended a conference at the Vatican with prestigious world leaders. We had been called, through *Fortune* and *Time* magazines, to identify private sector solutions for achieving more inclusive economies. This was a priority of Pope Francis, who granted us an audience. I also wrote an article for the *Time* about my belief in the need for new human-centered ways of measuring prosperity, evolving the current GDP metric. While there, I met with the most outstanding leader and pioneer of new thinking, Dov Seidman—he is considered the new Socrates for his work! No wonder why Nobel Prize winner, and one of my biggest hero, Elie Wiesel, obviously chosen him as the exclusive partner for the Elie Wiesel Foundation for Humanity Prize in Ethics in 2008. Seidman had written the *HOW* book ("Why HOW we do anything means everything") stating that "*we are in an Era of Behavior and the rule of the game have fundamentally changed. It is no longer what to do that matters but HOW you do what you do.*" If you aspire to be a leader, I strongly recommend knowing HOW and carefully, very carefully, read the book. It will lay down the foundation for enduring success. If companies would apply his incredible new thinking, then maybe also my "*soft*" *values, trust and reputation*, according to his theory, could have been considered my new *hard currency of success* for the future.

People kept assuring me that I would land well. Whenever I was faced with periods of depression, I reminded myself that this was the low part of the Kubler-Ross Curve: I couldn't stay trapped in pity for the present or fear of the future. In order to learn my life lesson, I needed to force myself to change. And being that fear has never ruled my actions; I began to feel that I was on a better track. There were reassuring moments and encouraging words that stayed with me. A former colleague at the company couldn't wait to meet me to make sure I could hear her supporting words, "Federica, you are one of the most visionary people I have met in my long career here." Juliette, a partner at a San Francisco private equity firm, told me that in Silicon Valley, "we value courageous leaders who take risks because that defines who they are—and we celebrate that entrepreneurial spirit." The sensitivity and support I felt from others during the first six months out of job helped me greatly. The messages and phone calls that I received were overwhelming. Many people and leaders sent me words of appreciation for my work and offered introductions or references if needed. That is America! People are extremely busy, but if you are in need, they rally for you. Americans teach you to keep experimenting and, most importantly, to move on. As quickly as possible.

I understood that support was essential in the process of making transitions. But as I began facing the question mark of my future career, I learned that I had to give myself what was needed. Along with plenty of self-support, I needed to make new decisions. Of course, now I was worried of making another misstep for the criteria I used to judge before whether things were right or wrong. Very few job interviews were coming in, and not the ones I was hoping for. I faced each way the winds of opportunity blew with care and thoughtfulness, trusting that my good intentions would lead me to the next best thing. Keeping the memories of all I had built to date in my eyes and soul would be what I would ultimately take with me as I dressed in perseverance for each interview. None could take away my brain, my heart, my purpose, nor my intellect. I was ready to defy the anger and disappointment with a brimming cup of compassion. When I turned down an opportunity that I didn't think would lift me up, I found myself being brave again. One opening seemed like it should have been an ideal fit. It was close to home, in New York, where I loved living. The job was one I could thrive in, since it was in the fashion field and—as a headhunter told me—I was ahead of the game. But that role pointed me backward and, most importantly, I did not have faith in the company's global CEO. This time my judgment was right as I learned a year later when that CEO was let go. Maybe if I had taken the initial offer I could have moved up to the top post; sometimes you need to take a step back to take two forward. However, I would have needed to bet on someone else's failure and have spent at least one year learning little. Instead, I spent that year improving myself, finding the refresh button, hitting it, and starting over. After several months, none of what I considered to be the right offers were presented to me in New York. I often thought that passing on that first opportunity was another mistake. After you make one mistake in your career choices, you can begin to question yourself too much. I had days in which I felt strong and positive, believing a bright future was to come yet, and other days in which I saw only dark clouds. But in retrospect, having the financial ability to look for a job truly gave me a tremendous learning opportunity. For the first time in my career, I had time to reflect. I learned more about my strengths and my weaknesses—about who I really was and about people who really supported me. I would never forget the kindness of a great executives who earlier in the process offered me a discussion about what I wished to do next. When one particularly successful woman, Mellody, called me, I was still in the mourning phase about what happened and was too soon for me to even understand the importance of that offer and even if nothing happened, that phone call was a sweet moment in that hash period, and I am forever grateful for that gesture.

It was becoming evident that I should look outside the box, not only in terms of new kinds of opportunities but also in terms of locations. The right door that opened for me could be someplace far from New York City. I decided then to travel across the US, Europe, Africa, and Asia to reconnect with the world again. To gain more flexibility and time to make the right decision, I started consulting. It was a great way to stay active. I was experimenting with what Kubler-Ross advised: Stopping resistance to change in order to arrive in a place of acceptance. It felt good. In fact, it felt right.

Evolving Leadership

As the months passed, I reflected more on visionary leadership. What is it? What skills could I perfect and add to my repertoire? I observed the role of the samurai. The Japanese samurai were the noble warriors of the military. According to a modern-day Japanese guide, "Samurais were supposed to lead their lives according to the ethical code of *bushido* ('the way of the warrior'). Bushido stressed concepts such as loyalty to one's master, self-discipline and respectful, ethical behavior." As I had concluded that I was the Chief of Me, I could be the master I'd stay loyal to, while self-discipline, respect, and ethics came naturally to me. I would work toward a greater inner balance, to be sure my future leadership would merge more with my visions.

And so it was, that while seeking a new project, a new potential employment, I could understand the qualities of the leader in a new light. I always believed that every word you speak, every thought you think, every dream you dream, shaped who you become. I was audacious in the pursuit of my dreams. I strategized, I took the expanse of the unknown and funneled it into words and actions. I have become known as someone who is transformational and leads with purpose. Dictionary.com defines the word *transformation* as "a change in form, appearance, nature, or character." It goes on to define *purpose* as "the reason for which something exists." My life's work so far is an illustration of purposeful transformation. I say this because of all the unlikely roads I have taken. I started in technology, went into high fashion, then to lifestyle and online. Every step I took, I took with purpose and persuasion. And as a leader, I have learned that true leadership is indeed about the evolution of the leader herself as much as it is about changing an organization. Staying awake to personal internal shifting allows a leader to shape the direction of a company almost as if with clay. Hands on. Passion heightened. Decision-making in every instant. Having molded a life setting and accomplishing one objective after another, I understand the nature of purpose and how it influences outcomes: I wanted the credit for doing my best, for inspiring people to give their best, so that we could collaborate in the making of a better company and the world. My thinking was enriched further by the amazing people I personally met in my local and foreign travels. Leaders at global leading corporations with sound success stories one can only see from afar. Listening to their words formed into questions and brief yet resolute statements or watching their firm and receptive body language that got me thinking to the Nelson Mandela's famous quote: "I never lose. I either win or learn." I used that quote in my "Sea of Clouds" remarks when two wonderful ladies invited me to speak at the WCD (Women Corporate Directors) chapter in San Francisco. Here is a brief extract of that speech:

> I was on my way out here yesterday and as the plane was reaching its flying altitude, we broke through a sea of clouds. When we got to the other side, what was cloudy below turned into sunshine above. The sea of clouds gave me a space to imagine. And imagination is something that has been near and dear to my life journey and as a professional.

...Look for opportunities. Seize the opportunities. Have an orientation point. And—Envision the non-obvious ... I have always been laser-focused on the things I chose to do in my life. This attention to details, both real and imagined, keeps me flying above the clouds.

...All it will take is time ... I mentioned time many times because when you have experience under your belt, you learn to trust your instincts despite the critics. You learn to act confidently despite the headlines. You bring forward your best attributes despite your fears. You act above the fray. As you are most likely aware, it took IBM's Lou Gerstner nine years to bring the failing company's market realization from $29 billion in 1993 to $168 billion.

...We needed time to meet and exceed expectations. Well ... My time at Lands' End was not long. When I stepped down a few months shy of two years, the company was just beginning to reflect on the envisioned changes we had set out to accomplish. Yet, differences amongst us lead to my eventual departure. Lands' End was the first company I didn't leave at the top of a successful curve. Yet, Lands' End has been a gift. As Nelson Mandela said, "I never lose. Either I win or I learn." I had brought enormous progress and innovation on many levels, and I have learned a lot from those months there. When you are at the top, many other things happen. You must learn how to get through tough times. Be kind, stay strong, and walk tall...

It is one thing to feel successful when you wear the title of CEO, but it is truly another thing to feel a greater success when you stand naked, as "just" yourself. It's what you build along the way that will count! And today, I feel stronger than ever before. Constant education and curiosity propel me above the clouds and into a richer meaningful life.

Learning to fall and getting back-up

In rough times, if you show your vulnerability and you are prepared for critics and suggestions, you can truly grow. But you can do this only if you are strong. Was I strong at that time? Well, not really. However, deep inside, my mind, my determination and my core were: I just needed to reuse those muscles. I built on past experiences but also learned from studying the careers of successful leaders, sports champions, and artists. It made sense that not even these people could reach the same level of success with every step, every match, or every album, performance, or painting. Sometimes great artists flop. Designers make times collections which people don't like. Their audiences believe in their work and still wait for what they will do next and give them another chance. It seemed there was something inside great visionaries that made them the leaders they were. I was coming to find out that their responses to setbacks built their characters. An amazing TV ad from Under Armor, featuring a defiant Michael Phelps battling to go back to victory, beautifully reminded us that "It's what you do in the dark that puts you in the light."

I had my own stumbling blocks in life, but up to this point, I was not truly ready to embrace them as part of my now and my future. Finally, I was beginning to understand their value. When I was invited to the premiere of Chris Perkel's documentary *Clive Davis: The Soundtrack of Our Lives,* based on the autobiography of the renowned music producer, it clicked like the snapping of a thumb and middle finger. I sat in the dark theater among a select number of carefully chosen audience members as the opening of the film appeared on the black screen. The silence in the room was awe-inspiring as the story of Davis' five-decade career as an award-winning maker of musical artists began. I could feel how every one of us was struck not just by his accomplishments, but more significantly, by his tragedies. Having lost both of his parents within a year from each other while he was a teenager, he was left orphaned like my mother and needed to live with his older sister in Bayside, Queens in New York City. He also focused his energy on education to give himself a better life. With full scholarships to New York University, he graduated magna cum laude and set his sights on Harvard Law School, where he also attended with a full scholarship. The film resonated with me like the gong of a bell tower in an ancient European town. And even the most astounding leaders, such as Davis, whose artists included the likes of Janis Joplin, Bruce Springsteen, Whitney Houston, Alicia Keys, Christina Aguilera, Kelly Clarkson, and The Notorious BIG, are all met with multiple hurdles in their lives. Davis was even fired twice! But as he said in an interview: "I have a very healthy respect for failure ... I do concentrate on what is required to be successful." And snapped my fingers! Respect failures! That's what it is!

I have since interpreted a visionary leader as one who deals with momentary failings with dignity, focusing on the future, and staying positive while continuing to engage with others. These were all the things I was trying to do and could possibly give me the confirmation that I would rise again. The prominent church pastor Andy Stanley has said: "Leaders can't stand the status quo. They don't lie in bed and dream of how things are. They dream of how things could be."

Learning from the research professor Dr. Brené Brown in her book *Rising Strong,* I understood that recovering from failure is essential in order not to be held back by your past mistakes from trying again. We can learn from being vulnerable, but it takes courage and requires us to risk. It is important to remember that there is a risk each time we try again, but we must be stronger than our fears. We can find strength in different ways. Besides staying kind to myself, close to my friends and family, and being vigilant, I was fascinated by all of Dr. Brown's books and stories of resilience. When you channel your insights from rumbling into positive changes, a revolution follows.

I was on my own mission to think higher as it wasn't any more about being in charge. No! It was about feeling the pleasure of coaching, goodwill, and enthusiasm of being a leader of the people. More than ever before, it was about developing others. With more time on my hands, I upped the ante on my philanthropy and started to transform my simple run-in real marathons, raising money for a foundation. I also got involved in Acumen, a nonprofit organization with the mission of changing the way the world tackles poverty. The privilege of knowing and working with the founder, Jacqueline Novogratz, was incredible. Her book *Blue Sweater* was the best company during my philanthropic trip to Tanzania where I run my first half marathon in Kilimanjaro. I actually understood Jacqueline's work in Kenya even better by reading her book in Africa. I started to read more inspirational books on leadership and resilience, like *Grit*, by Angela Duckworth, who tells us where the power of passion and perseverance can lead us. I had to learn that the passion and perseverance I used in my youth was needed again. I thought that life had given me enough troubles and that was it; I was going to thrive for the rest of my life. But that's not reality. You go through stages in which challenges are presented in different ways and the biggest issues, I understood, came when you didn't expect them. I was amazed by a friend when, after her 70th birthday, she told me "Darling, don't think this is the last challenge of your life! We only learn how to face them better with time and wisdom." I was in fact making the same mistake of thinking that I was now shielded from future struggles. That was not the right approach, I had to understand that I just needed to continue to use the muscles of inner throughout my life! And there isn't a leader who never felt despair at one moment or another. In the words often attributed to Winston Churchill: "Success is not final, and failure is not fatal. It is the courage to continue that counts." I was testing myself to understand if I had that courage and, ultimately, if I was a true leader.

With my reconfigured compassion, always a strong suit in my leadership and a new ally in potential future wars, I could fight the win-win fight with confidence to win again. I felt incredibly fortunate that my path to imagination was once again wide open. I was lucky to buy the last tickets to *Piaf! The Show* at Carnegie Hall—a musical tribute to the legendary singer Édith Piaf—and found myself tremendously moved by listening to her signature song, *"Non, je ne regrette rien"* ("I regret nothing"). I felt I had lived an intense life, full of experiences, and that I did not, in the end, regret having made mistakes too.

Defining Success

What is success? For many years, at first, I felt that the definition and measurement of success was obvious. It was, and still is for many, measured by the great leaps and achievements made in life. I was ticking that box. Indeed, after writing a visionary thesis in college, about the upcoming universal use of cell phones, I landed a position with Samsung. There I was—a woman in Italy, working for a Korean company in a technology field dominated by men. I had insight. I had a vision. Success was on my radar. I jumped into fashion and luxury in the consumer sector until I found my way to New York City as the President of Dolce & Gabbana USA and finally as the CEO of an American company. Mission accomplished! The stamp of success was on my lapel. I had envisioned my way to the top from a town of just 500 inhabitants. Just dreaming of living outside Santa Severa Nord itself had made some of my friends and family raise an eyebrow: "Where do you think you are going?" But I went. "I tis from where you come from that determine where you go." And I went with pride. A proud Italian. Born in Italy, Italian. Not Robert De Niro or Danny De Vito. Italian. Italian, Italian. I began to define my success not solely by the companies I worked for, but by the passion and purpose I attacked life with. After arriving in the United States, I embraced a new definition, which I gave to the writer Steve Mueller and which he published in a 2016 article on his "Planet of Success" blog. To summarize it here:

> "Success can come from a variety of different channels. It doesn't necessarily have to come exclusively from the work you do. Instead, when it comes to success, balance is what you should strive for. Success is not something that can be attained overnight. The pursuit of success is a journey that leads to wisdom and ultimately to success."

Since then, I have refined the definition even higher. A quotation attributed to various people, including Ralph Waldo Emerson, says that success is:

> "To laugh often and much; to win the respect of intelligent people and the affection of children; to earn the appreciation of honest critics and endure the betrayal of false friends; to appreciate the beauty; to find the best in others; to leave the world a bit better, whether by a healthy child, a garden patch or a redeemed social condition; to know even one life has breathed easier because you have lived; this is to have succeeded."

To that I raise a glass. That kind of success is what, indeed, I realized I wanted on my lapel!

In all our eagerness to make a good impression or fight for the right cause, we sometimes overlook the achievement that can be found in the smallest of places. I was raised in Italy, near Rome, a Catholic. One of the cornerstones of Catholicism is benevolence. In its truest sense, it means we look after the people in need, lending a helping hand. These acts are the gems on the royal crown. They are meaningful in the mundane. They are the open doors at the pearly gates. Which is why it is our duty to slow ourselves down and keep both eyes open when we are striving for success. It all starts with kindness and being a worthy citizen of the world, something that, in my opinion, ought to be taught in the first grade when we are most impressionable.

Shoveling off the loss from my latest challenge would need to be replaced with yearning—the yearning to work hard, make necessary sacrifices, and the yearning to dream again. I was on a path that could unlock the power of fundamental rewiring of my driving force. My success would lie in the words I have quoted here and in my seeing once again. I would stand on the rock of imagination with a strong spine to gain a better glimpse of the dreams that I had yet to reach. All the while, kindness would be the consideration I could offer myself to be sure that however I may have been led astray, my peaceful and generous nature could be what takes me on my way forward. There was much more still to achieve. I was young and energetic as a colt running in the field. I knew the freedom that a country like the United States could offer and I knew tradition as it ran in the rivers of my Italian country and European roots. For my personality and DNA, I understood that my next step needed to be something big. Something different. An unknown land, perhaps in Asia.

New horizons

To really be a global leader I indeed needed to know more about Asia and, of course, about China as it wasn't any longer just a developing country as I knew it was while I was growing up. In 2017 I began to focus my morning reading on Asia. Where were they strong? What were they lacking? Where did I fit in? There were the shiny red apples of my sweet dreams and the purple fruit of my plum plans. At that time, like every pioneer can experience, I felt that something was interestingly growing, and I was filled with an enthusiastic vision that so spurred my spirit. I wanted to feel I was discovering new horizons where I could learn. A place where I could leverage my talents and challenge my know-how. A land that would put me in unfamiliar environments, all the while knowing that my experience was the kind that was needed. I could not know for sure if Asia was a place I would land, but I knew where to direct my sense of purpose. For now, I would need to take in the moments of my sabbatical with patience.

One evening, at a dinner among friends, we were discussing about the famous best seller—and book banned in China—Jung Chang's *Wild Swans*, which describes the Cultural Revolution as seen by three generations and understood the critics from a gentleman on the Chinese culture for their way of doing business, their ethics, and their nonreciprocal ways in many instances. The hostess, who strongly disagreed with the Chinese regarding human rights issues, then sent us an article about Albert Einstein's travel diaries, published by Princeton University Press, which included a visit to China in the 1920s and I listen carefully some experts who were telling me that in China most of the civil society would need a decade or two to be at the level of the development countries, even if their economy is advanced and their infrastructures are now so modern. There was a huge disconnect between the two realities. Possibly having an experience right there, not just the exposure I had been having with some sporadic travels, could be for sure extremely challenging and definitely out of many people's comfort zone—at least mine—but also very useful at that burgeoning timing for the country. It seemed it was my turn to look more closely at this land to find out more.

I wanted to bring my family with me for a tour in Asia again so we could all learn together. This time, for my son spring break in March, we went to China and used this trip as a way to explore new places and learn more about a different culture. Curiosity again came in handy. In the different cities we intended to visit, I made sure we could have both the time to learn and to have fun. We landed in Hong Kong, a city we loved and which we used as a place to adjust to jet lag and meet old friends who live there; then traveled to Shanghai, where I met people to potentially work with; we ventured in Chengdu, where my son saw real pandas; after that to Xi'an, where Antonio could enjoy the Terracotta Warriors, and finally to Beijing, where we visited some historical places and meet someone I had been introduced to from the US We used flights, trains, subways, buses, taxis, and bikes, which we rented to try the sharing bikes system. The infrastructures we found were even more advanced than those in Italy. We visited monuments, science and art places, such as the 798 Art Zone in Beijing, played a traditional sport with the elderly people at the Temple of Heaven and practiced Tai Chi.

After returning to New York, I decided to participate in my second *Fortune* Global Forum. The previous year's event had been in Rome; the December 2017 Forum was scheduled for Guangzhou, in China. I couldn't believe my eyes when reading the list of prestigious attendees and speakers who would be present. Since my last name is Marchionni, I was listed in the same page of Jack Ma and Pony Ma. The founders of two gigantic companies, Alibaba and Tencent. Even if it was only a coincidence, I wanted to believe that some opportunity could be in the air and it was up to me to grab it. To attend a *Fortune* Global Forum, you must first be invited and then pay the conference fee as well as your travel and accommodation costs. Since I wasn't working for any corporation, I needed to make that investment myself, booking flight tickets to Guangzhou and a room which I chose to be at the same hotel where the Forum was being held. To make sure I was maximizing this trip, I extended my travel to Shanghai, where I could stay for two weeks meeting businesspeople, investors, and headhunters, since my longtime friend Milena was living there, and she could host me. At the conference, there were many foreign leading executives such as Tim Cook from Apple, Stefano Pessina from Walgreens, Bill Ford from Ford Motor, Carlos Brito from Anheuser-Busch InBev, Chuck Robbins from Cisco Systems, Henry Kravis of KKR, and many more. They were being interviewed while some were giving speeches: It was eye-opening mainly to understand the importance of China market for a lot of foreign companies. This confirmed that my instincts were correct, an experience there could be very significant for the Western world in my future.

At the conference, I learned many things, including what Dr. Kai-Fu Lee and Eurasia Group's Paul Triolo told a reporter from *Fortune* "the fact that China has more Internet users than the US and Europe combined could give China an unassailable lead in amassing the huge data sets that lie at the heart of AI innovation." Most importantly, it was becoming more evident the race on innovation from China after being a land of manufacturers and copycats. The shifting role was not really understood by the Western world till later on.

I also met interesting people, including Deborah Weigswing and Jay Walker, a researcher and the serial entrepreneur, also founder of Priceline. com. I was also impressed to learn about the private library he founded in Connecticut: The Walker Library of the History of Human Imagination which holds a collection of historic books and artifacts that show how we humans have advanced in science and art through the centuries—like an ancient "sky atlas" with a map of our solar system. I said to myself that I need to take my son to this library someday to inspire him with what a man can achieve in a lifetime!

At one of the evening events, I encountered a sophisticated woman who I had spoken with at the cocktail hour, not knowing who she was. Being kind and having a positive approach to anyone always helps. This woman happened to be seated right next to me at dinner, and I believe that she appreciated my being respectful and friendly earlier with no agenda. When I told her I was going next to Shanghai, she then generously introduced me to one of the most connected people in that city. The man's friend, Mark, welcomed me to Shanghai at a gathering he had previously organized with his friends so I could meet a number of influential people in one evening. They became my frame of reference there. Being able to stay in Shanghai for a longer time gave me a deeper perspective than tourists would usually have. I truly valued this opportunity and when my new contacts recommended more people I should have met, I made sure to connect to as many people as he was suggesting. One was an investor with an innovative approach for analyzing the markets. Richard was investing in companies that not only promised high returns but also represented the future: companies in e-commerce, delivery services, digital media, and similar fields. With time, he became a friend and my new go-to person in Shanghai—and, since he thought my experience and ideas could be valuable in China He was the one who introduced me to the founder of a company called Secoo, an online platform for selling premium fashions and lifestyle goods, along with a few stores throughout the country. It sounded interesting and I connected with Mr. Li on WeChat. On my last day in Shanghai, I went for a little sightseeing. I visited a Buddhist temple, the newly largest Starbucks opened in the world, and visited shopping centers, where I bought a pair of cool walking shoes at Shang Xia, the so-called "Hermès of China." On my flight back to New York in mid-December I reflected on everything I had witnessed and thought of how valuable it could be to have a working experience in that country to learn how to do business there as every company was looking to have a stronger Asia strategy—which China at the center of interest. I had planted a few seeds and needed to nurture them in the year ahead to see a potential blossom. I was fully engaged, energized, and determined, now having all that I needed to reignite the tools for big vision thinking. I arrived home before the Christmas holidays, in time to attend my son's recital at his school and take a vacation with my family. We needed to have some reunion time for me, my son, and his wonderful father—who had been letting me travel the world in search of myself while taking care of our beloved Gabriel. We had an amazing vacation in Tulum, Mexico, which lasted longer than planned as all flights to New York were canceled for a snowstorm. But we were not worried about anything anymore as we were all together.

The day before leaving Tulum I received an email from Secoo asking me to attend their Annual Gala in Beijing in January 2018. They said it would be an opportunity to meet everyone at the company within 48 hours. The next day I had my ticket to Beijing, where I booked, at my own expense, a place for two weeks after their Annual Gala as I wanted to continue meeting other people.

My second trip to China came just a few weeks after the *Fortune* conference and my time in Shanghai. All the way there, I envisioned the closing of a consulting agreement with the company. That Gala gave me tremendous insight into their drive and ambition, together with their ability to entertain and gather people toward common objectives. China is a country filled with challenges, but also a land of 1.4 billion people impossible to ignore. I was determined to learn more about them. The chance to be having a work experience in China thrilled me in the way that I'm told adventure-seekers feel when they hike along the spectacular cliff edges of the South Peak of Mount Hua. I had resumed the journey and, as in the hero's journey traced by Vogler, I left the abyss behind me, comforted by the affection and support of my group, resuming the path forward. But I was no longer the same as when I left. I had evolved. Everything helped me to have a wonderful experience and to evolve into *Fedy*, the real me.

The experiences I had lived through, going through darkness and pain, had made me stronger, more determined, and illuminated by a new joy and awareness. I could go back to exploring and imagining once again.

Some takeaways

For disruption and innovation to flourish, there needs to be an entire ecosystem geared to it.
Failures are steppingstones for future successes. We fall to learn how to rise again.
Accept the truth. Life gives us challenges and opportunities to learn bigger lessons.
Get a fresh start. Your past cannot hurt you if you let it go. Be the "Chief of you."
Stark abysses are real. Rely on self-love, self-esteem, and self-determination to get out of it.
Bo compassionate, have empathy. Learn to forgive yourself and others. It is important you focus on your goal and achievements as much as *how* you get to them.
Toughen up and move on. Takes the high road and lets deeds speak most of all.
It's not only about you. The purpose of life can be and shall be bigger than you. Go find it.
Redefine your success as you evolve. It can come from a variety of different channels.
Strategized, take the expanse of the unknown, funneled it into words and actions.
Work hard, make again necessary sacrifices, and yearning to dream again.

Seven: Envision the Future
Human Pillar: Possibility

> *"All truths are easy to understand once they are revealed. The point is to discover them."*
> Galileo Galilei

Young people are wonderful. They are forever imagining new possible realities, different from the ones in which they live. They see themselves being heroes, leaders, explorers, dancers, inventors, artists, teachers, and more. They create, in their minds, worlds of amazement that operate by rules and customs previously unknown. To the best of their abilities, they act out their dreams.

And then they "grow up." Or too often, they—meaning we—mature into diminished versions of the human possibility engines we once were. Of course, when we enter adulthood, it is necessary to be practical. But imagine this: What if gaining practical skills and life experience made us *more* able to envision, and realize, new realms of possibility? In fact, it does. If only we can recognize the fact and act upon it.

There are people who do this. There are some people mobilizing others to make new futures possible. It can almost seem as if they are being reborn in order to grow up again in a different way—hopefully, better than before. I chose to live and work among such people, carrying these questions with me: What enables them to do what they're doing? And what can we learn from them, which would help us to regrow into new possibilities in our own ways.

From Columbus to Marco Polo

Feeling like a life explorer, I was in full navigation mode as once was Marco Polo. In my constant amazement at everything I was about to discover in that land, I deliberately left out the judgments and things we already know about the Chinese regime because what was more interesting, at that time, was to understand and learn the speed of change in the country—along with other things that people who had not the opportunity to visit and work in China today could not understand. Indeed, a lot of people who were speaking and writing about China sometimes have not lived there or even traveled to mainland China. I wanted to understand how they really became what they are today beyond their regime. Accepting that we are all different in this world, even among us Europeans or Italians, let alone between West and East, I strongly believe that we should always seek higher levels of dialogue to bridge the gaps for certain higher purposes, the environment for example. Knowing better the different parties helps build bridges. As a "Roman," I know the importance of bridges: How crucial they can be in creating a positive impact through exchanges where new things can be achieved on both sides. Much of human history has taken place over bridges. There is an intense novel by Nobel Prize winner Ivo Andrić—The Bridge on the Drina—in which the protagonist is the bridge on which entire generations meet, those same peoples who later went to war. "Lunations followed one another, and generations quickly disappeared," Andrić writes, "but the bridge remained, unchanging, like the water flowing under its arches." Every place in the world has bridges waiting to be built and "other sides" of life waiting to be explored. If you have ways of making connections by moving between different countries, that is certainly interesting. But exploration can begin wherever you are today, right now. Every city or village shows a great diversity and richness of inhabitants. There are people employed in different jobs, who have different attitudes toward life and conduct their family existence and contacts with others in many different ways. Sociologists call them "subcultures." You can learn a lot from almost anyone, if you are willing to approach them and get to know them with an open mind. This is why it has been observed that innovation often occurs at the margins or "intersections" of various communities of people. Think about the music we listen to. Much of it is played on electronic instruments, invented by engineers and computer scientists working with musicians. You should listen to the simple story of Giovanni Giorgio, aka Giorgio Moroder, in his piece with Daft Punk about how he invented electronic music, *without preconceptions*. The music we now call hip-hop, invented by young black and Hispanic Americans in New York, has traveled all over the world: artists integrate it, develop it to make it their own, incorporating virtually every other style of music in their existence. Or think of a field such as biotechnology, a discipline in which (as the name suggests) various fields of knowledge come together to form something new. When we can find intersections and build bridges, we become richer people and our lives are potentially more fruitful, better equipped to imagine and create our own dreams and contribute to the realization of those of others. A visit to the Cathedral of the Immaculate Conception in Beijing gave me hope that, even in the most difficult and complicated situations, bridges and points of contact can be built. In fact, the cathedral was born from the work of Jesuit missionary and scholar Matteo Ricci who, around 1600, succeeded in linking the theories of Confucianism with Christian theology. Matteo Ricci was the first Westerner to be invited to the Forbidden City, an honor he had earned thanks to his scientific abilities, in particular his predictions of solar eclipses. He collaborated with the Chinese scholar and scientist Xu Guangqi to make the first translations of some Confucian classics into a Western language, the Latin of the time. Xu Guangqi, in turn, converted to Christianity and was apparently a man of great virtue.

Dream-plan: To Bridge Differences

Being a bridge myself as I always seek dialogue, in my moments of dreaming, I imagined that I could help people from very different nations expand their horizons simply with my own work and so, 750 years after Marco Polo's voyage, keep making sacrifices, I sunk my hands into my youthful spirit, helping western companies to expand their businesses in Asia and have a deeper understanding of the land that was getting more and more attention from western media. The company I joined had the aim of offering to Chinese consumers the best brands from around the world: fine watches, clothing, and other products from Europe, America, Japan, South Korea, Australia, and more. It was a place where I could start to make my little imprint. The time had come to say goodbye to my very dear land of Columbus and to reach the unknown land of Polo.

Missing home, while learning

At first, I went alone because, even if I wanted to give my son the opportunity to have an experience in Asia too, it was March, and he had to finish the school year in New York. To have time to understand Beijing I decided to stay in a downtown hotel. The rooms were spacious, and the people were always willing to give their best service. The reception area was elegant and quiet, with art on the walls that inspired dreamlike moods. On a large canvas reaching high and wide was a painting by Shao Fan who used teacups to present the Taoist concept of being truly integrated with the universe. The offices of the company at that time were located in the Galaxy Soho building. I always knew I loved architecture as much as art, but I didn't know until I arrived in Beijing how much that was so attractive to me. On my next trip to New York in May, after two months in China, I made sure to see great new buildings and interiors as well as great art. In addition to visiting the super-well-curated traveling exhibition "David Bowie Is," which was then at the Brooklyn Museum, I walked around and through the astounding, soaring spaces of the new Oculus train station, designed by Santiago Calatrava for the World Trade Center Transportation Hub. I needed to understand buildings like these better, now that I had seen many of the architectural experiments one can see in Beijing. I understood where the inspiration came from, but also the Chinese ambition, and New York was definitely a great example of great buildings and new experiment. Being Italian and loving opera, I was attracted to go to the National Center for the Performing Arts (NCPA) in Beijing too and I discover another beautiful structure called "the giant egg," a building that architect Paul Andreu designed to look like a drop of water in the middle of an ocean. It made me feel proud of my roots when I saw that inside almost half of that Opera Museum was dedicated to Italian works! I was happy to see that our culture was appreciated and celebrated. The curator of the Opera House was an Italian man, someone who I was able to meet after going to the theater many times. I was struck by his extraordinary devotion to opera, immense as the egg itself where the Opera House is located. He also transmitted his deep knowledge during lectures which he constantly held for fans, new onlookers, and students. While discovering new places, I couldn't help but notice the presence of cameras installed everywhere.

At the beginning of my stay, I traveled to the office in a Didi (the Chinese Uber) wearing a mask for the polluted air condition, which the active employees at my hotel helped provide. They also had prepared for me my cappuccino to warm me up along the way, a bottle of water to refresh and the *China Daily*, the Chinese newspaper written in English. My first meetings at the company couldn't have been more relevant. In those first days, the founder, Mr. Li, asked me to attend a dinner at Da Dong, a renowned restaurant, as he had a visit from potential investors. When I showed up, he asked me if I knew the investment company with whom we were having dinner. "I do!" I answered, smiling. When I met the chairman of that company, a bright Indian gentleman, and the general manager, a Chinese man with a PhD from Oxford, both from the Asian branch, I told them that I knew the global Co-CEO since he was based in New York, and I had met him previously. The dinner was very positive and productive, and they asked me if I was available for another occasion, as their Co-CEO was coming to Beijing for meetings.

In the following weeks at the office, I met with all the key managers. I had to evaluate the business and give my assessment and vision to the founder to help him expand his multi-platform omnichannel into a premium lifestyle offering. I started talking often with him about different aspects of the business and how he could improve in all areas—in warehousing, to enhance services; in retail, to elevate the company's overall positioning; in finance to improve profitability; in branding to raise awareness of brands among consumers, and more. At the same time, I was meeting with teams who were executing the company's projects and realized that I was probably the oldest person there, not just the only Western one! They were all very, very young. But committed and highly motivated. Their dedication and hard work were unparalleled. They had a youthful resilience that was unbeatable. Although they were well prepared for their specific jobs, they needed guidance and were thirsty to learn from someone who had exactly my experience. Within a short time, the role I would play in the company was clear: A coach for the Founder and a mentor to the teams. It couldn't have been a better opportunity since I was also learning, through them, all sorts of things about China—its culture and people, new sets of companies and competitors, their channels, and their go-to-market strategies. I understood what I had read in recent books about the country's evolution which now looked such a land of Metavese for foreigners. *Young China* by Zac Dychtwald's, *Betting on China* by Robert W. Koepp's, *The End of Chip China* Shaun Reins, *AI Superpower*, Kai-Fu-Li, *On China* by Henry Kissinger, and many more by Federico Rampini since his wide culture and deep knowledge of the places he lived make his work quite relevant.

The company had been working mainly with distributors and needed to attract more high-end brands to work directly with them. I knew almost all the key players, but this was not enough. We needed to have a stronger value proposition, and after assessing the business and the market, I came up with a plan that I discussed repeatedly with several people in the company before presenting it to the founder. The decision-making process I learned in the past was very different from what I saw happening in China. The time that people took to decide about something seemed endless. But when something was decided, the speed of moving into action was something I had never witnessed, and so was the speed expected for getting results. The pressure in China is unbearable because the competition is really fierce. I knew that I would work hard and that I would have to make important sacrifices. Bringing in new customers was crucial and keeping them was our best resource for maintaining momentum. Customer lifetime value was the company's most important KPI. Some interesting projects required working with external talents, too. Based on the information I was given; I hired a UK firm to create a strong company profile and investor pitch. The famous photographer and visual artist Chen Man, married to an American artist, helped me to create a new image for the company with an authentic flavor, but I was also able to meet people from different fields while socializing at different kinds of gatherings.

I had arranged for my son to come to Beijing during his spring break but since I had started working in early March and my son would arrive shortly after, I couldn't be with him in New York for his 10th birthday. Of course, before leaving the city, I celebrated with him a very special, meaningful, and unforgettable party with his best friends and then gave him a nice surprise on his actual birthday—which our friend Michelle helped me make it possible: Bringing him the gift he most desired at that time, a bow! But the real gift, maybe for me, was the letter I wrote to him that day.

6 March 2018

To Gabriel, the love of my life.

Right now, you are sleeping in New York, and I wish I could give you the good night kiss I love to give to you. In China it is morning, and I am writing from a temporary desk in Beijing where I am working. The office is located in the Galaxy SOHO building designed by Zaha Hadid. When I come here every day, admiring her work, I marvel at how far imagination can go and how positively human ambition can reach. You can Google the name of her and the building to understand what I mean (here in China people would say "Baidu" because Google is not allowed).

HAPPY BIRTHDAY my love!

I miss not being with you today and I want to make sure you know how much I adore you.

We already celebrated you in a fabulous way last week ("the best day ever" you wrote me in your card to thank me, and you couldn't make me happier!).

———

10 years ago, a beautiful child was born at 7 pm in Milan where we lived then. Both grandmothers were there, arriving from near Rome. Karen and Lawrence made a long journey from South Africa to be with us. My friend Cristiana came from Rome. With them and your wonderful dad, I was surrounded by love and support waiting to welcome you into this world.

An infant is a miracle that happens. All those who have had the privilege of having a child have certainly experienced the wonderful emotions that our heart, mind, body and soul create. You do not know that they exist until you have a baby in your hands. The joy of that moment was unprecedented and unparalleled. But the most interesting thing about life is that these emotions have grown with you every day and will continue to grow. I learned how wide and deep my heart was to love you as I do. I started then and continued to add love and more love and more love every day.

The first year as a mom was a mixture of joy and fear that something might happen, since you were born with a "intestinal duplication" and at almost 1 month you had surgery. People thought I was crazy at the time, keep going to doctors and interrogating them all the time. I was not! I had just developed an instinct, the maternal instinct, that made me save your life. I am always grateful to God for this gift; it is another reason why I strongly believe in Heavens, my love.

My life was full, committed to my work and my commitment to reach new heights every time, evolving as a person, as a woman, as an executive. Since you came into my life, I have become a better human being. The best result of life is our inner development! I better understand people, what they go through and the many sacrifices we all make to ensure that children are healthy, happy and full of opportunities. I have also become a better leader, understanding the importance of other people's time and the true priorities of life. As your mother, I understood my mother's love, what she did for me and how challenging I was to her as a child. She did a great job and with you I became a better daughter. Despite her limited education, she raised me with wisdom and a strong sense of learning and responsibility. It is no coincidence that I have a great work ethic! I had a nice party for your first year because it was also the end of fears, and I could give you a wonderful Christening. You grew up strong, happy, and beautiful. And so has my love for you grown. Every day is better than the other, every year more interesting than the other. I could write a book full of your stories and the happiness I felt having you in my life every day. To make sure I remember them all, I started taking pictures, which I did not do before (Daddy can confirm it!). But now I have memories of everything. We can go and review these photos whenever you want to know more about yourself and what you have done so far, because at this age it will be difficult to remember. So, I will continue to take photographs of you even if you don't like them! (Sorry ;-))!

The second year we were still in Milan, and I used to sing you a song about New York, a place where I always wanted to live. We were very happy in Milan and Grandma Franca lived with us, so I could still travel around the world for work without worries (sometimes, when I could, I brought you with me). She was a very loving grandmother, and she taught me a lot about how to deal with children, she had a special gift for that. None of my friends thought I made a good decision to have my mother-in-law in my house, but I knew it was the best for you, and YOU were the only thing that mattered to me. Grandma Ida, who worships you, always came to visit you in Milan and when we moved to Modena, she came to live with us. You had the best of both worlds: Grandma Ida was very good at playing with you and teaching you stories and things, while Grandma Franca dressed you for the day and made you eat all the food with no leftovers. In Modena you had fun with the whole family, and we celebrated a wonderful third birthday for you. Karen and Lawrence came too as they were truly an integral part of our lives. I enrolled you in the American school without knowing that soon I would live a dream come true: to move to New York! The song we were singing had become true for us! I could give you the opportunity to learn English very easily and to learn a different system and mentality, the one that is always positive—because in the American mentality it is enough to just do it (as the Nike's claim). I have organized some beautiful birthday parties for you over the years and, above all, I have tried to give you all the opportunities to become a wonderful adult in the future. Not only because you go to a good school but also because I could expose you to things that could better develop your heart, mind and soul. I have done, and will keep doing, my best to give you examples of people and situations that can inspire you and I have tried to be a good role model. Like you, I am not perfect, but I never stop trying to evolve and be better for you. No words can help me describe the depth of joy I feel when I am with you and in knowing that you are in my life. I adore you unconditionally, but I will never stop pushing you to be better. This is the responsibility that comes from the joy of being your mother. I can't just say yes to everything, let's keep playing and just have fun. I must correct you, educate you, teach hard work, even sacrifices, and it is intense work! But it is necessary to make you possibly a wonderful human being. You are already very gifted, full of talent and special things that God has given you and I wish you the strength, joy, and determination to continue building the best of You. I will always be there with love, care, joy and tenderness to make your foundation strong enough so you can spread your wings wide one day and fly to places you dream of experiencing.

Happy birthday, my love.

Forever yours,

Mom.

While in Asia

The timing of my arrival in China could not have been more significant for the historical changes the world was about to witness. The Chinese were rebuilding the patriotic pride of the Celestial Empire and were focused on what the nation could become. Later on, during my stay, I wasn't indeed astonished on how they reacted to the Hong Kong protest, as it was only a confirmation of how confident China felt in its endeavor and long-term plans for the country. Every day I observed the ambition of the Chinese and the patterns of their life in the cities. They were people who worked and studied hard, competed fiercely, and succeeded or failed and retried. Of course, I could see the many differences from the West, many truly difficult to accept. China has a culture of its own, and as I said, my goal was to understand more deeply their economy and its evolution since that understanding, I was convinced, would undoubtedly be useful for any project I was going to undertake in the future.

The Chinese regime was definitely a key asset to that evolution but, I was convinced, there was more. What were the decisions, the abilities, the strategies, and other key elements that made them progress so much in such a short span of time? Attending management meetings in the office and realizing how surprisingly open the debate was—strictly behind closed doors. Internal opposition was avoided publicly to "save face." Being behind closed doors when important things must be discussed is part of the Chinese culture: You can feel it everywhere, even when you go to restaurants. Most of the restaurants have private rooms, and not just one or two, but many. "The face" is a concept in China that I began to know better while working there.. It is most crucial to their culture. A new friend had helped me to understand it. An elegant, intelligent, and kind lady, married to an Italian businessman and benefactor, she made me realize that in their culture, public reputation is everything. None discuss politics, ever—especially the ones who have foreign friends.

Since my arrival, I had noticed that even in international hotels, the Chinese had not enough staff who could speak English and rarely were they fluent: The language barrier was much bigger than I had thought it would be since, at work, young managers were good English speakers having studied abroad. Obviously, everywhere I went there were only Chinese characters: In cafes, in supermarkets and shopping malls, on street signs, everywhere but someone taught me how to scan the characters with *WeChat* and get an immediate translation. It was the greatest survival lesson! Once I mastered it, life became a bit easier. Many other survival lessons came later, including the use of another app to get an instant translation when people were talking. This became my safe way to attend dinners where I was the only foreigner, without needing a person to interpret for me constantly. *Mr. Translator*, from Tencent, was the companion I needed to help me understand at least some of the conversation around me. It was the highest evolution of voice recognition! A visitor can easily be dazzled by how widely everyone is embracing mobile technology or how many people are into app creation. Just as people have used social media in the West to create their own personal brand identities, here they were also trying to build their own mobile apps, their own personal online shops, and more.

I met a few times a business partner in his beautiful places where I could admire his taste in design and furnishings—they were an expression of sophisticated wealth. His oldest daughter, the oldest of three children (not just one), had graduated from Stanford and was opening English schools in Asia. He invested in many different fields such as health and food. Apparently, investing in health care is normal everywhere but what struck me was his investment in people's *mental* health. He also thought he should focus on companies making cheaper but good-quality consumer products as he expected to see increasing demand in the lower price ranges and further success stories like Pinduoduo. A visionary for sure, since not too far from when we met, the economy started to slow down.

On July 6, 2018, tensions between the United States and China escalated to the point that it began to be called a "trade war." One day, I was dining with some intellectual people who told me that "when you fight, it's good. You confront each other: it's a way to get to know each other better." Well, I think it's always best to avoid fights, but after that dinner, I realized the relevance of these comments. Indeed, the trade war made known to the world the trust and power that China had created within its country, and its growing ambitious. Business between the two countries became unimaginably more complicated, not only for big companies like Apple but also in regard to many simple realities. When industry leaders asked me at the beginning of the trade war if it would have an impact on the luxury business, I told them that in a short time it was not possible. They did not believe my comments. They thought I was an optimist. I certainly am one, but the results achieved in China by LVMH, Chanel and Hermès in 2018 and 2019, with most companies raising their business expectations in that region, showed that I was more in tune with the situation because I was there experiencing it. Working in China allowed me to understand, in a faster and deeper way, what was going on; the difficulties that my experience might have entailed, as a blonde foreigner working in Beijing in a Chinese company, were perhaps similar to what one goes through in a "PhD" study. I think I also learned the meaning of the word Zen, because if I hadn't had built patience and tolerance—and truly in the highest abundance—I would never have been able to survive there and get my fair share of the wins in negotiations.

Understanding nuances

In Shanghai, the people I met were younger and more international. Many of them had studied and worked abroad, some in the UK, others in Canada, many in the United States, but they all had come back to their roots because, they thought, there were many opportunities in China. This country "is more efficient," they kept telling me. Anything you need, you can find or make it. From all the people I was meeting, I learned about how things were going. And in the big cities, it is important to look beneath the cutting-edge modern trends that are so visible everywhere. A closer look revealed how deep the Chinese traditions are for them too, even the young generations. I believe that this mix of efficiency and traditions helped drive their entrepreneurial spirit and their reborn patriotism.

Another important thing to grasp is the country's vast diversity. Among the people I met, there was Andrew, a bright gentleman who made me understand that people often mistakenly think they understand China by traveling in a couple of cities. Shanghai is certainly an international one, foreign-friendly and one could say "more similar" to New York, but the differences between China's cities and provinces and the people who live in many far-flung places are wider than we may imagine. As it is true of Europe, the United States or India, China is a very complex and varied reality, and only by having a humble and curious approach can one avoid making mistakes in business. Many companies have had problems with some of their initiatives and needed to apologize to the Chinese. With the rise of a new nationalism, global brands needed a greater commitment to understanding China's culture to avoid offending their sense of sovereignty. China was also undergoing changes in its culture and understanding these was as crucial as capturing the new fashion trends. I had learned this well in the United States when I was hit in the midst of a cultural change. I now felt much more equipped with experience and tools to avoid such problems.

Besides differences in business, language, lifestyle, and entertainment, another difference for most foreign people in China is simply the food, and Italians are certainly spoiled in the matter. When I went to Paris on a trip to secure the approval of an important investment for the company, the founder celebrated the meeting at a prestigious Chinese restaurant in the city as he prefers Chinese cuisine whenever he can get it. In previous years Chinese wanted to learn Western food styles, etiquettes, and ways of socializing, the new nationalism has led many entrepreneurs to spread and teach Chinese traditions and culture, including food.

China in general, and Beijing and Shanghai in particular, were becoming theaters of big international meetings and events in which, it was necessary for world leaders in business to participate and build network. In China, relationships are truly important, *guanxi*, as they call them. A particular impression I had through meeting people at some of these events, was that the divisions between Chinese competitors and their founders inside the region seemed almost inexistent compared to the unity everyone maintained among themselves outside the country. Their internal competition is fierce, but they seem all united for the good of the country and able to put aside individual differences. Is that only because of the regime, I was questioning that a bit after being in some homes.

The most talked-about subject abroad which I had also heard, was the "Belt and Road" initiative or New Silk Road, a massive infrastructure project that showed China's ambition globally. Instead, I was not familiar with the Beijing Summit of the Forum on China-Africa Cooperation (FOCAC) until I saw some delegations from African states in the same hotel where I was staying. But in 2019 it was already the seventh of these summits! Our hotel became as controlled as an airport guarded by security agents at the entrance. In the elevator, I once met some of these gentlemen and I noticed how they seemed comfortable and in a good mood. I understood them because many spoke French, a language that I learned during my time at college. After that summit, I forced myself to watch the movie *Wolf Warrior 2*, a Chinese production action movie. I do not like films of this genre, but I wanted to understand why this movie had become a national bestseller. The film confirmed my perception of how China was approaching not only America but also Africa and how it was seeing its "*friends*" and its "*enemies*" to be defeated, a bit like the American movie *Rocky IV*, where Rocky Balboa challenges the Russian Ivan.

While I was working in Asia, many things have happened that will be read in the history books of future generations. I am sure that my son will always remember our times in the East, including our trip to his favorite land of Japan at the time of their cherry blossoms and, above all, at a moment when Japan celebrated the new Emperor, Naruhito. A once-in-a-lifetime event!

Terrifying news

Traditionally, during the Chinese New Year, all companies close for the Spring Festival holidays. As I was coming off a period of hard work and satisfaction from securing major contracts for the company, I decided to take a holiday on my own. Miraculously, I chose not to stay in China. I was going to stay in Asia though as I didn't have the strength to endure another twelve-hour jet lag back to New York City. I was going to America anyway next month for meetings and, most importantly, to see my son. I brought him back to New York after a school year in Beijing where I didn't see him happy. I made this decision on his eleventh birthday, watching how much he missed his school, his friends, and his home, so I gave him the present he wanted the most. I was making bigger sacrifices missing him in my daily life, traveling back and forth till I potentially find a new job back in the United States when my contract was going to be ending.

For that Chinese New Year, I went to Indonesia and my holiday was set to be an unforgettable experience, but it was not for the reasons I thought. There were reports of a virus that had struck Wuhan—the danger of which was yet to be determined. The Chinese authorities required everyone to wear a mask: It was no longer just an optional precaution, as when air pollution was high, but it began to be an obligation at all times. While I was on a boat, lost among beautiful Indonesian islands, my assistant contacted me asking me to fill out a questionnaire that required me to enter my health status, my symptoms, and my exact GPS location. How strange, I thought. All employees had to do it, she pointed out, it was a request from the authorities. Every day. I immediately understood that something important was about to happen and I called my friend Francesca, who had stayed in Beijing during the Chinese New Year, to ask her for more information. Although there were no sick people in the capital, at least not yet at that point, she described a surreal atmosphere. She told me that even the delivery men—who normally buzz the streets carrying all sorts of things, as people in China use online ordering for most needs—didn't even carry water anymore. Supermarkets were starting to run out of supplies, including rice, and the incessant traffic on the streets was suddenly gone. Beijing was deserted. I breathed in her fear and tried to figure out if she was exaggerating.

On WeChat, Chinese people started posting pictures of notoriously lively hotels with the lights off: no one was there anymore. Talking to my fellow travelers, all Westerners, about what was happening in China, I realized that there was an incredible gap between what I perceived through my contacts with people in Beijing and their understanding of the problem at that time. Even though newspapers and online news were reporting on the virus issue in China at the end of January 2020, no one seemed to be really alarmed by it. My instincts told me to be on the alert and urged me to take a risk: Not going back to China after the vacation and possibly losing my job. I wrote to my boss and told him that I didn't think it made sense for the company to have me back to Beijing after Chinese New Year. Even if I was going to stay out of the country regardless of his wish, I let him decide what was best for the company. Mr. Li allowed me to work remotely.

On February 3, no one returned to the office in China.

In just a few days, Secoo organized what became a new way of working: the smart working. There were calls in the morning to teams to set goals, online meetings to move projects forward, and phone calls to give us all a sense of closeness. It wasn't really important at that time to sell more products and do business the way it had been done up to that point. The real need was to give a sense of continuity, of normality, because as the days went by, it seemed that life had been snatched away from us. I had very strong feelings, I felt the pain of the devastation of the daily deaths. I worried for all the families who had lost their loved ones in the worst possible way, without a final goodbye. An atrocity within an atrocity. One of my team members had lost her father to a cancer he had been battling for some time. Neither she nor her mother had been able to say goodbye and attend his funeral. Each death caused whole families to suffer, and grief spread as fast as a virus.

We did not know at the time that what was happening in China would happen to everyone in the world and that we were about to experience a pandemic. There was no clarity in those days about the origin and transmissibility of the virus, and there were different theories, but only one certainty: You had to monitor your body for two weeks without symptoms to feel confident that you did not have Covid-19, as the disease was called. The two weeks spent in Indonesia were truly a miracle for me. When at the end of February, I read the tragic news and saw the shocking images of what was happening in Italy, I felt a call I had never had before: I wanted to return to my homeland. I called my former bank manager, Luigi, who lives in Codogno, where the virus in Italy had originated. His words were heartbreaking. In the small street where he lives, four people lost their lives. Bergamo was mourning so many victims that all of us Italians had become "Bergamaschi," especially after seeing the devastating images of coffins being transported on military trucks. It seemed to me that the virus had the effect of a nuclear bomb. The lives spent, the gloomy atmosphere, the despair, the fears, and the inability to move. Many families were separated for months by the impossibility of traveling, because countries, one after the other, had closed their borders and airlines no longer flew. Lucia, the consul in Guangzhou, saw her children again after more than two months and her husband after six! I understood her very well and I cared about all these situations because I knew how difficult it was to be away from one's loved ones, especially young children.

The many manifestations of humanity by my compatriots filled my heart with love and hope. The songs from the balconies, from the rooftops, from the Duomo in Milan, where Bocelli sang in an empty cathedral on Easter Sunday, were small but necessary relief. The composure of everyone in respecting the rules of lockdown and the many demonstrations of solidarity of the whole country toward those in need inspired the whole world. Italians can teach a lot about humanity and civility whenever they want. In the meantime, the pandemic was spreading like wildfire, making us realize how vulnerable we all were, even those who thought they were immune or who had attacked Italy because of its rigid reaction and strict containment measures. Gradually, states across America began to suffer from the virus. Every country in the world fell into the same abyss. The daily death toll was chilling. The entire world had to deal with an experience that changed the lives of all of us forever. When dealing with tragedies of this magnitude, it is easy to lose heart. Depression is not just economic for a country; it is first and foremost mental and human. We are weakened by the collapse of our certainties and points of reference. There were times when I had to think of the virus as a world war, perhaps because this made me feel paradoxically privileged compared to the generations before us. They had lived through the horrors of previous world wars with the constant fear of attacks, with the dead buried under the rubble, without food, without communication with loved ones, without love. Instead, staying at home and having the time we never had before, we began to do and think about new things. I asked myself a thousand questions in search of answers that I hoped would be helpful. I read everything I could to reconstruct history, to trace its cycles and find possible solutions that would lead to a stronger sense of humanity. How had our grandparents and great-grandparents fared after the wars? How had our parents grown up in the years of reconstruction? What could we learn from their past? How could we face a future so uncertain and almost impossible to imagine?

As governments began programs to rebuild their economies, we all had a chance to better understand our lives and our priorities, to ask ourselves how we really wanted to live, what kind of world we wanted to create and pass on to our children. The psychologist Francesca Morelli wrote a touching reflection on what was happening that went around the world. It began, "*I believe that the Cosmos has its own way of rebalancing things and its laws when they are upset.*" It was time to realize that we all owed it a debt and that the time we have can be used differently than we had learned.

The meaning

Many people today live in a situation of uncertainty never experienced before. Everything has become more complicated; it takes three times as much effort to achieve the same results today than it used to. In some way, all of us today (all over the world) experience similar feelings, fears and difficulties. Human resilience, especially in these times, is the most important essence and hope is the real source of energy. There is an even deeper realization that we cannot walk the paths of the future without inspiration. Committed leaders feel more compelled to contribute to the causes for which they fight. It is in these moments, when we are caught up in a greater cause, that our value to our fellow human beings multiplies. Will the younger generation express their opinions and priorities in ways that go far beyond "likes" on social media? When I listen to the words of the song '*Stand Up for Something*' by Andra Day, I feel that only by acting with a deeper sense of life do we achieve meaning. In my own small and determined way of working, I always pushed companies to think ahead, with strategies and product offerings that not only positioned them for success but made them think about their responsibilities while doing business. Business of impact is the key to moderate leadership. The impact of COVID-19 caused companies all over the world to start talking about how essential it was for people at the top to have a more positive purpose and impact on the companies they serve, as far as their employees, their customers and, of course, their shareholders are concerned. Finally, I began to see that what I had always believed in - leadership that puts people first - was really emerging.

I returned to Italy even though it didn't seem like the safest option at the time, but I wanted to be with my mom and my brother. As everyone, my son could no longer go back to school and had to continue learning online. For each travel at that time, you were forced to have a quarantine, I decided to do it in the place where my life had originated, in Santa Severa. In the days of isolation, I listened to classical music because I needed to think more deeply: from Vivaldi to Beethoven, from Morricone to Verdi. After the usual fourteen days locked in my room to work, read and think a lot, I took a bike ride. I took my son to see the little house where I had attended elementary school, and as we walked through the few streets of the town, I showed him where I had spent my childhood. Having had the time I never had, I allowed myself to visit all my uncles and cousins, proud of my success and at peace with their lives. I spent many hours with my brother, whom I found more caring than ever, happy with his wife Elena, and full of interests and hobbies. It was wonderful to get together as great and evolved people, though in different ways. Before leaving Santa Severa, I visited "my castle" by the sea and found my spirit and imagination again. "*I am here*", I sang to myself, as if I were Cynthia Erivo when she beautifully interpreted that song at the Tony Awards. The warm and special welcome in Milan by my new neighbor Valeria, who was almost unknown to us, made me realize that my son, in his European experience, could add to his already matured knowledge of the world, the poetry, the depth and the beauty of simple, kind, authentic gestures. These are things that we must always remember and value, even building a strategic project around them. I was becoming aware of my more centered and balanced values and identity and eager to restore more *humanism*.

It is said that necessity drives humans to invent and thus to progress. But need is not the only driver of invention. Our human nature drives us to reimagine, rediscover, and reinvent, and we can use it to project ourselves into the future in ways that are not obvious. As soon as it was possible for me to travel to China, I returned to negotiate my exit from the company. My three years were nearing their end, and I could feel satisfied with what I had learned and built in that time.

I wanted to commit to a more meaningful cause.

What we become is not stationary. We don't reach the end of the rainbow to stay there. We want new dreams, and we need new projects. Tomorrow must be created with concrete plans. All of us will have a role to play, continuously, with discipline. There are so many useful things waiting to be done, and I knew that if only I would direct my focus to other types of projects, I could feel more useful. The virus made us realize the urgency of concrete actions to preserve our planet. Sustainability was a compelling cause, necessary for our survival. It is up to us to implement the changes we want to see. It's not just about doing what we want but also about feeling responsible and taking action.

Every single action counts.

We are not necessarily going to become Gandhi, Mandela or Mother Teresa of Calcutta, but we can and must do our part if we want to see a new humanity emerge and promote more ethical leadership throughout the Universe. Space included, because it is also in that dimension that our future lies. In orbs we don't fully know and are exploring, in areas where there will be new achievements. No real success can be achieved if this possibility is not passed on to others, if it is not shared.

One morning, while reading one of the many newsletters I subscribed to, I found an advertisement about a non-profit organization based in Denmark, Global Fashion Agenda, that was looking for a new CEO. GFA was a non profit organization championing sustainability in the fashion industry. The role would require another change, a significant amount of study and commitment. When I realized that the mission could significantly contribute to people's lives and the help to protect the planet, I decided to take on the task. I didn't think twice about the opportunity of advancing sustainability, particularly in the fashion industry, which I knew well. I sat down at my desk and wrote a letter explaining my choice, listing examples of what I had done six years before (all public, so it could be checked) and what I believed in. Shortly afterwards I started a series of interviews to assess if my experience and vision was in line with the Board's objective. Securing the role, in March I signed a new contract for a new job located in a new city, Copenhagen. My Easter in 2021, at the beginning of April, had a different sense of celebration and anticipation knowing that the next day the press release for my new role would be sent out. I felt reborn, more committed than ever, happy to be able to help accelerate change in an industry I had come to know in all its twists and turns. The time had come to apply my leadership to address sustainable growth, respecting the environment, the people and all communities involved. Helping this industry and its leaders reverse its climate impact, protect biodiversity, set priorities, and push them to make bold decisions – with the ultimate goal to even changing their business models – for reducing greenhouse gases was for me the right cause at the right time. Once again, I could confirm that what is not obvious today will be obvious tomorrow. Maybe that's why I had to go through the Lands' End experience where I put sustainability as one of the first priorities. The choices I made in the past were taking shape today. Søren Kierkegaard, Danish philosopher, said that "Life is to be understood by looking back, but it is lived by looking forward." We must make an effort to imagine and project ourselves into the distant future, even though we know that it is difficult to predict what will happen tomorrow. Long-term planning helps to achieve ambitious goals in all areas. Warren Buffett and Jeff Bezos, in their annual letters, have often urged us to think long term, identifying seven years as ideal time frame in business. What is the right time frame for a country project? Ten years, twenty? And for us? The ability to imagine the unthinkable will continue to give us new ideas on how to continue enriching our lives, if we are allowing new possibilities.

Some takeaways

Leave out judgments and preconcepts if you want to understand something unfamiliar.
Even in the most complicated situations, bridges and points of contact can be built.
Assess business, the market, your team, and your ideas to come up with a strong plan.
Go with company pace for decision making and execution, not just yours.
Coach and mentor but also allow reverse mentoring to stay current at your work.
Disagreements can bring greater clarity. Agree to disagree. Bring unity to stay stronger.
Increase your patience and tolerance when differences are higher than ever faced before.
Each culture has a vast diversity inside, looking for nuances to avoid missteps.
Uncertainty is the new norm. Defining your priorities and find significance in your life.
Big ambitions require long-term planning, but you can make a difference with small steps.

Infinity: Envision a new Beginning
Human Pillars: Reinvention

> *"We have not inherited the world*
> *from our fathers, but we have borrowed*
> *it from our children, and we must give it*
> *back to them better than we found it".*
> Ancient Masai saying.

The pandemic had a tremendous effect on every industry, including fashion. It has disrupted value chains, caused the closing of many of the world's retail outlets and created a new level of public awareness over health, safety and the fragility of the planet. It has forced brands and upstream players to take difficult decisions every day, from managing cash flows, to rethinking distribution models and acting to protect the health of employees and consumers alike.

At the same time, consumers were becoming increasingly engaged with sustainability topics, including social issues and climate change. Many were showing their willingness to reconsider how, when, and what they buy. Sustainability was also attracting increasing attention at the executive level. A rising number of asset and wealth managers had mandates that prioritize companies that pass sustainability thresholds with ESG becoming a point of reference. The pandemic has spurred policy makers to refocus on sustainability, with various regional and national authorities linking post-COVID recovery efforts to sustainability objectives.

These systemic issues were also apparent in the growing impact of climate change. We needed to take coordinated actions on the greenhouse gas emissions (GHG) contributing to climate change, to avoid crises such as heatwaves, rising sea levels and damage to ecosystems that are vital to our future and support a transition which was just for people around the world, including the global south. People started to understand that there is not a planet B.

How can I help?

As soon as the America opened its boarders and was safer to travel, I went back to my beloved New York City where I could also have a vaccine. I was impressed by the speed of which health companies that came together with various players to give us hope and freedom again. We needed to regain trust to be together without fears and get humans once again. Simple gestures weren't possible anymore. No shaking hands with businesspeople, no hugs with friends, no kisses to relatives. Social distance was needed during the pandemic but it was not easy to keep for too long. We needed to move on. Therefore, despite the global debates about the effectiveness of COVID-19 vaccine and the questions about which one was less harmful, with no hesitation I took my shot for the first available slot I found in Chelsea, hoping for no side effects. Indeed, I was supposed to attend the first online Board meeting a few days later with the Global Fashion Agenda (GFA) as newly appointed CEO. I woke up earlier than usual and my enthusiasm kept me awake as I went through the five-hour meeting and luckily, I had no fever nor side effects. While on the videocall with new colleagues, I immediately understood that being an outsider in GFA could gave me the chance to bring new ideas to accelerate impact in a non-for-profit organization.

After my appointment, I immediately wanted to contact the co-founder and former CEO of GFA to express my gratitude for having started something so meaningful and for deciding to leave – as her departure gave me the opportunity to step in and bring the mission forward. I learned from previous experiences that it can be good to have a meeting and possibly establish a dialogue, with the former CEO of the organization you're going to lead - and I believe this is valid also for other positions. Of course, you shall expect the first conversation to be far than easy at times, but believing in the importance of bridges, building a good relationship, can help not only you in the job, but also the team, the Board and the partners that built relations with the organization because of the previous leader. I had a great call with Eva who truly appreciated my gesture and understood my vision and passion, so we promised each other to meet in Denmark once travelling was possible. We went out for lunch at Victor Café, the place where fancy Danes dine. We established a wonderful dialogue, and I told her that I would cherish her "baby", GFA, and bring it to the next level by growing its impact and global reach.

Before my first day in the GFA office, I went to buy some Italian wine – since I was told that it is normal for Danish people to gather right afterwork and enjoy a beer or a good wine – and I added several books, plus a puffy red heart. I offered these books to the team to encourage them to keep learning and being inspired. Not all the books were about global warming, some of them were about fashion and some about humanity, like *Sapiens* from Yuval Noah Harari. Among the books, there was one titled *Everything Starts With Creativity*. I told the team that I would give the organization, the team and its work my heart and creativity. I left that book and the red puffy heart next to my desk to remind the team about that promise even while I wasn't present in the office but online or at some external meetings and conferences.

Most of the team members were already working with lots of dedication but it took a while for them to adjust and believe in the change, in a new strategy and my leadership. I didn't come from the activism world, I came from a business world, and that came with prejudice in this environment. Another one to add on my long list of prejudices I have dealt with during my life! Danes are progressive, free-thinking and not afraid to speak up so understanding and adopting their culture was an additional challenge for me - besides the need to elevate GFA to the next level and make it a global forum and platform. I must admit that I didn't expect such a cold welcome to go from a competitive world to a non-for-profit organization since I only wanted to give back, share my expertise, develop the organization to its full potential, mentor people - and be mentored by them as well. But trust wasn't there, and it needed to be built step by step. It took a while to gain an open door from a very skeptical team. I often felt in meetings they needed to push back to my suggestions just to impose a different stance regardless of their real views. The only way to be able to move things forward was to not respond to their pushbacks and not put up walls. Since I was confident in my approach, I tried to create trust and a culture where they felt comfortable to voice their point of views and that we could agree to disagree at times to ensure a constructive dialogue could lead to a better and more formative outcome. They didn't make it easy for me at all and I am sure they felt exactly the same as I am a demanding leader always aiming for excellent results in each project or initiative. However, being in a different stage of life, I knew I could overcome all these challenges of negativity and professional and personal criticism with a higher level of maturity and wisdom. I often went home feeling discouraged and worried that I had chosen the wrong career move again. Nevertheless, as always, I don't give up easily, and this time I was not only much more experienced, but the Board was supportive in giving me the time and the chance to transition into a new course, including the co-founder. During the time of resisting the change, seeing my dedication, my sincere openness to listen to everyone, my fresh mindset, inclusivity, accessibility, flexibility, and understanding, I worked with them to build patience, determination and the necessary trust.

After having successfully led some projects with the team, there was a new spirit of empowerment and development and an appreciation that we belonged to a stronger organization with more ambitious goals. Ultimately, I wanted to bring the joy to our work and working together – which was reflected in their cooperation and passionate dedication to the cause we were all working towards.

With the pandemic still impacting on our lives, even in a Nordic country devoted to wellbeing, the work-life balance was increasingly more relevant. I granted the team an additional week off to the already generous holiday allowance, and I also decided to encourage office gatherings and even yoga classes to keep up the team spirit, morale, and culture of both personal and professional development. Learning that even the biggest organizations (our peers) working with similar missions were working remotely, I decided to implement a more flexible remote working policy to retain and keep attracting great talent, which I also benefited from during the following years. We were in a cozy office space, in an area – called FMG – with beautiful, cobbled courtyard full of pink roses and blossoming trees. Inside, the GFA office was a large space with several desks. Though beautiful, this office felt too isolated. Right across the street, alongside the spectacular canals, there was an office area, called BLOX, that belonged to the same landlord who rented out our space and offered several offices and co-working spaces. BLOX is a beautiful modern building full of new and established enterprises; I believed that moving GFA to this environment would enable them to feel part of a bigger cause since you are working alongside many intelligent and vibrant people that you could interact with in the corridors, the kitchen areas, elevators and, of course, in and out the several meeting rooms. With the aim to expand our vision, I proposed to move to BLOX in a smaller office space to pay less than our previous rent but with the opportunity to use all the common areas, have exchanges with other people who worked for different companies around us and feel part of a bigger picture instead of being isolated in a cozy but often half empty space. In the end, everyone was proud of the change and loved to overlook the beautiful canals of the pretty Copenhagen from the big BLOX windows.

There wasn't a day in which I didn't express to everyone I was speaking with how beautiful the city was. Copenhagen is so well maintained, incredibly clean, efficient in all the public transportation and services and gives you lot of options to sightseen, eat and hang out. There are so many museums to visit, theaters to go and it's full of restaurants where people eat outside in the summer days. Many shops are very chic, and the architecture is truly sophisticated. No wonder why it is called the Paris of the Nordics! The summer is marvelous to enjoy the long days when the sun only sets after 10pm. In July most people take off, but the city is still full of people – mostly tourists – since the Danes are back in August when school starts, and life is back to the Fall mode. Even if everyone speaks English, not speaking Danish is quite a barrier for making Danish friends, besides the differences in habits and culture. They love to mingle with their longtime friends and family and if you are new, not married to a Danish or not knowing the language it takes a while to be invited out for dinner or other activities to share time after work. I was lucky to have reconnected to my friend Cristina and her husband Massimo who were helping me settling in the city at the very beginning. The winter there is made for "hygge", a Danish expression to mean a warm atmosphere to enjoy the good thing with good people - also because the sun won't be seen much from the fall and people stay inside. The energy around town while walking in the winter is a lot quieter, and people use that time to "illuminate their soul". I loved that concept and the solitude to reenergize, I always make sure that I have time - in silence - at least once a week, normally on Saturdays. Loving also an active social life, during Fall and Winter when the office space becomes almost empty after 5pm on workdays, and no one to hang out with in the evening after work or at the weekend, I felt the emptiness of the long dark hours. Even if I always found interesting things to read, watch, listen and do, for the first time ever in my life, I experienced the taste of loneliness. I joined a gym, used the extra time to reconnect with longtime friends, and watched some interesting TV series after cooking better meals to treat myself. Always lighting candles and listening to music, my source of joy.

Meeting a real Princess, now a Queen.

I often had the privilege to meet brilliant people in my different jobs since they exposed me to all sorts of minds around the world. Important designers, businesspeople, talents, artists, celebrities, billionaires, and politicians. I even met a few Presidents of the United States while working in America. But I never met and worked with the Royals, with a real Princess. During the hiring process, one day the GFA Chairman informed me that he was organizing a meeting with our Patron, Her Royal Highness (HRH) the Crown Princess Mary of Denmark, the future Queen of Denmark (she became Her Majesty the Queen in January 2024). The (former) Crown Princess's long-standing patronage demonstrated continued support for promoting a sustainable and responsible fashion and textile industry and it was essential that we met.

The Royal Danish family is very symbolic in Denmark, as the country still loves formalities even if they are very progressive. I read the subject of that email many times. I couldn't believe it! I was living in a new country, working in a new job and I was invited to meet their Princess?! How was I

supposed to speak to her? What subjects should I touch on? How do I make
a good impression? What if she doesn't like me? I am not Danish; I am
Italian born, a New York resident, and a global citizen, will that be a limit?
I had a million questions in my mind which were doing ping pong with the
excitement of the feeling of high honor. Not only because she was a Crown
Princess but because she truly represented many things I admire in a woman. A real person who has been a positive figure on the world stage, a person
with a strong academic background and, off duty, someone who protects her
private life. While I was scrolling coverage of the Royals, I noticed that she
looked always composed, with a natural elegance and wearing appropriate
looks for every occasion. I had the impression that what she was wearing was
less important than the causes she was supporting, and that impression was
not only mine. The Crown Princess was and still is highly respected, fully
engaged with several organizations for which she served as Patron with a
range across various areas of support.

Our meeting was at one of the four buildings which form the Amalienborg Palace, called Frederik VIII's Palace, where the Royals live with their
four children: Prince Christian, Princess Isabella, and the twins Prince
Vincent and Princess Josephine. When I was walking in the square passing the Royal guards before entering the Palace, once again, I couldn't stop
flashing back to my humble childhood and time at the Santa Severa Castle
by the beach and thinking of that girl full of dreams who was envisioning
her future outside a Castle, was finally getting inside and that was due to
many reasons, but mostly thanks to my hard work, self-belief and the wish to
make a difference. I breathed a few times, taking in the feeling of immense
gratitude to the heavens for an opportunity which people could often only
dream about. I then kept going, pretending I wasn't nervous, but I was!
When Her Royal Highness Crown Princess Mary of Denmark entered the
room, I was obviously feeling under pressure. I was hoping to be understood
on how important it was for me to be accepted not being Danish - as I am
sure HRH had to pass many judgments at the beginning, including the one
of the very popular Queen Margarethe II, her mother-in-law. How it must
have been for HRH - being an Australian girl from a wonderful but normal
family- to be accepted by the Queen - a phenomenal woman, very popular in
her country, known for her strong sense of duty, her incredible personality, a
large generosity, with a unique talent? I was hoping HRH could then relate
to my humble feelings, but I went there very prepared for the meeting with
ideas and back up presentations. HRH warm approach that put me at ease
and was very knowledgeable about the work GFA was doing and was giving
me suggestions, inspirations, and insights. I was impressed and it made me
want to redouble my commitment to a job with a purpose. HRH patronage

started right at the beginning when GFA originated, in 2009, when COP15 came to Copenhagen and there was no mention of fashion on the climate agenda. HRH told me that she wanted to accelerate actions to reach the day when buying a piece of clothing, "sustainability was a gift with purchase." The meeting went well, and we started to prepare for the next Global Fashion Summit. HRH is also supported by an extremely knowledgeable and talented team, including her private secretary. It has been a delight to work with HRH team who so gracefully expressed appreciation for our work.

From that very first meeting, I was honored to be welcomed by such a dedicated and inspirational Patron and her genuine support has resonated with me throughout the years that have followed.

A new Agenda

The fashion industry, which we all love, is a multifaced industry. On the one hand, it is a powerful engine for global growth and development, but it is also one of the largest, most resource intensive industries of all. To help understand the role of this particular industry in combatting climate change and transition into a more equitable world, we need to put things in perspective. We need to start by understanding that since the beginning of the industrial revolution for all industries, which we could assume started around 1750, all human activities have increased by 50% the quantity of atmospheric concentration of carbon dioxide, CO_2. This is one of the six greenhouse gases emissions (GHG), but it is responsible for the vast majority of global warming. The second biggest GHG is methane, which mainly originates from agriculture and waste and lasts in the atmosphere for approximately 12 years - while the carbon dioxide, CO_2 can last thousands of years! That is why you have been mainly hearing about CO_2 emissions which come mostly from the combustion of fossil fuels and cement manufacturing, from fertilizer production and deforestation. According to a GFA publication released in 2018 called *"Fashion on Climate"*, the fashion industry accounted for 2.1 billion tons of CO_2 emissions. As scientists predicted years ago, the CO_2 emissions contributed to lifting global temperatures since the Industrial Revolution and their increase put our lives in danger. Only recently have people truly understood its risks with stronger evidence of real catastrophes such as fires, droughts, flooding, and stronger storms among many other events. The implications of these effects were enormous since they disrupt many supply chains and systems, including food, logistics of any goods, workability, and livability too. And these adverse impacts could become even more severe over the coming years if we weren't starting to drastically reduce the GHG footprint. The evidence was all around us – devastating events, driven by extreme weather conditions, have been frequent and destructive – from the blazing wildfires in LA, to the surging hurricanes in Cuba, Mexico and Florida, to the catastrophic floods in Spain, Bangladesh, Pakistan, China, UK, and so many more. We have also seen countries around the world reach historic records for their soaring temperatures, with unimaginable effects on working conditions in manufacturing countries.

Dream-Plan: To Create a Systemic Change

While I was embarking on this new venture, I realized that the global garment production was forecast to increase 63% by 2030 - the equivalent of 500 billion shirts – therefore also the current business model of the fashion industry was unsustainable and needed to change. Though progress has been made, we needed to be much more ambitious and urgently implement changes to accelerate the systemic transformation that was needed to meet the Paris Agreement. GFA was able to raise awareness of the need for sustainability in the fashion industry and for fashion leaders to prioritize it in their businesses. I was determined to expand on that and move from addressing not only "why" sustainability was the journey every company needed to embark on but also help them define "how" to take that journey and "what" specific initiatives companies could undertake. I was proud to be leading change, as change is deeply rooted in my DNA, and it is needed in the fashion industry too: to bring positive progress for us all, positively impacting the industry we all love. Indeed, we could help form a thriving industry that creates prosperity for people and communities, reverses climate change and protects biodiversity. But for this to happen, more actions were required immediately. Drawing from my personality, and the previous CEO roles, I had extra pragmatism and the necessary skills to better understand the real challenges and hurdles that companies should have been able to overcome in order to push for more actions. Sustainability was a daunting task, and unpacking the solutions was key to every stakeholder: from brands to manufactures; from politicians to citizens; from academia to students; from investors to innovators; and more. In my first assessment to the Board after 30 days in the job, I was glad to impress the GFA Board of Directors – an extraordinary group of experts in different fields of the sustainability agenda and wonderful people - with a fast-learning grasp of a complex eco-system and told them the role I envisioned GFA, as a multi stakeholder initiative, could play in the future to bring about a systemic change. I used the same approach of searching, digging, reading, analyzing, and connecting dots that I had mastered throughout my career and my passion for being a bridge. I am a bridge, I kept telling people, so they could understand the need to start walking on the other side to meet somewhere.

I found a lot of materials to read and learn from and felt overwhelmed by the technicality, the myriads of names, organizations, and initiatives I needed to become familiar with. But I always liked challenges and simplifying complexity, so I was often reading after work hours too and even on the weekends, to make sure I could truly speak the same language and make a difference in a substantial way. I started by reading many sustainability reports, the policies available, the existing frameworks, reports and more. Not only the materials created by GFA - such as the *Pulse of the Industry*, the *Fashion CEO Agenda* and the *Fashion on Climate* reports – but also the work done by Science-Based Targets, CDP (Carbon Disclosure Project), DJSI (Dow Jones Sustainability Indicators) and more. I felt at times buried by these materials, but I strongly wanted to speak with knowledge to my new peers and – most importantly - bringing the inspiration needed to the leaders of the industry. GFA was working with some of them, and, among many, we could count on the support of the pioneering players. I wanted to make sure our cooperation was stronger and more meaningful and immediately engaged in interesting conversations with them.

GFA new strategy

Though sustainability was a buzzword in 2021, GFA was facing the additional challenge of being sustainable itself. Indeed, the organization was known for bringing together people in one of the most authoritative conferences about sustainable fashion called "Copenhagen Fashion Summit". However, the pandemic paralyzed this activity for two years, so no summits were held in the city and no visitors were traveling to meet in person. Even if GFA was able to deliver online content to keep up its thought leadership, we realized that people were tired of Zoom meetings and online conferences.

My new beginning had a rough start not only for the immense efforts on studying new materials, the adjustment into a new culture and work environment, but also because I needed to revamp a struggling financial situation after the pandemic. I must admit, as mentioned earlier, that I had days where I questioned why I was getting myself into a complicated world with not much reward. Everything was judged differently, even from the most imperfect people. I was tempted to give up but then I spoke to one of the most admired executives in the field and she gave me the first boost of energy. A very respected figure in the sustainability world, was appreciating my vision and was openly supportive. Her initial support was essential in helping me drive the change in the industry. When I got the invitation to speak at COP26, I started to understand that the level of influence I was going to have was higher than ever before. I went in Glasgow prepared and full of grit to make our voice heard as well. There, I met with other company representatives, and once they understood my approach, they offered their commitment to accelerate action. I returned to Copenhagen with a much clearer picture of the world, the sustainability agenda, the role we could play and my role as a changemaker. Understanding the value of GFA work and its potential to transform an entire industry for the better, I worked incredibly hard to protect the team, avoiding layoffs and immersed myself in the great mission at hand. Ultimately, I was there to make a difference and have a greater purpose, so I felt strongly that I was in the right place at the right time, despite the various challenges. And that felt so good!

With the GFA Board, brilliantly managed by a sharp and gentlemanly Chairman, Thomas Tochtermann, and the talented GFA team, we took time to define a new strategy, vision, and mission to improve sustainability performances. We decided that to lead the change, GFA needed to be "on a mission to accelerate impact in the fashion industry" by inspiring, educating, influencing, and mobilizing all stakeholders. By doing so, GFA needed to reach the new vision of striving for a "Net Positive fashion industry by 2050" which we envisioned for the people and the planet. We wanted indeed an industry that would give more to the planet, the global economy and society than it takes from them. We designed our futuristic home: at the top, the vision and mission, below our tactics (four pillars to deliver on our promise: Publications & Programs; Policy & Advocacy; Media & Event; Academy & Development) and at the bottom the source of income to sustain our work (grantors, partners, etc.). GFA was spearheading the fashion industry's journey towards a more sustainable future mainly through our summits, which we positioned at the center of our four pillars. I took time to explain our strategy internally making it very clear to understand our goals and our way. With the team, I then met all the different stakeholders to learn and confirm that we needed to move from the "why" to "how" and "what" so we could evolve from being a conference and a trusted forum to a global platform with concrete impact, working with the entire eco-system not only to educate, advocate and mobilize the industry but also to implement action.

Our summit was and is a powerful tool to help implement action as it helps to mobilize the industry. I wanted to reach a broader audience of thousands of stakeholders including not only brands but also innovators, manufacturers, investors, and more. I was aiming to get more global, having the summit internationally as well, so we could tackle more issues closer to the different stakeholders – such as the places where materials were coming from and manufactured - and convening major fashion industry decision makers to really be the nexus for agenda-setting discussions on the most critical environmental, social and ethical issues facing our industry and planet. We could become a solution provider providing several tools to the industry at large. I asked the Founder first and then to Board, always after getting my leadership team's consent first, to change the name of the Copenhagen Fashion Summit to Global Fashion Summit. To my surprise, they all agreed, and we started planning the first one for the following year as a test. The forum was renamed to manifest the organisation's global outlook and reach. Global Fashion Summit was going to build on the 13-year history of the renowned Copenhagen Fashion Summit by strengthening its representation and connections with diverse perspectives from across the world. Therefore, the Summit would be hosted in various key cities in the future, in addition to its flagship edition in Copenhagen.

We were only at the beginning of the needed change since what we really needed to achieve was (and still is) systemic change. Addressing complex challenges and interconnected issues, can only be attained with a systemic change which starts by catalysing, enabling, and supporting the transition. There were important challenges to face including to effectively prosper, de-coupling growth from its negative impacts, on resource consumption and re-imagining the evolution of growth-based systems. This was not the biggest challenge for the fashion industry but the biggest challenge for our planet and societies as I firmly believed in a broader cooperation even between different industries. I was strongly pushing GFA to engage with key stake-holders to increase our influence on the industry transformation, our ability to identify business opportunities, using our position to remove barriers and enable pre-competitive collaboration, demonstrating more concrete actions, pushing innovation to flourish and more. GFA could indeed pave the way for countless tangible outcomes that could advance sustainability in the in-dustry. With the team and the support of our esteemed Board of Directors, we started to design and implement impact programs. These were projects focused on topics such as circularity and renewable energy that facilitated pre-competitive collaboration among stakeholders across the value chain to identify solutions and work with local implementation partners to put them into action.

Alliances for a New Era

While I was at COP26, in Glasgow, there were protests on the street by young people. The choice of Glasgow as the place to reunite people at COP after the pandemic was, from my point of view, very strategic. To transform industries capital was essential and the finance institutions needed to be more protagonists. I also think that Scotland not only offered a backdrop where the finance and the energy transition were flourishing, but it is also the second region of the UK per GDP and often debates its right to independence, so hosting the global forum there was a symbol of unity. The excitement of the people meeting each other after so long gave everyone a tremendous boost of optimism.

There I was inspired to create the theme of our next summit which was going to be the first for me in person to host and attend and the first for the GFA community after the pandemic. I wanted to call it *"Alliances for a new era"* and envisioned to include in our dialogues voices that represented the entire spectrum and price point of our industry, including the companies who weren't currently focused on putting sustainability as their first priority. When I presented the idea to the team, the Board and the different stakeholders, they were eager to embrace this approach and that truly started to become my very first mark at GFA together with the globalization of our work. To walk the talk of building alliances, the first I initiated were the ones with GFA and the UNFCCC Fashion Charter and another with the Financial Times which were both possible thanks to my relationships. While with Fashion Charter the relationship was most recent, the one with the FT was built in the past – mainly with the FT Live department. I met Lindita, the Fashion Charter Secretariat General at Glasgow and appreciated her approach very much, so I decided to invest in growing our relationship to support each other's work. My objectives were clear and focused on accelerating impact, so I wanted to stay closer to changemakers around the world, support them with educational programs to decarbonize the supply chain and to expand our Fashion CEO Agenda toolkit to as many CEOs and C-suites as possible.

The preparation of the Summit took a toll on all of us but the cooperation amongst the team manifested the spirit of belonging and fellowship, where everyone was helping and lifting each other up during the high and low moments. Sustainability is hard and often the resistance of certain stakeholders may dampen the team's fantastic enthusiasm, but not mine. I became the rock they could lean on, baring all the negative and difficult tasks and conversations, supporting them each step of the way to stay motivated. Watching them at work and on the ride towards our journey motivated me. It started to feel as though I could channel my energy to them and vice versa. I enjoyed working with them all and I kept telling the team that we couldn't get anywhere without their support, professionalism, cooperation and grit. We arrived at the summit as a strong team and together we made a strong impact. Under the theme 'Alliances for a New Era', Global Fashion Summit: Copenhagen Edition 2022, we endeavored to form previously inconceivable alliances within the fashion industry and examine atypical cross-industry alliances, in a bid to accelerate the transition to a net positive reality. Hosted the grand setting of the Royal Opera House in Copenhagen, the event convened almost a thousand leaders from brands, retailers, NGOs, policies, manufacturers, and innovators to drive urgent action. The theme underlined all elements of the Summit content. On the main stage during plenary sessions, we had high-level keynote speeches and panels to bring together speakers that are often perceived as direct competitors to have transparent conversations about their mutual challenges and collaborate to discuss the actions needed to tackle the urgent issues. The programme also included other industries such as transportation, food and energy, not only to consider the challenges that are similarly experienced in other sectors and learn from successful solutions that are being demonstrated outside of fashion but because they were intertwined too. Beyond the stage content, the Summit theme was put in practical terms by mobilizing leaders to implement immediate actions through newly formed partnerships with solution providers and other industry players, setting long-term industry commitments, hosting leadership roundtables, and creating binding industry agreements that could provoke progress based on its sustainability performance level. At the same time, we hosted the Innovation Forum, which presented a curated exhibition of the world's most promising sustainable solutions. Participating brands were able to connect with exhibitors covering the entire value chain – from innovative materials to on-demand manufacturing. The forum's Matchmaking service offered small and large fashion businesses the opportunity to advance their sustainability journey by being matched directly with relevant solution providers. I opened the Summit dressed in a white suit, the same outfit I was wearing for the formal announcement of my appointment and during the summit recorded online the previous year. When everyone was seated inside, I went outside for the most important welcome. It was early June and despite the drizzly and windy weather, my heart was glowing like a summer's day when our Patron, HRH the Crown Princess of Denmark (now HM the Queen) arrived. We went to the stunning theater, a modern building along the Honsebrolobet canal, not far from Amalienborg Palace and right in front of the beautiful Marble Church. I walked almost numbed since I was going to give the opening speech in such a huge stage. I used to speak in important places and institutions, but the stage of The Royal Opera was the biggest and most frightening I had ever walked on. Even with a soft light, my eyes could see the hundreds of people filling the big theater, from the parterre to the balconies, with representatives of the entire industry I had been serving for so long. And right in front of me was HRH, and several Ambassadors in Denmark from around the world including the one from Italy. I was scared to say the least, but with so much control and confidence faking, I delivered a strong speech which resonated with the audience and the media. I reminded the five most important priorities for the CEOs - smart material choices, resource stewardship, circularity, better wage systems and secure work environments - and gave examples of the existing solutions which could have been leveraged to accelerate the transformation towards a net positive industry. Indeed, we published the *GFA Monitor* to guide fashion leaders towards a net positive fashion industry and told the audience that the report presented consolidated guidance according to the five core sustainability priorities. Building alliances through shared industry knowledge, each priority included expert insights from GFA's Data Partner, and its Impact Partners, one for each priority. We also announced the launch of the Global Circular Fashion Forum (GCFF), a global initiative to spur local action in textile manufacturing countries to accelerate and scale recycling of post-industrial textile waste. With that program, we could convene stakeholders across various circular programmes and regions, sharing knowledge and building upon best practices in an effort to achieve a long-term, scalable, and just transition to a circular fashion industry. The first project run in Bangladesh demonstrated the potential to scale the recycling of post-industrial textile waste to create new textiles, so we were aiming to establish similar programmes in other regions, beginning in Vietnam and Cambodia. Once I finished my ten-minute speech, I had the honor to introduce a special speaker to deliver the welcome address, something the audience was looking forward to hearing each year since the first Summit. HRH gracefully addressed all the issues the industry was challenging. She then took the time to visit the Innovation Forum asking the right questions to the companies who were exhibiting to learn and encourage innovation to flourish.

The Summit content was designed to be the boldest yet and focused on topics and honest discussions with more voices. The programme covered topics from 'What even is a sustainable brand?' to 'subverting fashion's historical exclusion', to the 'metaverse impact and decentralised futures.' Attendees who were representatives of companies from brands of all price point spectrum, heard from over hundred speakers who at that time were heling powerful roles in key companies and NGO. From Kering to H&M, from Neiman Marcus to Zalando, from Nike to Ganni, from Isko to Lenzing and many more. I said to everyone that fashion is about change, you can let it happen, or you can make it happen. And of course, we wanted to make it happen! The wonderful GFA team was truly on top of everything, and the Summit was a great success at all levels. We had a Board of Directors meeting the very next day and, while we were overwhelmed and exhausted, we were rewarded by the positive feedback received by the entire community and our fantastic Board.

The same year, in November, we hosted outside of Copenhagen for the first time in its 13-year history, the Global Fashion Summit in Singapore and assembled many stakeholders representing manufacturers, garment workers, retailers, brands, suppliers, NGOs, policy, and innovators to spur industry action. This edition too was centred around the theme 'Alliances for a New Era', building on dialogues from the June edition in Copenhagen and gathering leaders from across the entire value chain to elevate diverse voices and foster alliances within the fashion industry and beyond, to drive sustainable impact.

Going to Singapore was ensuring that we were going to be closer to manufactures, we facilitated even more conversations within the supply chain to discuss crucial challenges and opportunities to work collaboratively with brands on equal terms. 'Scope 3' was becoming the new buzzword since it refers as the value chain emissions. Singapore was also a way for my team and for the GFA eco-system to broaden the vision, action and impact. The jet lag for me was brutal as I was coming from NYC. But off I was in Singapore now proud of giving my team the opportunity of seeing more of the world than our familiar places. The programme featured bold panels, case studies, masterclasses and leadership roundtables reflecting on topics including 'Data Scarcity: A Crisis of Measurement?', 'Disruption for Better Wage Systems', 'Community and Circularity', 'Connecting the EU Textiles Strategy with the Value Chain' and 'Our Energy Transformation Moment'. The first international edition of Global Fashion Summit marked a special moment for us. I wanted to champion the changemakers instead of hammering the bad companies. The fashion industry is nuanced, highly complex, and technical. In a world fraught with greenwashing, sustainability education and research is needed on an on-going basis to ensure claims are substantiated by up-to-date and reliable data. In my speech that day, I outlined the crucial need for accurate and robust data to substantiate sustainability claims and credentials but acknowledged that the focus on finding 'perfect' data cannot be allowed to stifle progress. As the focus was shifting from words to deeds, we called for ambitious and much-needed actions that not only reduce harm but also deliver positive impact for the environment and societies. That day, we also announced a new alliance with BBC Storyworks Commercial Productions to launch a film series on BBC.com. The new series, called "Fashion Redressed" presented human-centric stories focusing on both social and environmental sustainability in the fashion industry. It was released to a wide audience the following year and we continued to develop this alliance further.

Ambition to Action

Regardless of what people believe politically, the World Economic Forum is a place where people meet and discuss crucial topics in formal and informal settings. After having a sweet family vacation in Vienna where we experienced a lot of culture from music to the arts, on January 2023 I went to Davos not only to represent GFA but also to receive a special award. A friend of GFA offered us to stay in her cozy place located right in the center of the beautiful Swiss village so we could walk everywhere we had meetings and panels to attend. Beside dining with great people such as William McDonownell, the author of *Cradle to Cradle, Remaking the way we make things,* on January 21st, I received the World Woman Hero Award for my commitment to gender equality. I had known the CEO of the World Woman Foundation for several years, and she witnessed my journey and commitment towards female equality. The fashion industry is female-dominated with nearly three-quarters of all garments workers worldwide being women. Nevertheless, many women are disproportionately affected by gender-based discrimination in the workplace. With my work in the past, I was always striving to address the issue of gender equality. Now at GFA, among the targets, we wanted to help increase wages of textile workers to living wages (many of which are female), decrease the gender pay gap starting from the European value chains through a cross-sectoral programme. All of these led me to two special moments: the one in Davos in January and a very special one in NYC. Indeed, in March, a month USA used to raise awareness for woman equality, the World Woman Foundation asked me to ring the bell at Nasdaq to open the market. The experience of being in a respected room for such a significant moment made me feel humbled and extremely honored for the recognition I was receiving. While I wasn't there to list a new company in the stock market, I was there for a very significant purpose. After ringing the bell with many women who were coming from different walks of life asking to accelerate the closing of gender pay gaps among many inequality issues, we went to take pictures outside, in Time Square. In the huge screen was displayed the sentence "Nasdaq welcomes Federica Marchionni, 2023 World Woman Hero Honoree & Global Fashion Agenda CEO". Picture my heart in that moment. A shot I loved and posted on LinkedIn was perfectly capturing my feeling. It is me praying the Heavens with an immense sense of gratitude for the opportunities I had and the wish that women would be able to live safe and free as men can do. Definitely a big ambition which I was determined to bring into action.

That year we decided to call the Summit theme 'Ambition to Action'. Major objectives for sustainability action were in place. Yet across the globe, industries were not on track to meet them, and pathways of improvement were often unclear. The Summit intended to galvanise partners and participants to transform ambitions into concrete actions that could drive the industry towards more sustainable practices, both socially and environmentally. Under these premises, the event presented content experiences focused on tangible and evidence-based impact, with over half of the programme dedicated to educational and action-oriented business case studies. The Summit also facilitated more than ten strategic roundtable meetings that brought together executives and policymakers for productive dialogues on how to address pressing sustainability issues and act accordingly. With the upcoming policy expected to influence the fashion industry even further this year, earlier in February I went to the European Commission in Brussels to discuss circularity. The EU is, and still is, focused on the Green Deal and GFA was leading important meetings to help shed light on the ongoing pieces of legislation under discussion both within the EU and worldwide. The industry went from being a non-regulated one to an industry into the focus of regulators globally, starting from the EU. At the summit, it was important to address the need of harmonization since raw materials, such as cotton or wool, are produced in a part of the world (for example in Brazil and Australia), transformed into a garment or accessory in another region (mostly Asia for the fast fashion and Europe for luxury), consumed in another (from USA to China to everywhere in between) and wasted in landfills in another different part of the planet (mostly Africa and Latin America). GFA therefore launched the Global Textiles Policy Forum, a platform for governments and textile industry associations from around the world to align an ambitious sustainability pathway for industry and the global policy frameworks needed; raise and amplify supply chain voices and spread the likely impact of the EU Textiles Strategy outside of the EU. With GFA also launched a new policy matrix to summarise the key legislation going on around the world implicating the textile industry to help companies navigate into this more complex world.

In an effort to educate marketers, media and influencers, we also showcased *The Sustainable Fashion Communication Playbook*, at the Summit - a guide for fashion communicators made by UNEP and UN Climate Change to align efforts to sustainability targets. It showed how to take action through countering misinformation, reducing messages perpetuating overconsumption, and redirecting aspiration to sustainable lifestyles. Another landmark report presented at the Summit was made by the University of Cambridge Institute for Sustainability Leadership (CISL), the Fashion Pact and Conservation International as it mapped out how the fashion, textile and apparel industry could implement the first science-based targets for nature.

Furthermore, I was really excited by the GFA's newly launched Next Gen Assembly programme produced with the Fashion Values Programme and presented by one of our partners. The young members were able to candidly share their perspectives and stories with industry leaders during a roundtable and produced a reflective report informed by insights gained at the Summit. Last but not least, we presented industry leaders to the CTI Fashion Initiative to drive circularity in fashion. Led among others by WBCSD (World Business Council for Sustainable Development), the latest alliance had the ambition to establish harmonized metrics, standards and best practices, anchored by the Circular Transition Indicators (CTI) for measuring impact, fostering accountability and advancing sustainable value creation. I was filled with a sense of hope following the Summit which was truly focused on turning the aspirational to the actual – championing evidence-based actions that can redesign our business models with net positive at the core, improve the livelihoods of the millions of garment workers and protect and enhance our precious ecosystems. Since I joined GFA, I had also the ambition to work closely with a globally renowned leader in logistics that aims to deliver a more connected, agile and sustainable future for global logistics. That year, we finally announced our new partner, demonstrating another strong action to the ecosystem. Indeed, to accelerate circularity we need to utilize more sustainable logistic alternatives too, and later we published a *Reverse Logistics* report that was supported by an open online masterclass on the topic. Last but not least, while GFA was focused on companies which produced a lot of volume, to increase their sustainability performance, I wanted to highlight the key role of luxury in inspiring positive social and environmental progress. So, it was an achievement for me personally to be able to interview executives from companies that are not normally associated with high street fashion. We had a great discussion, and I was glad they too chose our summit to share their views. Onstage while speaking about leather, I mentioned the opportunity to keep innovating to possibly use new materials – a topic we decided delve into more the following year after calling more experts, innovators, startups, and activists. Among GFA targets, we wanted to push for the adoption of animal-derived fibers (such as down, wool, alpaca, mohair, leather) from preferred sources by 2030 and reduce the use of virgin polyester by 45% by 2030 as well as the use of conventional cotton and conventional manmade cellulosic.

In keeping the goal to build more alliances, for the first time, the Summit also spanned across the category of watches and jewellery, thanks to the Alliance with the Watch & Jewellery Initiative 2030. While certain issues are specific to this category, the overall sustainability agenda could be aligned together with the fashion to mobilize greater action and impact. Another

important alliance was inked with an American organization which was focusing a lot of its work with measurements in manufacturing companies, and
we could leverage each other's work. We decided to host our international
summit together, this time in Boston. This gave me the opportunity to bring
into the conversation companies and leaders with whom I had interacted in
the past while living in America. On a personal level, I used the weekend to
reconnect with my son, who I had moved back to the United States to study
near Boston, a perfect environment for his growth while his father, after a
life threatening experience, decided to live in Puglia, but we all reunite for
the holidays.

During one of the key meetings with our esteemed partner earlier in my
time at GFA, we decided to pursue a project that was very ambitious, and
we were proudly able to announce it later that year at COP28 in Dubai. It
was about a wind groundbreaking energy project in Bangladesh which was
projected to reduce emissions by ~725,000 tonnes annually. Since more than
70% of the fashion industry's GHG emissions come from upstream activities
and current operations predominantly rely on non-renewable energy sources, changing the industry power supply to renewable energy required new
infrastructure solutions at scale. If development is successful, operations are
expected to commence in 2028 and would have an approximate capacity of
500MW, making it the first utility-scale offshore wind farm in the far east
and is expected to contribute to substantial job creation, stabilise energy supply, and reduce emissions. Our Chairman, Thomas Tochtermann, worked
very closely to bring this ambitious project to fruition and we could also
demonstrate how a collaborative approach on sustainable financing solutions
could go hand in hand to overcome industry-wide challenges.

In Dubai, where my team was experiencing a new world and mindset, as
we were in one of the most important fossil fuel regions, I met several key
business players who were cooperating to make a positive impact. There
was something magical that happened in Dubai for different reasons including, to my surprise, the request to moderate a session at the LVMH Life
360 Summit in Paris, which they called "Ambition to Action". I couldn't be
prouder that GFA had inspired as a thought leader of one of the most important fashion groups. The panel was a discussion about collaboration and
together with LVMH, the CEO of Martell and Champagnes Mumm and
Perrier-Jouët, the President of Maison Hennessy, the brilliant Pascal Mo-
rand from Federation de la Haute couture et de la mode, there was Chanel
too. We discussed joint forces in an effort to implement more action in the
supply chain. The event was held at UNESCO followed by a beautiful dinner in which I understood I was able to reach the cloud nine once again but
reinvented. I celebrated my birthday on December 23rd, 2023, feeling that,

I was indeed, "*back in the race*" (as Frank Sinatra, and now also Lady Gaga, sang on "That's life").

Unlocking the next level

Going back to NYC in a cold January made me get closer to the dear friends I made during my time in the city over the years. Not only my best friend Desiree, but also Bill, Ron, Shellie, Teresa, Milton, Sherrie, David Michelle, and – from the Italian community living in NYC - Francesca, Giovanni, Claudio, Daniela and many more. My new work was also giving me the chance to build new meaningful friendships, such as ones with Julia, May, and Simon. I enjoyed having inspiration to conceive bigger, more ambitious and impactful projects. Since one of my goals was to globalize the work GFA was doing, I pursued the opportunity to collaborate with a Turkish start-up created by a pioneer in sustainability. Their Chairman, also owning the biggest supplier of denim, developed a textile-to-textile company to increase circularity and help eliminate waste. I went to Istanbul to ink a three-year partnership and on my way back to NYC, I joined another partner who was scouting the startups in Riyadh, Saudi Arabia, for their Innovation Award which they announced the next year. My experience in Riyadh was different than I anticipated. I wasn't obliged to wear the veil and could go by myself around the city. The people I met were highly educated, including women who all spoke good English. The ambition I sensed was not different from the one I experienced in China, and I wondered if they were pushing themselves over the lines accepted in the current economic world order. Something only time will tell, and it will be interesting to watch Saudi Arabia's journey as they are focused on diversifying the economy to be more sustainable.

Back in the Big Apple, I was busy preparing for the upcoming 2024 summit. The event's theme, *Unlocking the Next Level,* impelled participants to urgently act on the learnings from the forum to support the implementation of solutions to reach both near and long-term goals. Under this premise, the Summit presented content centred around evidence-based impact, with much of the programme dedicated to educational and action-oriented business case studies. Among many organizations, we cooperated with the American Apparel and Footwear Association which hosts a gala every year to fundraise for the CFDA Foundation. Textile policies were at a critical juncture, with an exponential rise in regulations requiring alignment, collaboration, and education among stakeholders. GFA played a key role by harmonising policy positions, facilitating dialogue between policymakers and value chain actors, and providing guidance through publications and masterclasses. As CEO of GFA, I was selected as one of the honorees and recognized with the 'Eco-Steward of the Year' at the prestigious American Image Awards. The evening of the event I met a wonderful woman, who was honored as the 'Person of the Year'. We knew about each other's work, and I was truly pleased to meet a Danish CEO in the USA. She had successfully grown in the company and arrived in the evening with her beautiful family and key members of the company. That day we learned sad news that somehow made us bond even more. Indeed, the Børsen, a beautiful 17th century building situated next to Christiansborg Palace, the seat of the Danish Parliament, has set on fire. A tragic event happened during some renovation work they were doing inside. The good news was that no one was hurt. GFA was planning to host important meetings the day prior our summit inside the Børsen so we moved the meetings to the modern Danish Architect Center. The closed-door sessions brought together curated groups of high-level stakeholders to openly discuss relevant barriers, share learnings, and to build collaborations to support the implementation of solutions. The summit roundtables addressed topics such as: 'Scaling Circular Textile Systems', 'Pay Equity Interventions in European Value Chains', and 'Impactful Influence'.

The year 2024 was very special to GFA as it marked the 15-years since the first Global Fashion Summit (formerly Copenhagen Fashion Summit) and has since established itself as the leading forum for sustainability in fashion. During the opening, I mentioned that for 15 years GFA has used the Summit to activate impact and forge new initiatives while educating and mobilising the fashion industry and because of that, sustainability has moved from a peripheral concern to a central focus becoming an agenda-setter even in boardrooms. However, I underlined, the pace of sustainability progress has not accelerated enough to respond to our changing world and this year's Summit was focused on identifying the barriers to 'Unlock the Next Level' and accelerate further implementation. In my point of view, we had reached a polarisation point where the geopolitical environment around us was threatening to stunt our progress and I wanted to emphasise that we needed to unite to meet the 2030 and 2050 agenda. I said, "*whether we differ in geographies, cultures or political mindsets, sustainability must be a unifying bond among all of us*". Each and every company needed to depart from business as usual and intentions needed to meet determination. I eagerly called for fashion's systemic transformation.

The Summit championed evidence-based strategies poised to reshape the business ethos, placing net positivity as the overarching goal. The pivotal anniversary was offering a special moment to not only to take stock of the evolution of the sector and the progress made so far, but, most importantly, to look ahead at what actions urgently needed to be implemented in the near term, and the gaps that must be filled to accelerate industry transformation. With deadlines for pledges made over the previous 15 years looming, GFA was mobilizing the industry to implement further actions that ambitiously address societal and environmental impacts and challenge the existing paradigm. With the goal to inspire the audience to "*rise up*", a stunning performance act opened the summit with dancers who were all dressed in white dynamically moved a piece of fabric that was draped across the stage. The fabric was illuminated with projection of planet Earth and displayed homages to the pioneers who walked our stages 15 years prior. The production team has always done a great job, as well the rest of the GFA team, but this particular moment excelled and was more moving and powerful than ever before. I had the privilege to take part in the opening sequence and when, dressed in a white suit too, I took the dancer's hands to bow, I felt truly blessed by the Heavens.

We structured the summit program around unlocking solutions to fashion's biggest sustainability barriers, no matter where an organization was on its sustainability journey. Sessions included: 'Fragmented Futures: Fashion's Policy Agenda', 'Luxury, Leather, and Land', 'Towards a Binding Agreement on Wages', 'Pathways to Indigenous Partnership', and 'Ending Oversupply. We invited Indigenous people to represent their communities – which are often impacted by issues in the fashion value chain such as deforestation, inequality and cultural appropriation. Another highlight at the Summit was the *Trailblazer* program. Innovation is a fundamental component to transforming the current fashion system to one that benefits people and the planet. Yet, to truly achieve impact on a scale, innovation and investment go hand-in-hand. In a time of significant economic challenges, it was more important than ever that the fashion ecosystem prioritises investment in early-stage solutions so that we could bring them to fruition and make them last. Through this programme, supported by a partner, GFA strove to help innovation thrive. GFA first presented an open call for solution providers addressing different challenges across the fashion value chain to apply for the programme. Applicants were reviewed and shortlisted by an esteemed jury. Eight shortlisted innovations were enrolled in a group of Trailblazers, receiving feedback and investment pitch training from industry experts and our partner. At the summit we revealed the winner who won an equity investment, commercial and operational support to help bring the innovation to scale.

The end of the conference, where I finally felt confident and in control, was designed to boost key messages, one was delivered by the Brioni CEO who launched the slow luxury manifesto and the other by Patagonia CEO, one of one the companies most committed to the environment and combatting climate change.

Overall, while the entire Summit community felt that we wanted to be more advanced after being 15 years on in activating impact, we also realized that sustainability had become a priority, but the operationalization needed a faster track to make a just transition in time with all the pledges and agreements. We celebrated our anniversary with a special artist, Lucky Love, who beautifully delighted us with his *"Tendresse"*.

GFAmily

The GFA team is made up of young and enthusiastic employees who have great talent in their own fields. When I joined GFA, I understood the full potential of the leadership team and my biggest satisfaction was being able to develop them and also lift up the rest of the team which are the backbone of the organization. I always carefully listen to my team's needs, from the leaders to the most junior members to make them feel empowered for the contribution they gave, and they were going to still give to GFA. I am a demanding and ambitious leader, but I have given opportunities to grow and experience different things to each and every one, leading them to new heights. I always strive to give the best example and in moments of need, they knew they could count on me. I exposed the leadership team to the Board and to the strategic partners many times and offered them new opportunities to experience more. We truly felt we had become not just a team but a collaborative community and started to call ourselves the GFAmily. I cannot list everyone here but a few of them deserve a mention since most of the work mentioned above was driven by them and I was glad to have been able to promote them and their work. Holly, who started as a Senior Sustainability Manager, was promoted first to VP and then CSO. She worked tremendously hard and led all the publications and impact programs (some of which I have mentioned). After many years with GFA, she decided to take a sabbatical and travel the world on a sailing boat joining her husband, something I also wish to do one day in the future (probably when my son will be busy working). Maria Luisa, our VP of Public Affairs, started also as Senior Public Affairs Manager and was promoted three times. She grew our work on policy very professionally and was able to bring together several organizations at different tables with many voices and stakeholders. Alice, from a Senior PR Manager, became my Chief of staff and the Director of Communications, wonderfully leading a team of focused and committed people to disseminate and highlight the work of everyone else; Cristina, recently promoted as a Director of Impact, who helped create the Innovation

Forum and the Designer Challenge among other initiatives; Faith who was brilliantly working with the rest of the team and all our eco-system to bring the summit program to life leading GFA Content; Signe, the talented Head of Operations & Events who was making her magic for perfectly producing all our summits; and Dana a mom of three beautiful children who became VP of Partnerships for her talent, skills and empathy with people.

The summer after the summit in 2024 was getting by too quickly and for some of us at GFA was busier than ever. Not only because Jonas, a veteran of GFA who I had also promoted to COO during my time, decided to leave to dedicate more time to his daughter (and I was focused on taking that role till I onboarded later on Lennart, the new COO), but also because we had four of our employees in maternity leave. I was very glad that our GFAmily was growing and, being a mother myself, I supported all the colleagues who were living one of the most important times in theirs. For me, the GFAmily was extended to our Board too, people who I deeply respected and to whom I was grateful for their guidance and support. With time, I also develop an incredible partnership with our Chairman, and I had the pleasure to even meet his beautiful family – a dream one to have. Thomas has a wonderful wife and daughters who have clear ideas, skills and dreams which I admire. We met in different places and always loved our conversations and interaction. Each time I only wished I had more opportunities to enjoy their amazing company. Thanks to GFA , I found a great friend, Annamaria. An intellectual stylish lady, a wonderful mother, an Italian accomplished architect in Denmark and more. She is quite a special and unique woman with a generous heart, (she even married three times) and who made me feel more welcomed in Copenhagen even opening her beautiful home where she often hosts friends. In our evening conversation after work, she always gave me a wise, powerful and graceful perspective becoming for me an inspiration for the way she lived and still live fully her life in her eighties!

In the pursuit of bringing more action, during Climate Week NYC, we organized a GFA Assembly at a partner's offices: Nike. Indeed, after meeting their VP of Sustainable Manufacturing and Sourcing, I understood she wanted to do more in a collaborative approach and decided to host something together to spur new initiatives and actions. Many stakeholders were attending this important moment in NYC, and we could maximize our impact by being in a place where key partners were either based or travelling anyway. It was also a great opportunity for me to welcome my team to the city where I was living and was so dear to me. We brought together different organizations dividing them into four different rooms to discuss and move forward on what was started during our summit. The most important discussion was about circularity and Extended Product Responsibility (EPR). EPR is a policy tool which shifts pressure on producers to take responsibility for the entire lifecycle of their products (including end of life management). So, a particular focus of the conversation at the GFA Assembly centred on proactive strategies to operationalise EPR given the regulatory requirements that will mandate action from all actors within the industry. Industry leaders expressed the need for a roadmap, harmonization and GFA could play an important role in creating a project to support it. Another task on to add to our very busy agenda. In response, we developed a new *Mapping to Global Extended Producer Responsibility* educational report where we sought to provide a non-exhaustive overview of existing EPR schemes at the global level. The ultimate objective was: 1) to identify the requirements of the different schemes and push for global harmonization to reduce compliance costs for companies, and 2) to avoid fragmentations that slow down the introduction of effective global waste management. Despite the recent attacks to ESG and the broader sustainability agenda, climate change is unfortunately underway and everyone started to realize that sustainability is not a trend that can fade away. It is here to stay as an essential part of our work and life to be taken even more seriously, scaling innovative solutions to create resilience and competitiveness.

Through all of GFA's work, we were and are mobilizing, educating, advocating, and influencing the entire fashion industry by driving collaboration and guiding action – all led with the vision to transform the industry to one that is net positive. Because we believe that

"if we can change fashion, we can change everything."

Feeling fulfilled should not have you sit back and only enjoy the rewarding moments. For sure, we must enjoy. But then? I need to envision myself from now till I will be an old lady, like my beautiful mom now is. I hope that despite the growing age, my attitude of envisioning will stay active, and my head will be full of dreams.

Dream-Plan: To create New Dream-Plans.

Continuing to dream is fundamental because it is our dreams that propel us forward, with every millimeter of our being. The only power we need has already been given to us. It resides in our inner strength and human pillars. The obstacles we face are just that: obstacles. They are not dead ends. We are creatures made to go further. We were created to evolve into infinite possibilities.

Some takeaways

Understand macro shifts and have larger lenses in reading world changes.
Configure your new codes when major shocks happen and impact your daily life too.
It may be good idea to possibly have a dialogue with former employees in the same position.
Ask what you can do in the new context and how you can help to bring value.
New realities can give new opportunities, find the one that speaks to you.
Reinvention can happen if you decide to give yourself a chance to start over.
Accept the highs and lows of the new beginnings, as if you are a start-up, using wisdom.
Be a positive force for yourself and learn how to overcome lonely moments.
Live always with a great sense of gratitude and never take things for granted.
Give the people you manage opportunities to grow and empower them.
Share not only decision making and leadership but rewarding moments too.
Never stop dreaming and chase something which brings a smile to your soul.

Bibliography

Andrić, Ivo, *The Bridge on the Drina*, The University of Chicago Press, Chicago, 1977.

Angelou, Maya, *Phenomenal Woman: Four Poems Celebrating Women*, Random House, New York (NY), 1995.

Brandt, Richard L., *One Click: Jeff Bezos and the Rise of Amazon.com*, Penguin, London, 2012.

Brown, Brené, *Rising Strong: The Reckoning. The Rumble. The Revolution*, Random House, New York (NY), 2015.

Brown, Brené, *The Gifts of Imperfection: Let Go of Who You Think You're Supposed to Be and Embrace Who You Are*, Hazelden, Center City (MN), 2010.

Chang, Jung, *Wild Swangs, Three Daughters of China.* Harper Collins, New York (NY), 1991.

Collins, Jim, *Good to Great*, Random House Business, New York (NY), 2001.

De Bono, Edward, *The Use of Lateral Thinking*, Penguin, London, 1967.

Doerr, John, *Measure What Matters. How Google, Bono, and the Gates Foundation Rock the World With OKRS*, Portfolio, New York (NY), 2018.

Duckworth, Angela, *Grit: The Power of Passion and Perseverance*, Scribner, New York (NY), 2016.

Dychtwald, Zak, *Young China. How the Restless Generation Will Change Their Country and the World*, St Martins Press, Ney York (NY), 2018.

Gallmann, Kuki, *I Dreamed of Africa*, Viking, New York (NY), 1991.

Gladwell, Malcolm, *Outliers: The Story of Success*, Little, Brown and Company, New York (NY), 2008.

Goleman, Daniel, Boyatzis, Richard E., McKee, Annie, *Primal Leadership*, Harvard Business School Press, Cambridge (MA), 2001.

Hamel, Gary, *Humanocracy: Creating Organizations as Amazing as the People Inside Them*, Harvard Business Review Press, Cambridge (MA), 2020.

Heath, Chip, Heath, Dan, *Decisive: How to Make Better Choices in Life and Work*, Crown Business, New York (NY), 2013.

Huffington, Arianna, *Thrive*, Harmony Books, New York (NY), 2015.

Johnson, Spencer, *Who Moved My Cheese? An Amazing Way to Deal with Change in Your Work and in Your Life*, Putnam Adult, NewYork (NY), 1998.

Kahneman, Daniel, *Thinking, Fast and Slow*, Farrar Straus & Giroux, New York (NY), 2011.

Kissinger, Henry, *On China*, Penguin, New York (NY), 2011.

Koepp, Robert W., *Betting on China. Chinese Stocks, American Stock Markets, and the Wagers on a New Dynamic in Global Capitalism*, John Wiley & Sons, Hoboken (NJ), 2012.

Kübler-Ross, Elisabeth, *On Death And Dying*, MacMillan Publishers, London, 1970.

Lee, Kai-Fu, *AI Superpowers. China, Silicon Valley, And The New World Order*, Houghton Mifflin Harcourt, Boston (MA), 2019.

Marchionni, Federica, "It's time for a new measurement of prosperity", *Time Magazine*, https://time.com/4587494/ marchionni-measuring-prosperity/.

Novogratz, Jacqueline, *The Blue Sweater. Bridging the Gap Between Rich and Poor in an Interconnected World*, Rodale Press, Emmaus (pa), 2010.

Rampini, Federico, *L'impero di Cindia. Cina, India e dintorni*, Mondadori, Milano, 2007.

Rein, Shaun, *The End of Cheap China: Economic and Cultural Trends That Will Disrupt the World*, John Wiley & Sons, Hoboken (NJ), 2012.

Rein, Shaun, *The War for China's Wallet: Profiting from the New World Order*, De Gruyter, Boston (MA), 2017.

Rubin, Gretchen, *The Happiness Project*, HarperCollins, New York (NY), 2009.

Seidman, Dov, *How: Why we do Anything means Everything*, Wiley India Pvt. Lim, 2011.

Sinek, Simon, *Start with Why*, Portfolio, New York (NY), 2009.

Sutherland, Jeff, *Scrum: The Art of Doing Twice the Work in Half the Time*, Random House Business, New York (NY), 2014.

Thiel, Peter, Masters, Blake, *Zero to One: Notes on Start Ups, or How to Build the Future*, Ebury, London, 2015.

Vogler, Christopher, *The Writer's Journey: Mythic Structure for Writers*, Michael Wiese Productions, 2007.

Zeihan, Peter, *The Absent Superpower: The Shale Revolution and a World Without*, Zeihan on Geopolitics, 2016.

Zeihan, Peter, *The Accidental Superpower. The Next Generation of American Preeminence and the Coming Global Disorder*, Twelve, New York (NY), 2016.

Acknowledgments

I sincerely want to express my gratitude to all the people I have met on my journey. From the residents in Santa Severa to those of the cities in which I have studied, worked, lived, and traveled.

All of them, in their own way, have contributed to my evolution. Even those who created obstacles instead of helping me overcome them, because they pushed me to go beyond my limits, making me a stronger person.

Of course, special thanks go to my whole family and to all those who have touched my heart with affection, support, and positivity. Without their presence, I wouldn't be human and real as they had shown me.

I would also like to thank those who I have not had the pleasure of meeting in person but who have been an important source of inspiration. From artists to Nobel prize winners, to savvy and successful business people to the simplest people who struggle every day in their daily lives. I was often reminded that beauty is everywhere.

Thank you. Thank you very much to everyone. You made me.